Meteorology.
natural History Editor.

H Earthquakes, Volcanoes, Storms

Unesco Essays —
1st vg. xlib —

VIOLENT FORCES
OF
NATURE

Robert H. Maybury

Editor

Published in Cooperation with Unesco

LOMOND PUBLICATIONS, INC.
Mt. Airy, Maryland 21771
1986

Library of Congress Catalog Number: 84-82537

ISBN: 0-912338-37-7 (Clothbound)
       0-912338-38-5 (Microfiche)

Most of the papers in this volume were prepared originally for publication in the United Nations Educational, Scientific and Cultural Organization journal, *impact of science on society,* Vol. 32, No. 2, copyright by UNESCO.

Index prepared by C. J. Swet.

Printed in the United States of America

Published by
Lomond Publications, Inc.
P.O. Box 88
Mt. Airy, Maryland 21771

Table Of Contents

Publisher's Note

This is the fourth volume that we at Lomond Publications have produced in cooperation with the United Nations Educational, Scientific and Cultural Organization (Unesco). The basis for the book is a particular issue of Unesco's quarterly journal *impact of science on society* which took as its theme the taming of nature's violent forces. The editor, Robert H. Maybury, has maintained a continuing interest in the subject and expanded *Violent Forces of Nature* with timely reprints as well as certain articles specifically produced for this book.

Much of the literature on disasters is a grim recounting of death and destruction. Significant studies have been made of various natural disasters in an effort to predict their occurrences. Nonetheless, as the contributors to this book remind the reader, prediction is only partially successful. *The most significant factor in reducing the devastating effects of the earth's cataclysmic events is, more often than not, preparedness, not prediction.*

In a collection of internationally written articles such as this, a publisher is faced with a troubling variation in spellings. While English language spelling conventions vary considerably, most alternatives, however, are widely known and accepted. In this case, the publisher has decided against attempting to edit the different articles to adhere to American English spelling conventions, believing that even so seemingly trivial changes can tamper with the integrity of an author's tone and style.

The publisher is very pleased to have had the opportunity to once again bring an important addition to our book list and to have had the privilege of working with Jacques G. Richardson (Unesco, retired) and Robert H. Maybury (Unesco, World Bank) assembling, editing and disseminating the valuable insights discussed by the authors in these papers.

PREFACE

There is a gentle side to Nature, to which the most characteristic human response is perhaps the lyric expression of the poet. Hence, we find these words by Byron:

Dear Nature is the kindest mother still
Though always changing, in her aspect mild.

Childe Harold, ii. 25

There is also, of course, a violent side to Nature, one displayed through a great diversity of fierce and destructive phenomena—earthquakes, volcanoes, tsunami, avalanches, landslides, cyclonic storms, lightning, floods, fires, and so on. When Nature strikes out at us through these violent forces to wreak havoc on our homes and buildings, our roads, bridges and dams, our farms, crops and animals, and to harm or even kill human beings, we recognize how vulnerable we are to this violent side of Nature. Our most characteristic response is understandably fear and terror.

But just as understandable is our capacity, as human beings, to go beyond the negativism of this emotional response to the positive activity of engaging in scientific study of these violent forces of Nature. Such study is carried on in the hope that, as the secrets of Nature's violent side become unveiled, the vulnerability of humankind to these violent forces will somehow be reduced.

In this book, we have brought together accounts of scientific studies that exemplify this positive response to Nature's violence. In chapter after chapter, our authors, many as front-line research investigators, report what science has been able to discover to date about Nature's violent forces. We learn that plate tectonic theory—sections of the earth's crust moving around on an underlying molten base—provides an increasingly valid explanation of seismic and volcanic events and holds out hopes that eventually we shall be able to predict these reliably.

We learn much about Nature's violent use of water: how it can pile up as snow on a mountainside where, through a variety of metamorphic changes, it becomes ripe for an avalanche; how, as an ocean, it can be piled up by the impulse of an earth tremor to form a huge and destructive wave; how as a river it can overflow its banks to turn a floodplain into a watery nightmare; and even how its scarcity can bring devastating drought to millions of people and animals.

Finally, we learn how Nature can turn the climate against us, twisting the winds around a vortex at velocities exceeding 270 km per hour, flinging lightning bolts at us at a rate of millions per year, and fanning the resulting fires until losses to the ecosystem reach as high as 25 kilograms per hectare.

In introducing this series of scientific reports, Dr. Fournier d'Albe, a scientist with a long career in international organizations, places in proper perspective this whole matter of probing Nature's secrets in order to reduce our vulnerability to violent forces:

> It has to be remembered that no amount of knowledge or planning will be effective in reducing risk without the understanding and cooperation of the whole population concerned . . . . Scientists and engineers have a vital role to play in discovering means of protection against the violent forces of nature. The extent to which society puts this knowledge to effective use *depends upon its social, political, economic and even religious values: in other words, upon its culture.* (Italics mine.)

Accordingly, we have brought together under Part V, headed *"Preparedness and Rescue,"* some accounts of the efforts being made to organize society so that effective use can be made of the scientific knowledge of Nature's violent forces in reducing the vulnerability of people to these forces.

If we were to make an appropriate dedication of this book, it would have to be to two groups: first, to those scientists who are pressing the struggle to unveil the secrets of Nature's violent side through their studies and expeditions, and second, to those public spirited individuals who are dedicating effort to awaken the general public to the need for cooperation and effective organization that can use scientific knowledge to lower risk and vulnerability to Nature's violent forces.

Robert H. Maybury

A natural hazard is what is imposed upon us by nature. It is, and probably will remain, beyond human control. It can however be studied and assessed scientifically. Vulnerability, on the other hand, depends entirely on the nature and physical characteristics of the elements at risk, and is thus, in theory at least, subject to human control. But no amount of knowledge or planning will be effective in reducing risk without the understanding and cooperation of the whole population concerned.

Reducing Vulnerability to Nature's Violent Forces: Cooperation between Scientist and Citizen

E. M. Fournier d'Albe

The author is a British physicist born in 1921, who obtained the doctorate in philosophy from Oxford University. After military service during the Second World War, Dr. Fournier d'Albe served as a technical expert dealing with atmospheric physics, working in Mexico and Pakistan in behalf of Unesco (1951-1960). From 1960 until his early retirement from Unesco in 1979, the author was responsible for Unesco's programme concerned with natural catastrophes, and from 1974 until 1979 he was Director, Division of Earth Sciences, Unesco. Since that time, Dr. Fournier d'Albe has continued to serve as a consultant to Unesco and other specialized agencies of the United Nations. He can be said to have organized, almost on his sole initiative, a global "earthquake watch," and the publisher and editor of the present volume are most pleased to count Dr. Fournier d'Albe among its contributors.

The past few decades have witnessed a gradual change in ideas and attitudes relating to natural disasters. The traditional view was that these are "acts of God," unpredictable and inevitable. All that could be done was to rescue, relieve and assist the survivors of a disaster to re-establish a normal life as soon as possible. Only in recent years has it been realised that, although nothing can be done to prevent the occurrence of earthquakes, eruptions, cyclones and other violent natural events, there is much that can and should be done to protect life and property against them. This new attitude is gradually, but still too slowly, spreading from the scientific and engineering community to the spheres of government, public administration and public opinion.

A symptom of this change of attitude was the meeting convened in Geneva in July 1979 by the Office of the United Nations Disaster Relief Coordinator (UNDRO). It was attended by scientists, engineers, physical planners and representatives of many United Nations agencies, who in their report put forward a new conceptual basis for action aimed at reducing the vulnerability of human beings and their works to the violent forces of nature. Because action must be based on ideas, and ideas must be expressed in words, the definitions of the concepts involved are worthwhile quoting here:

- *Natural hazard* means the probability of occurrence, within a specified period of time in a given area, of a potentially damaging natural phenomenon.

- *Vulnerability* means the degree of loss to a given element at risk or set of such elements, resulting from the occurrence of a natural phenomenon of a given magnitude; it is expressed on a scale from 0 (no damage) to 1 (total loss).

- *Elements at risk* means the population, buildings and civil engineering works, economic activities, public services, utilities and infrastructure, etc., at risk in a given area.

- *Specific risk* means the expected degree of loss due to a particular natural phenomenon; it is a function of both natural hazard and vulnerability.

- *Risk* means the expected number of lives lost, persons injured, damage to property and disruption of economic activity due to a particular natural phenomenon, and consequently the product of specific risk and elements at risk.

These definitions establish a clear distinction between the several mutually independent factors which determine risk.

The natural hazard is what is imposed upon us by Nature. It is, and probably will remain, beyond human control. It can, however, be studied and assessed scientifically. Estimates can be made of the probabilities of events of various magnitudes affecting given places in given periods of time. Maps can be prepared showing the way in which different hazards (earthquakes, volcanic eruptions, floods, wind storms, landslides, avalanches, tsunamis, etc.) vary from one place to another. This is the task of the scientists who specialise in the study of these phenomena. Such maps are useful, even if little is known about the vulnerability of human constructions, because they permit the quantitative comparison of the risks attendant on siting a given structure in various alternative locations.

Vulnerability, on the other hand, depends entirely on the nature and physical characteristics of the elements at risk, and is thus, in theory at least, subject to human control. It is the task of engineers and architects to design the buildings and structures in which people live and work in such a way that they resist successfully the forces of nature to which they are exposed. In most cases, this is now technically possible.

In principle, therefore, the risk of damage and consequent loss of life can be controlled and reduced, either by appropriate design and construction or by avoiding construction in areas subject to phenomena against which no protection is possible (e.g., glowing avalanches, lava and mud flows from volcanos).

In practice, however, there are many difficulties, not the least of which stems from the fact that, for many years yet, the majority of people in hazardous areas will have to go on living and working in buildings and structures which are not proof against the violent phenomena to which they may be exposed. In such cases it is important to evaluate the risks as accurately as possible, to take precautions to reduce eventual damage and loss of life as far as possible, and to prepare detailed plans for evacuation, rescue or relief in the event of an emergency. This is not an easy or a popular task, for it is difficult to assess the vulnerability of existing buildings and the expenditure of public funds on measures to protect against an event that may never occur is not generally regarded as politically rewarding.

On the other hand, new settlements, new buildings and public works can, thanks to recent advances in science and engineering, be planned and constructed henceforth with better knowledge of the natural hazards and of the means of reducing vulnerability. At the stage of physical and economic planning, the additional costs (if any) of siting a new development in a less hazardous area can be balanced against the reduction of risk achieved by doing so. At the stage of urban planning, settlement and development can be restrained in the more hazardous zones; water and power supplies, drainage and communication networks can be planned so that damage to one link in a network does not put the whole system out of action; city layout can be planned so that access and escape routes are not blocked in the event of an emergency. At the stage of design and construction, the adoption and enforcement of appropriate building codes can do much to ensure that buildings and structures have a satisfactory degree of resistance to earthquakes, wind and other forces likely to affect them.

Here again, however, experience has shown that what may be easy to say is often difficult to work out in practice. One of the problems most commonly encountered is a difficulty, or even absence, of communication between scientists and engineers on the one hand, and planners and civil authorities on the other. Scientists and engineers have developed their own technical languages which are not readily understood by those of other professions. It must also be said that few scientists or engineers take the trouble to discover and understand the nature of the problems faced by administrators, planners, and architects, or of the decisions that these are obliged to make. For instance, a scientist, unless he goes further than his knowledge justifies, will normally express hazard and vulnerability in terms of the probabilities of occurrence of natural events and of the consequent losses. Such statements are difficult to translate into the "yes or no" decisions that have to be made by the public authorities: whether or not to allow settlement in a certain area, or whether or not to order the evacuation of a threatened zone. There are real technical problems here, and an urgent need for dialogue between the professions concerned.

Finally, it has to be remembered that no amount of knowledge or planning will be effective in reducing risk without the understanding and cooperation of the whole population concerned. Public information and education are an essential, though often forgotten, element in any attempt to reduce these risks, and the public must be involved in all stages of planning. Otherwise, people will fail to understand why they are being advised, or even compelled, to accept restrictions or to take action which may appear inconvenient or unnecessary, and such action will be thereby less effective.

The articles in this book all deal directly or indirectly, from various points of view, with these questions. They will be of interest to people in many walks of life, for the attitudes and responses of a society to the threat of natural disasters throw into sharp relief the nature and structure of that society. Scientists and engineers have a vital role to play in discovering means of protection against the violent forces of nature. The extent to which society puts this knowledge to effective use depends upon its social, political, economic and even religious values: in other words, upon its culture.

PART I

Earthquakes

The Pacific plate and the North American plate slide past each other in fits and starts—these jerks producing earthquakes, which will in time (12 million years) locate San Francisco and Los Angeles side by side. In the face of public apathy to the threat of a large quake, scientists and officials press for neighborhood-level preparedness plans and promote further research on quake prediction.

Chapter 1
Quake Readiness: New Solutions Cut Across the Fault Lines

Marshall Ingwerson

Marshall Ingwerson is Los Angeles correspondent for the Christian Science Monitor, *covering national and regional issues in southern California and the Southwest. A native of Los Angeles, he received his B.A. in English from Principia College in southern Illinois.*

California's Crustal Plates Sliding

In 12 million years, barring unforeseen twists, San Francisco and Los Angeles, now about 400 miles apart, will sit more or less side by side.

Picture, then, riding the Bay Area Rapid Transit (BART) down Sunset Boulevard from Nob Hill into Beverly Hills, and then perhaps a monorail to Disneyland's Matterhorn. Newspaper columnists like the Bay city's Herb Caen and L.A.'s Jack Smith can carry on their quibble over which city is more livable and compelling across the backyard fence.

Obviously there is plenty of time to work out the details. Meanwhile the two cities move closer at an average speed of about two inches a year. They are each riding the edge of a moving plate of the earth's crust, and it can be a rough ride.

Like cars with sticky clutches, the Pacific plate and the North American plate slide past each other in fits and starts. They catch on rough spots along their uneven edge, the San Andreas fault zone, which cuts from just south of the San Francisco peninsula down into the Gulf of California. Then the sides break loose and spring forward to catch their pace.

And thus the sunny cities of the southern California coast slip and

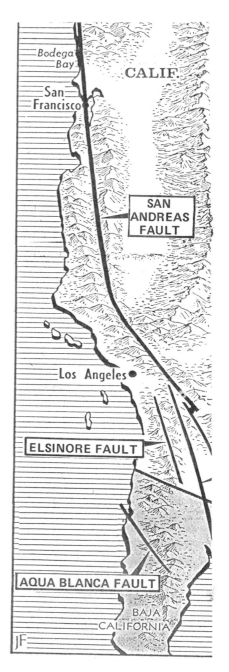

jerk northward—pulling Baja California along with them—while the rest of North America slides south.

This is the general drift of things behind the most lively earthquake zone in the contiguous United States.

It is also, of course, a huge oversimplification. But it's the framework from which explanations hang. Of the dozen or so plates that make up the earth's lithosphere, it is the restless Pacific plate—ringed by the Aleutians, Japan, New Zealand, and California—whose squirming causes the big majority of the earth's temblors.

Lately, southern Californians are being warned they are due any year for a big breaking loose of a locked southern section of the San Andreas. A great earthquake is on the way, many earth scientists say. And they stress that southern Californians are not ready for it. But they can be. Like New Englanders who build their houses to withstand the winter wind, Californians are slowly learning to build their cities so that the earth's clumsy shiftings don't have to mean disaster.

Clarence R. Allen of the California Institute of Technology (Caltech) here—one of the elder statesmen of earthquake research—flatly says it: "We can solve the earthquake problem. And we are fairly well along the road to doing that."

Public Apathy the Weakest Link

The struggle is to inspire a people to action over a risk that is not so tangible, not so immediate, to most of them. It's a puzzling priority: an imminent danger that may wait half a century.

It's an abstract notion, a great earthquake, except to those who have felt big temblors before. And in the meantime, lawns need mowing and cars need oil changes and daily life presses on.

Although southern Californians are more keenly aware of the earthquake threat now than at any time in the past decade, public apathy is still the weakest link in the readiness effort, remarks Richard Andrews, director of the year-old Southern California Earthquake Preparedness Project.

The focus of attention is sharpening. The preparedness project—a government-backed effort to set up earthquake-response plans from the neighborhood level up—is a case in point. New earthquake scenarios by the state geology department give local planners a much-needed common ground to work from. Atlantic Richfield Company recently sponsored a major conference on earthquake preparedness for business leaders in the region.

"Unprecedented," comments Dr. Andrews. "Not too long ago, respectable people didn't talk about this publicly."

Yet the U.S. is not spending much money—around $100 million a year for earthquake prediction and preparedness nationally, contrasting with Japan's more than $300 million a year over the next five years in just one region. Focusing on the quake-prone Tokai district southwest of Tokyo, the Japanese project ranges from building tsunami, or tidal wave, walls to stockpiling food and water underground. The American effort is lackluster in comparison.

The Earthquake Hazards Reduction Act—the chief U.S. program—is so far scheduled for about the same funding next year as this year, approximately $60 million. There is, however, a requested $3 million extra. This is for a study on how to set up a seismic instrument network in southern California to continuously monitor by computer the most active faults.

Dr. Andrews's basic assessment: "It is unlikely at the present level of expenditure that we can provide a short-term warning of a major earthquake."

Prediction Research Disappointing

Technology can't prevent earthquakes, although this is not beyond imagining. Some faults could theoretically be kept slipping along smoothly without big jolts by injecting water. The expense and the legal tangling would be formidable.

Better to be ready for the rumble when it comes, say experts. Hence the urgent question: When is it coming?

There are still some good, live leads in the field, but prediction research so far has been disappointing.

Like a window under the steadily building pressure of a hydraulic ram, explains Thomas L. Henley, professor of geophysics at the University of Southern California, a locked fault finally cracks at its weakest point, at a flaw. From this first break, the crack spreads along the fault at a couple of miles a second, fading as the tension of the shifting earth is relieved.

"If we knew what the stress distribution in the earth was, we could predict earthquakes pretty well," observes Dr. Henley.

But stress deep in the earth can't be picked up by remote sensors the way starlight can. Stress monitors would have to be on the spot, deep underground along a fault, and this is very expensive.

So seismologists have spent the past decade sleuthing after those more slippery clues that come to the surface. Five years ago scientists held high hopes. That was the year the Earthquake Hazards Reduction Act passed Congress, fueling an almost mission-type study effort.

The search took some exotic twists by earth scientists' standards. Researchers probed all kinds of unexplained changes tied to underground movement—in radon gas burbling from the ground, water level in wells, animal behavior, electrical resistivity in rocks, twisted or distorted land surfaces, and micro-earthquake swarms.

They are still probing these anomalies, but their connections to earthquakes have been more fickle—or at least harder to find—than expected. None of the clues have yet provided reliable signals of when the ground is beginning to move, and no one is too certain whether they will.

In a sense, scientists are coming to think there are no shortcuts to predicting earthquakes. They can't interpret clues without a better picture of how an earthquake works.

"My own opinion has changed in the last few years," admits Dr. Allen. His well-traveled briefcase plopped on a stray chair is a reminder that a geophysicist is an outdoor academician. He is chairman of the National Academy of Science's Earthquake Prediction Evaluation Council. "We put instruments all over the state without knowing what we wanted to do with them," he says of the networks of seismic monitors set up by Caltech and the U.S. Geological Survey, among others.

He now thinks seismologists need to fill in their basic understanding of earthquakes before they can read the earth's next move. Five years ago, he says, "we were overly optimistic."

Geological Ancient History Uncovered

But another line of research has far exceeded the hopes of five years ago. The geological ancient history that Kerry Sieh, a young assistant professor at Caltech, uncovered in a dried-up swamp near Palmdale now supplies the best idea scientists have of when to expect the next great shake.

For 2,000 years this bog left layers of sand and peat on its floor, which lay smack across the San Andreas fault where it passes nearest Los Angeles.

The layers left stripes, from a cutaway view. And the stripes were broken and offset along the fault where earthquakes had shifted them out of alignment. Since peat sediment can be dated using carbon 14, the stripes held the history of 2,000 years of earthquakes.

In that time there have been a dozen great earthquakes (those that score around 8 or higher on the Richter scale). They have come roughly every 150 years, with spans averaging between 125 and 225 years. Since the last one, the Fort Tejon earthquake of 1857, it has been 125 years.

In the meantime, six or seven meters of slip has stored up on this section of the fault. That much slip in an earthquake would register 8 or more on the Richter scale.

The Federal Emergency Management Agency puts the probability of a great quake coming in any given year now at 2 to 5 percent. Dr. Allen thinks this is a little high, based as it is on some creakings and groanings of the earth that no longer bode as ominous as they once did. He estimates a 1-2 percent annual likelihood, or a 20-30 percent probability in the next two decades.

More mysteriously, Dr. Sieh did similar excavations further south on the San Andreas last year, and found that this section has been quiet for 560 years. This "seismic gap" now has around 10 meters of slip stored up and no geological clue has surfaced to explain how often it breaks.

Apparently the movement of the earth along the San Andreas is highly uneven from region to region, Dr. Sieh notes, like an "uncoordinated centipede."

Tallest Buildings Safest

All appearances to the contrary, the tallest buildings in Los Angeles would be among the safest in a great earthquake.

"You'd get quite a ride," smiles George W. Housner, professor emeritus of engineering at Caltech and an eminent researcher in earthquake engineering. But the skyscrapers wouldn't fall down, he says.

Brick buildings, on the other hand, are virtually certain to fall down, Professor Housner says. There are some 8,000 unreinforced brick buildings in Los Angeles County, many of them housing lower-income families.

Much of what Dr. Housner and his colleagues know about how buildings withstand earthquakes they owe to the hard shaking that caught San Fernando, a northern Los Angeles suburb, by surprise in 1971.

Engineering models are one thing, but "the real test comes," says Dr. Housner, "when you get a good shake. In 1971 we found we were deficient."

The San Fernando quake was unexpected by geologists. It stemmed from an overlooked complication on the San Andreas. Southern California, to move northward, must turn a corner, squeezing around the deep roots of the Sierra Nevada and San Bernardino Mountains. In negotiating this "big bend" in the San Andreas—east and north of Los Angeles—the earth behaves something like a stale brownie crust and crumbles up along lesser faults throughout the region.

The San Fernando quake was an instance of the "big bend" pushing the San Gabriel Mountains up and over the Los Angeles basin.

At 6.6 on the Richter scale, scientists now agree that San Fernando gave as vigorous a shaking as an earthquake can muster. Bigger earthquakes don't shake any harder at the epicenter than a 6.5 quake does. The difference is that a bigger quake will shake longer and shake a larger area. So this made San Fernando a fair test of what happens in the eye of an earthquake. Since this chastening temblor, and largely as a result of it, the Los Angeles area has become better braced.

Now straps have been attached to 75 percent of the area's freeway overpass sections, which previously rested unattached on overlapping ledges to allow for expansion and contraction. In 1971, some of them fell down. Two hospitals collapsed. Today hospitals are subject to the same safety code that has battened down the state's schools. California dam owners must now upgrade their dams until they pass earthquake muster, since the San Fernando quake damaged one nearly to the point of bursting over the heavily populated San Fernando Valley.

The city of Los Angeles decreed last year that its several hundred unreinforced brick buildings must be strengthened or condemned. These have been considered vulnerable to earthquakes since the 1933 Long Beach quake, the one that first earned temblors notice in building codes.

The codes have come a long way. Structures of 16 stories or more must now be built on the basis of a computerized, dynamic analysis of their potential behavior in an earthquake, according to the Los Angeles building code. In contrast, the first earthquake codes of the 1930s required a building to be able to bear a lateral shove equal to 10 percent of its weight. This kind of a shove, Dr. Housner points out, is nothing at all like the shock waves of an earthquake.

Hunched over a manual typewriter in the corner of his book-lined office, Dr. Housner—chairman of the National Research Council's Committee on Earthquake Engineering Research—is drawing together a major review of the state of this research. Overall, he is optimistic.

There are key gaps in our knowledge, such as how big pieces of communications, manufacturing, and computer equipment might fare when shaken up. "But looking at it over the years," he says, "the research has made it into the codes."

"The real question in design is: What's the worst shaking you can get?"

Nuclear power plants and dams are designed to withstand the strongest of all possible earthquakes. But to design everything to that standard would be far too expensive. Dr. Housner points out that builders now spend $30 billion a year in seismic areas for earthquake preparedness. So tightening of standards spells considerable costs.

Earthquake Concern Given Boost

California is not the only earthquake zone in the U.S., but it's the most lively and the easiest to understand.

East of the Rockies, it's different. Temblors of a given strength carry farther through the ground in the East, says Clarence Allen. In the spongier geology there, faults don't break the surface.

"We have some hints in Missouri," he says regarding the geology of earthquakes there. "But we're still floundering around in Charleston. No clue in Boston."

Although California is where the quake action is in the U.S., Japan and China are much more seismically active. Accordingly, earthquakes get much more public attention in the Far East. China suffered one of the worst disasters in earthquake history in the 1976 Tangshan quake. Tangshan was a large city built of unreinforced brick. The Chinese don't have the sophisticated technology of the West, but they have some 10,000 scientists studying earthquakes and 100,000 amateurs keeping seismic data. Japan has technology and manpower.

"If there is a major breakthrough (in seismology), it could as easily happen in Japan," says Dr. Allen, chagrined at the prospect of the U.S. slacking in its leading role.

Earthquake concern here was given a boost, Dr. Andrews, of the preparedness project, figures by the debate over the mysterious Palmdale Bulge and the erupting of Mt. Saint Helens.

The Palmdale Bulge, a swelling up of a massive area of southern California between 1959 and 1974, may have been an error in surveying measurements. But some say it could be another decade before we know for sure. There have been several possible earthquake precursors, like the bulge, which California has creaked and groaned with in the past few years. But none has been followed by a significant earthquake.

Dr. Allen, meanwhile, looks down the road 20, 30, or perhaps 50 years to a time when Californians will have learned to live safely on the edges of their slipping and jerking lithospheric plates. Then, he told a recent conference of Los Angeles businessmen, they can write to friends in the East, "Come on out to California and enjoy one of nature's spectacular phenomena with us."

Defining geological plates in earthquake regions has helped scientists to group earthquake prone regions into four categories. Although plate tectonics has made it possible to predict, with some accuracy, where earthquakes are likely to occur, it still does not provide us with many clues as to when seismic activity will occur.

Chapter 2
Earthquakes and Plate Tectonics

Henry Spall

Henry Spall is a geophysicist with the U.S. Geological Survey at its national center in Reston, Virginia. He is editor of the Survey's Earthquakes *and* Volcanoes *and is currently Deputy Chief of the Survey's Office of Scientific Publications.*

The world's earthquakes are not randomly distributed over the earth's surface. They tend to be concentrated in narrow zones. Why is this? And why are volcanoes and mountain ranges also found in these zones, too?

An explanation is to be found in plate tectonics, a concept which has revolutionized thinking in the earth sciences in the last ten years. The theory of plate tectonics combines many of the ideas about continental drift (originally proposed in 1912 by Alfred Wegener in Germany) and sea-floor spreading (suggested originally by Harry Hess of Princeton University).

Plate tectonics tells us that the earth's rigid outer shell (lithosphere) is broken into a mosaic of oceanic and continental plates which can slide over the plastic aesthenosphere, which is the uppermost layer of the mantle (Figure 1). The plates are in constant motion. Where they interact, along their margins, important geological processes take place, such as the formation of mountain belts, earthquakes, and volcanoes.

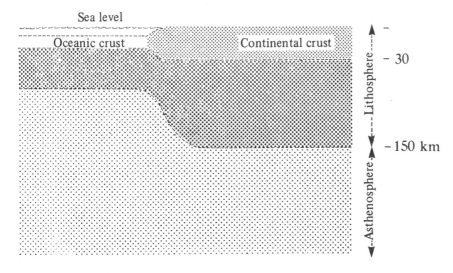

Figure 1. The oceanic and continental crusts are parts of the lithosphere.

The lithosphere covers the whole earth. Therefore, ocean plates are also involved, more particularly in the process of sea-floor spreading.

This involves the mid-ocean ridges, which are a system of narrow submarine cracks that can be traced down the centre of the major oceans. The ocean floor is being continuously pulled apart along these mid-ocean ridges. Hot volcanic material rises from the earth's mantle to fill the gap and continuously forms new oceanic crust. The earth's surface consists of a mosaic of crustal plates that are continually jostling one another (Figure 2). If the earth is not to be blown up like a balloon by the continual influx of new volcanic material at the ocean ridges, then old crust must be destroyed at the same rate where plates collide. The required balance occurs when plates collide, and one plate is forced under the other to be consumed deep in the mantle.

Most of the geological action—mountains, rift valleys, volcanoes, earthquakes, faulting—is due to different types of interaction at plate boundaries.

How are Earthquakes Connected with Plate Tectonics?

Most of the earthquakes are confined to narrow belts and these belts define the boundaries of the plates.

Plate tectonics confirms that there are four types of seismic zones. The first follows the line of mid-ocean ridges. Associated with this type of seismicity is the volcanic activity along the axis of the ridges (for example, Iceland, Azores, Tristan da Cunha).

The second type of earthquake associated with plate tectonics is the shallow-focus event unaccompanied by volcanic activity. The San Andreas fault is a good example of this; so is the Anatolian fault in northern Turkey. In these faults, two mature plates are scraping by one another. The friction between the plates can be so great that very large strains can build up before they are periodically relieved by large earthquakes. The 1906 San Francisco event was caused by breakage along the northern end of the San Andreas fault.

The third type of earthquake is related to the collision of oceanic and continental plates. One plate is thrust or subducted under the other plate so that a deep ocean trench is produced. In the Philippines, ocean trenches are associated with curved volcanic island arcs on the landward plate, for example, the Java trench. Along the Peru-Chile trench, the Pacific plate is being subducted under the South American plate which responds by crumpling to form the Andes.

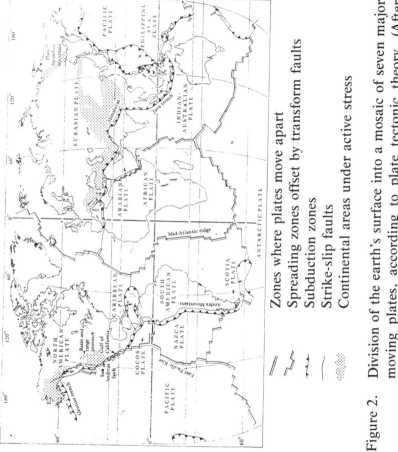

Zones where plates move apart
Spreading zones offset by transform faults
Subduction zones
Strike-slip faults
Continental areas under active stress

Figure 2. Division of the earth's surface into a mosaic of seven major moving plates, according to plate tectonic theory. (After Warren Hamilton, "Plate Tectonics and Man," in *U.S. Geological Survey Annual Report*, p. 41, U.S. Geological Survey, 1976.)

The fourth type of seismic zone occurs along the boundaries of continental plates. Typical of this is the broad swath of seismicity from Burma to the Mediterranean, crossing the Himalayas, Iran, Turkey to Gibraltar. Within this zone, shallow earthquakes are associated with high mountain ranges where intense compression is taking place. Intermediate- and deep-focus earthquakes also occur and are known in the Himalayas and in the Caucasus. The interiors of continental plates are very complex, much more so than island arcs. For instance, we do not yet know the full relationship of the Alps or the East African rift system to the broad picture of plate tectonics.

How can Plate Tectonics Help in Earthquake Prediction?

We have seen that earthquakes occur at the following three kinds of plate boundary: ocean ridges where the plates are pulled apart, margins where the plates scrape past one another, and margins where one plate is thrust under the other. Thus, we can predict the general regions on the earth's surface where we can expect large earthquakes in the future. We know that each year about 140 earthquakes of magnitude 6 or greater will occur within this area which is 10 percent of the earth's surface.

But on a worldwide basis we cannot say with much accuracy when these events will occur. The reason is that the processes in plate tectonics have been going on for millions of years. Averaged over this interval, plate motions amount to several millimetres per year. But at any instant in geologic time, for example the year 1982, we do not know exactly where we are in the worldwide cycle of strain build-up and strain release. Only by monitoring the stress and strain in small areas, for instance, the San Andreas fault, in great detail can we hope to predict when renewed activity in that part of the plate tectonics arena is likely to take place.

In short, plate tectonics is a blunt but nevertheless strong tool in earthquake prediction. It tells us where 90 percent of the earth's major earthquakes are likely to occur. It cannot tell us much about exactly when they will occur. For that, we must study in detail the plate boundaries themselves. Perhaps the most important role of plate tectonics is that of a guide to the use of finer techniques for earthquake prediction.

Do volcanoes and earthquakes give us signals as to their upcoming activity? Scientists find that monitoring hydrogen outgassing preceding seismic events shows an increase in H_2 levels, thus providing evidence of probable seismic activity.

Chapter 3
Chemical Signals May Help Predict Volcanoes, Earthquakes

Reprinted by permission, *Chemical & Engineering News*, January 7, 1985.

Increases in H2 have preceded seismic events; scientists monitor hydrogen outgassing, radon levels for evidence of upcoming seismic activity

Data from monitoring stations in the continental U.S., Hawaii, and Japan all suggest that volcanoes, earthquakes, and other major seismic events give off detectable chemical signals before they occur. Used in conjunction with seismic monitoring techniques, these chemical signals could one day play an important role in predicting and preparing for geologic disasters.

"We're not sure yet of all the circumstances that have to be met for us to be sure of our predictions," geologist Kenneth A. McGee told the International Chemical Congress of Pacific Basin Societies, held in Honolulu last month. "But we are most encouraged by what we have found so far," says the deputy scientist in charge of the U.S. Geological Survey's Cascades Volcano Observatory in Vancouver, Wash.

For several years USGS scientists have been monitoring volcanic areas—such as Mount St. Helens in Washington, Kilauea and Mauna Loa in Hawaii, and the Long Valley Caldera in California—for hydrogen gas emissions and transmitting these data to the Cascades observatory for daily analysis. Since 1980 they also have been monitoring active earthquake faults in California to see if seismic activity in these regions can be correlated with earlier hydrogen release.

"Available data suggest that hydrogen gas is released from a volcanic system in a smooth diurnal pattern during periods of low seismic activity," McGee explains. "On occasion, however, this pattern is punctuated by large pulselike increases in hydrogen emission lasting up to several hours. Most of these gas events appear to be associated with either eruptions or distinct increases in seismicity, and they occur typically a few days prior to the eruption or seismic event." During one of these pulses, hydrogen emissions can rise to more than 10 times their diurnal level.

McGee believes the hydrogen escapes from deep within Earth when movements within the magma cause microfracturing of the crust below its surface. The seismic energy released during such microfracturing is probably too low to be detected by most geothermal monitoring techniques, but such microfracturing is often followed by larger fracturing of the crust, and, shortly afterwards, by volcanic eruption.

For example, in late December 1982, monitoring stations at the summit and along the east rift zone of Kilauea volcano in Hawaii picked up an anomalously high value for hydrogen outgassing, and on Jan. 3, the first in a series of outbreaks of lava occurred in that volcano. Since then there have been more than 20 additional outbreaks of lava from that volcano, all associated with the same fracturing of Earth's crust.

Almost all of the seismic events that have occurred at or near monitoring stations were preceded by increases in hydrogen gas emissions, McGee says, although sometimes hydrogen emissions rise and no detectable seismic event follows. McGee does not find these "false positives" disturbing, however. He thinks they may signal real, microfracturing events that were never followed by larger, more serious fracturing of Earth's crust.

Data from 15 monitoring stations along active, earthquake-producing faults in California suggest that hydrogen outgassing may also be a useful indicator of earthquake activity, says Motoaki Sato, a geochemist with USGS in Reston, Va. "We have accumulated enough data in the past four years to say, with a reasonable amount of confidence, that monitoring of hydrogen may help us understand the triggering mechanism of a damaging earthquake in tectonically active areas," Sato says. He is careful not to claim that hydrogen monitoring data are reliable enough now to be able to predict when and where earthquakes will occur. However, he says, "the first step towards accurate forecasting is to understand how a large earthquake is triggered."

Sato has his own hypothesis of what triggers an earthquake. It is based on hydrogen monitoring data as well as other geochemical and geophysical information about earthquakes. Plate tectonic theory helps explain how mantle convection can create stress in the seismic belts of the world, and how that stress facilitates the loss of heat from Earth's interior. In addition, the recent discovery that Venus has no surface features associated with plate tectonics and also no water on its surface suggests that water plays a role in making plate tectonics possible.

Sato proposes that the hydrogen anomalies that occur prior to large earthquakes are triggered by plastic intrusions of a type of rock called serpentinite into fault zones. Serpentinite is formed by hydration of igneous rocks rich in magnesium and iron, and hydrogen gas is generated in the process. "Serpentinites, as slippery as the name suggests, are known to move around comparatively easily," Sato explains. "As substantial amounts of serpentinites are squeezed into the fault zone, the fault becomes lubricated, and eventually the fault blocks slip with a jolt in the direction of the existing stress dictated by plate tectonics," he suggests.

The hydrogen monitors used in both of these projects were developed by Sato in the 1970s. The sensor is essentially a small hydrogen-oxygen fuel cell that generates a voltage across a load resistor when hydrogen molecules hit the external electrode surface. Oxygen is supplied to the interior electrode from a high-pressure cylinder, so no electrical power is required to operate the sensor. Data are collected at least once every 10 minutes and transmitted to central data banks for analysis.

Japanese geochemists also are monitoring hydrogen gas emissions in several seismically active regions of Japan to determine their usefulness as predictors of seismic events. Hiroshi Satake and coworkers at Toyama University, for example, have been monitoring hydrogen in soil gases at the Atotsugawa and Ushikubi faults since 1981. Both are active fault zones in north central Honshu. About 1,000 measurable earthquakes occur each year along the more active of the two faults, Atotsugawa, although most of these earthquakes have a magnitude of less than 3.

The biggest earthquake to occur during the observation period, a 7.7-magnitude earthquake on May 26, 1983, was preceded by elevated hydrogen levels on May 18 at three of five monitoring stations.

Hydrogen levels at the remaining two stations did not peak until June 5, nearly two weeks after the earthquake, pointing out some of the potential difficulties in using hydrogen gas emissions to predict earthquakes. Satake thinks that the hydrogen detected at these sites was produced during the earthquake itself, not beforehand, by reaction of groundwater with fractured silicate rocks. Because of the structure of the particular fault zone, the gas did not reach the monitoring stations until June 5. The time of discharging of hydrogen can vary greatly from one fault to another, he suggests, making only some of them useful for predicting earthquake activity.

Hydrogen is not the only gas geochemists monitor for evidence of upcoming seismic activity. Donald M. Thomas, a geochemist at the University of Hawaii and the Hawaii Institute of Geophysics, has been working with colleagues there and at the University of Auckland, New Zealand, to monitor radon concentrations in soil gases at the Kilauea volcano in Hawaii. This monitoring, which has been taking place since

1979, is less extensive than the hydrogen monitoring program. Nevertheless, radon, too, looks like a promising indicator of upcoming seismic activity.

Radon, an inert gas, is naturally present in crustal rock, Thomas explains. Changes in stress on the rock deform it very slightly, allowing radon to escape. "Apparently there is a critical point at which the radon release increases substantially, after which the earthquake occurs," Thomas says.

Radon is radioactive, emitting alpha particles, which can be detected by sensitive films. The geochemists monitor its release by placing strips of these films in inverted plastic cups buried vertically at least 40 cm in the soil. The films are exposed for periods ranging from two to eight weeks at each monitoring site.

One of the best examples seen in the Kilauea study of radon's potential for predicting earthquakes occurred in 1983 when radon emissions at the Kaoiki fault monitoring stations rose substantially from about August to November, reaching the highest levels ever observed at these stations. In November, an earthquake of magnitude 6.7 occurred in this fault zone, with its epicenter about 17 km from the monitoring station that recorded the greatest radon anomalies. These anomalies occurred at least three weeks prior to the earthquake.

Radon concentrations appear to rise during volcanic eruptions, too, Thomas says. Unfortunately, the rise seems to occur simultaneously with the eruption so that radon concentrations may not be useful as a predictive tool for these events.

Greater attention to geophysical, geochemical and biological anomalies is lending increased reliability to the methods and techniques of earthquake prediction. But this technical advance must be accompanied by improved understanding of public behaviour in the face of a warning if lives are to be saved when an earthquake occurs.

Chapter 4
Earthquake Prediction and Public Response

K. Kitazawa

K. Kitazawa, a Japanese geophysicist, was educated in physics at the Gakushu-in University in Tokyo, where he received a Ph.D. degree in physics in 1968. After carrying on research on submarine geophysics (mainly geomagnetism) at the Ocean Research Institute of the University of Tokyo, he joined Unesco in 1976 first with the natural-hazard programme and, more recently, with the Intergovernmental Oceanographic Commission.

Introduction

Interest in earthquake prediction has increased rapidly in the last twenty years following early efforts along this line initiated by seismologists in the United States and Japan. A proposal for earthquake prediction research first appeared in Japan in 1962 and in the United States in 1965. After experiencing severe earthquakes of magnitude 6.8 and 7.2 at Xingtai, about 300 km southwest of Beijing, in March 1966, the Chinese Government initiated a national programme for prevention of earthquake losses.

It is noteworthy that in the early stage these projects were called earthquake-prediction research projects, but soon dropped the word "research." This may have been encouraged by the notable success of the Chinese in predicting several major earthquakes of magnitude about 7 in 1975 and 1976 on which basis effective civil defense actions were taken. The truth is of course that completely reliable techniques of earthquake prediction cannot yet be said to exist. Efforts to make reliable forecasts of seismic vulnerability use both historical data and the rapidly developing knowledge of the physical mechanisms of the earth's crust. The relevant earth sciences recently showed the possibility of using careful observation and analysis of phenomena to achieve high precision in indicating an imminent earthquake.

Phenomena that are forerunners of an earthquake—geophysical, geochemical, and biological anomalies—have been the subject of reports for many years. The recent rapid buildup of networks of observatories in earthquake-prone areas has greatly increased the rate of detection of these anomalies (which are listed in this article). The relation between precursor time and magnitude of a quake is shown in Figure 1. Much interest attaches to this relationship but its exact formulation and the physical meaning of precursors still eludes us, a reminder that it has perhaps been premature to drop the word "research" in the title of these efforts at prediction.

Earthquake Prediction Experiences in China

Following the major earthquake at Xingtai, China established a national earthquake programme with the dual aim of preventing loss of life and mitigating property damage. Earthquake prediction was given high priority and wide publicity by the Chinese Government. This

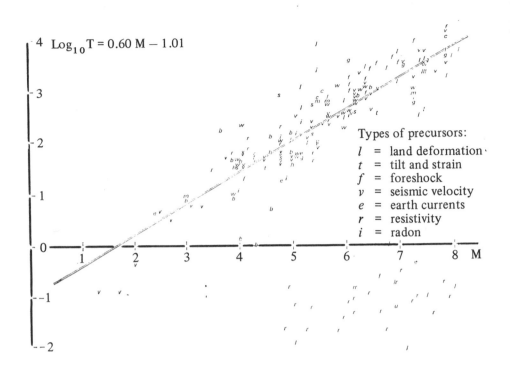

Figure 1. Relation between precursor time (in days) and magnitude of main shock.

ensured not only adequate financial and administrative support for the programme, but convinced the people that a working programme of prediction was necessary and feasible. This programme is being carried out not only by a few specialists but also by a large number of ordinary people: farmers, factory workers, students, etc.

An essential part of the prediction scheme is the State Seismological Bureau created in 1970. This bureau, composed of institutes of geophysics and geology, is the responsible body for basic research on seismology.

In the period 1975/76, Chinese scientists predicted four disastrous earthquakes of magnitude about 7. The most remarkable results of the Chinese earthquake programme are its success in issuing imminent predictions and in taking appropriate decisions for evacuation of inhabitants. Among successful predictions, the Songpan-Pingwu (Sichuan) earthquake of August 1976 is noteworthy. Imminent predictions were made for the different earthquakes, the second occuring six days after the first and the third appearing thirty hours after (each at different epicentres).

The following descriptions of two examples of Chinese efforts at earthquake prediction underscore the great difficulty in ensuring practical application of these predictive efforts. Even in China, where a strategy on such predictive work has been adopted, the methods of prediction are still in a formative stage.

The Haicheng Earthquake of 4 February 1975

The town of Haicheng, with a population of about 100,000, in Liaoning Province in northeast China, was struck by an earthquake of magnitude 7.3 at 7.36 p.m. (local time) on 4 February 1975. Damage in Haicheng and adjacent towns was extensive but very few lives were lost even though the area was highly populated. This was a result of the successful prediction of the earthquake by Chinese scientists and of appropriate action by the local authorities in evacuating inhabitants to safer surroundings. This is the first time in the world a destructive earthquake had been predicted with a certainty great enough to enable civil actions to be carried out. Although there are other examples of earthquake prediction around the world, only in China has proper action to save lives been taken. Most of these other examples were merely the presumptions of scientists.

In the case of the Haicheng earthquake, the prediction was a systematically conducted effort allowing administrative measures to be based on scientifically certified information. The level of risk was determined at periodic intervals, when increasingly accurate estimations of the time, place, and magnitude of the earthquake were made. Three stages marked this prediction effort, as the following account shows.

In 1970 or earlier, the State Seismological Bureau identified Liaoning Province as a high earthquake-prone area. This might be considered as "long-term prediction." This was largely the outcome of basic seismic studies, especially those on the migration of earlier large earthquakes in the area. Because this area was of high industrial importance (a centre of heavy industry), the State Seismological Bureau urged fuller investigations including geologic and tectonic surveys, long-base-line measurements of tilt and gravity, and also geomagnetic surveys. Additionally, fourteen new seismological observatories were installed in the area between 1970 and 1974.

In June 1974 the local seismological commission pointed out on the basis of deformation studies that a strong earthquake might occur in the northern part of the Gulf of Bohai within one or two years. A "medium-term prediction" was then issued by the Revolutionary Committee of Liaoning Province. A public information campaign was activated, disseminating basic knowledge about earthquakes, particularly about the origin of earthquakes. The need for wide co-operation throughout the region in aiding earthquake prediction was stressed. For example, abnormal behavior in animals (snakes, housemice, dogs, horses, etc.) were to be reported. This elicited an overwhelming response from the public.

On 20 December, the Revolutionary Committee of Liaoning Province was told to expect an earthquake of up to magnitude 5, at which point the committee announced a "short-term prediction." Two days later, an earthquake of magnitude 4.8 occurred near Kiaoyang (70 km north of Haicheng) but since tilt and other anomalies continued to increase after seventeen months of tilt anomaly, it was considered that this quake was not yet the one predicted.

In mid-January 1975, the State Seismological Bureau held a national meeting on earthquake prediction when it was concluded that an earthquake of magnitude 6 or more could occur in the area of Yingkou-Gin Xian in the first half of 1975. Reports on abnormal animal behaviour, on groundwater levels, and on the rising or lowering of well-water levels continued to come in with increasing frequency. On 30 January, the ground tilt at Shenyang Seismological Observatory suddenly changed its direction from southeast to southwest. Beginning on 1 February, an increase in the number of micro-earthquakes occurring in the Yinkon-Haicheng area was noted. These increased gradually until noon of 4 February. The morning hours of that day were marked by earthquakes of magnitude of 4.3 and 4.7 and at noon the micro-earthquake activity suddenly decreased. At 2 p.m., a general warning was issued and inhabitants were moved to the evacuation camp. The main shock of magnitude 7.3 hit the area at 7.36 p.m., as quoted above, with little loss of life occurring, thanks to these public safety measures.

The Tangshan Earthquake of 28 July 1976

In contrast to the successful example above, the following is an account of failure in predictive effort. A catastrophic earthquake of magnitude 7.8 struck Tangshan, a city of about a million inhabitants located 150 km east of Beijing, at 3.43 a.m. (local time) on 28 July 1976. It was reported that 98 percent of the residential buildings and 90 percent of the industrial structures in the city were completely destroyed. Loss of life from the earthquake was estimated by authorities to be about 240,000 with 164,000 people severely injured.

It is widely known that, in this instance, no imminent earthquake warning had been issued. Long, medium, and short term predictions had, however, been announced on the basis of geophysical aspects. In June 1974 the State Seismological Bureau had called a meeting to discuss the possibility of future earthquakes in the northern China-Gulf of Bohai area. The meeting found that anomalies in the leveling, gravity, and groundwater level, as well as the tendency of westward migration of seismicity in the area, all pointed to a destructive earthquake in northern Bohai. At the same time, the possibility of a magnitude 5 or 6 earthquake in the Beijing-Tianjin area within a few years was pointed out.

A "medium-term prediction" had been made in mid-1975. Remarkable changes in ground tilt, radon content in groundwaters, level of wells, etc., had been observed in this period. The State Seismological Bureau advised the government authorities concerned that a destructive earthquake would occur in the area of Tianjin-Beijing-Tangshan within two years, and advised that necessary measures to reduce earthquake hazard should therefore be taken at each factory.

A January 1976 study of seismic activities in the region by the Provincial Seismological Bureau found the earthquake-prone area too widely spread out to focus on any particular areas for issuance of an imminent warning. However, there were obvious increases of geophysical and geochemical anomalies in the ground conditions in early April. Also, an earthquake of magnitude 6.3 occurred about 300 km west of Beijing on 6 April, followed two weeks later by a magnitude 4.4 earthquake 70 km to the south at Tranjin. No remarkable seismic activity was observed in the Tankshan area, however.

On the other hand, various anomalies which could be considered as precursors of earthquakes were observed in the Tangshan area. Two weeks before the 28 July earthquake, a sudden increase and decrease in radon content in groundwater were reported from an observatory situated 130 km from the epicentre. Furthermore, over 2,000 cases of anomalous animal behaviour were reported, 80 percent of them appearing only one day before the major earthquake.

Even though a seismologist team observed these remarkable precursors before the earthquake, no imminent prediction was issued. The following reasons have been given for this: (a) most of the macroscopic anomalies appeared rather late in comparison with the Haichen earthquake; (b) no remarkable foreshocks were observed; and (c) anomalies were observed in a wide area and their appearance mode was complicated.

International Experimental Sites for Earthquake Prediction Research

Although research on earthquake prediction has been carried out by a large number of scientists in many countries, the present stage of methods and techniques for predicting earthquakes is still at the trial-and-error level with no absolutely certain strategy anywhere in the world. Scientists gathering at the Unesco symposium on earthquake prediction in April 1979 broached the need to create a truly international experimental field for earthquake prediction study in which different research teams could work together. For instance, some of the precursors are clearly observed in one area but do not appear in other places owing to the differences in the nature of an earthquake and to variations in geological and geotectonical conditions. In the experimental field, teams of scientists would identify the precursors considered most effective to predict an earthquake.

These scientists therefore recommended that, in order to accelerate the collection of high-quality observational field data required for progress in earthquake prediction, Unesco should develop a mechanism enabling countries to offer highly seismic areas of their territory for long-term study as international experimental sites. The group also requested that such experimental sites be located in regions where large earthquakes are expected within the next ten to twenty years.

The idea behind these international experimental sites is to encourage broad participation by teams from different countries in the study of a given area followed by a comparison of their results. Such sites can become prototypes for experimental work in other regions. One outcome of these experimental studies should be the more rapid improvement of prediction techniques than would otherwise be the case.

This recommendation for international experimental sites was further considered by an ad hoc working group of ten seismologists which was convened jointly by Unesco and the International Association of Seismology and Physics of the Earth's Interior (IASPE) at the July 1981 General Assembly of the association in Ontario (Canada). The ad hoc group considered that, in general, the availability of background and base-line information is very important from the long-term viewpoint. They asked that, in the selection of experimental sites, attention be put on three classes of geotectonic settings: subduction zones, transform faults and intra-plate areas. The characteristics of seismicity and other conditions are substantially different in the three classes of setting, and to this extent, different experimental problems will be encountered.

The ad hoc group specified the main considerations to be taken into account in choosing experimental sites:

- High seismic activity and high potential for large earthquakes

- Availability of a geological map

- Availability of a geotectonic map and neotectonic map

- Good bedrock conditions for installation of instruments

- Adequate earthquake catalogues (instrumental catalogues for at least ten years and historical catalogues)

- Possibility of drilling bore-holes

- Site to include an adequate area of land ($10^4 km^2$ minimum)

- Possibility of using telemetry

- Accessibility and transportation

- Availability of the following ancillary materials:

    — seismic zoning map;
    — hydrological map
    — previous geodetic surveys

Seismotectonic conditions should be such that earthquakes more than 6 in magnitude are expected, since this is the threshold above which earthquakes may have a great impact on human society. The importance of prediction, of course, increases with the density of population in the high-risk region. The objective of research at experimental sites is not, however, primarily to make practical predictions but to advance the study of precursory phenomena through international co-operation.

Whilst it is important to establish experimental sites in each of the three principal types of geotectonic areas, the project as a whole should aim at concentrating rather than dispersing the available international resources of research equipment and manpower.

Techniques Available for Experiments

The ad hoc group listed the following techniques relevant to earthquake-prediction research and suitable for application at the intended experimental sites:

- Crustal deformation techniques

    — repeated levelling and trilateration (the advent of space-age geodesy should facilitate such studies in the future)
    — tilt and strain
    — repeated gravity measurement as microgal* sensitivity
    — tide-gauge observations

    * Unit of gravity.

- Seismological techniques

    — space and time distribution of earthquakes
    — investigations of foreshocks
    — acoustic emission

- *In situ* stress measurement

- Electric and magnetic techniques

- Groundwater measurements

- Animal behaviour

The ad hoc group also specified the need for meteorological stations, for data centres, and for laboratory studies of properties of rocks from a site.

Guidelines for International Co-operation

At the conclusion of its consideration of the experimental sites programmes, the ad hoc committee turned to the issue of general guidelines for agreement on international co-operation, including procedures for exchange of data and publication of research results, access for participating scientists to experimental sites, and import and export of equipment.

In particular, the committee considered it essential to draw up guidelines for the formulation, evaluation and communication of earthquake predictions to which host countries and participating institutions would be asked to signify their agreement. This matter was then presented to the IASPEI Assembly, which among its resolutions passed one calling for the world seismological community to develop a code of practice on the formulation, assessment, and communication of earthquake predictions, especially when the crossing of international boundaries is involved.

Social Aspects of Earthquake Prediction

Once an earthquake prediction has been issued, it cannot be "business as usual" for the community so forewarned. Unfortunately for all concerned, too little is known at present about the underlying socio-psychological phenomena stirred up by this warning or about the techniques and administrative measures for carrying out effective civil defense. Little is understood about how and when such a prediction should be released to the public, particularly through the mass media. A recent episode in Peru illustrates the problem of our ignorance along these lines.

In early 1980, an individual scientist predicted that a gigantic earthquake of magnitude about 8 would occur in the offshore subduction zone along the Pacific coast of South America in mid-August 1981. He positioned the event to occur near the city of Lima, Peru, and to run south for about 1,400 km. A while later he fixed the date of this quake as 10 August 1981.

This scientist was an experienced experimental physicist and based this particular prediction on his studies of rock fracture, carried out in his laboratory as well as through observations at mining sites. He indicated that the major earthquake would be preceded by a series of minor forerunning quakes of about 4 in magnitude.

As it turned out, in the period leading up to the date of the predicted large quake, the worldwide seismological observatory network failed to record any of the suggested forerunning shocks, although the local Peruvian network did detect two tremors very much smaller than his prediction.

In January 1981, the Peruvian Government sought the advice of the United States National Earthquake Prediction Evaluation Council concerning this scientist's prediction of a giant earthquake in mid-1981. The council indicated that this prediction was based on speculative and vague evidence and should therefore be disregarded. Despite this advice, Peruvian society continued to give credence to the prediction. On a day when one of the foreshocks was supposed to have occurred, the city of Lima was peculiarly quiet, many of those with the money to do so having arranged to travel elsewhere. Even the visit to Lima on that day by the vice-chairman of the United States Council and his reassurances given through the local press had little or no influence with the believing public. It is now historical record, of course, that 10 August came and went without the occurrence of the predicted cataclysm.

Conclusion

Earthquake prediction techniques are still at a formative stage requiring widespread and intensive co-operation among scientists in advancing knowledge of these techniques and methods. The international co-operative investigations that should be possible through the proposed programme on experimental sites are expected to speed this advance of knowledge considerably. At the same time, study must also be given to the socio-economic aspects of issuing earthquake warnings in a community. Such studies should be pursued by those in government responsible for organizing civil defense measures in times of disaster or, better, disaster warning, to ascertain just when and how a warning should be issued and communicated to the public.

The relationship between scientific prediction and public information is a delicate matter as the Peruvian episode above reveals. There it was clearly a case of inadequate consultation between government and mass media. There are other instances known of a foreign scientist making a prediction to a local community. In Japan, a group of civil defense officers and local members of the press have studied this problem of information and hazard warnings and, after a year of discussion, have reached a temporary agreement on a so-called thirty-minute rule, which holds the mass media to observe a thirty-minute delay in reporting any prediction supplied to them by the earthquake evaluation committee.

There is no question as to the responsibility of scientists to study natural hazards, not only earthquakes but also volcanic eruptions, landslides, and so on. Scientists should be entirely free to pursue the study of these phenomena by whatever methods and procedures they find necessary. Moreover, the scientific community has an obligation to evaluate these studies and to reach consensus on the gravity and nature of any danger to the public they see. In few countries, however, are scientists required to inform government authorities about such dangers, particularly about predictions they have validated. It is a most urgent matter to evolve guidelines on this co-operative relationship that must exist between the groups involved in natural-hazard prediction: scientists, both natural and social; government authorities, especially those concerned with civil defense; and the mass media, press, radio, and television.

References

Earthquake Prediction and Public Policy. Washington, D.C., National Academy of Sciences, 1975.
Gere, J.; Shah, H. (eds.). *The 1976 Tangshan, China, Earthquake.* San Francisco, Earthquake Engineering Research Institute, 1980.
Proceedings of the International Symposium on Earthquake Prediction. Terra Scientific Publishing Company, Tokyo and Paris, 1981.
Public Information Aspects. *Disaster Prevention and Mitigation*, Vol. 10. Geneva, United Nations Disaster Relief Organization (UNDRO), 1979.
Rikitake, T. *Earthquake Forecasting and Warning.* Tokyo, Dordecht, the Netherlands, Center for Academic Publications and A. Reidel Publishing Company, 1982.

Land subsidence, or land surface settling, is a natural phenomenon which occurs all over the world. It often results also from man's activities, such as the extraction of water, oil or gas from underground sources. But whether of natural or man-made causes, the effects of land subsidence are almost always undesirable, ranging from minor changes in the landscape to major damage to structures or the environment itself. Often, these deleterious effects do not become evident until long after their cause has been set in motion.

The author explains some of the processes involved in subsidence, and then reviews examples of sinkings drawn from a variety of sites and situations around the globe.

Chapter 5
Land Subsidence: A Worldwide Environmental Hazard

Laura Carbognin

Laura Carbognin is statistician and senior scientist in the Division of Geology at the Institute for the Study of the Dynamics of Large Masses of the National Research Council (CNR) in Venice, Italy.

Reprinted with permission from *Nature and Resources*, Vol. XXI, No. 1, January-March 1985, Copyright 1985, UNESCO.

Land subsidence is the surface sign, and the last step, of a variety of subsurface displacement processes. The word "subsidence," in its common use, merely indicates vertical, downward movement independent from the causal mechanism of its occurrence, areal extent, or rate of movement.

Land subsidence is associated with natural causes that constitute the geological history of the affected area (geological or natural subsidence) but it can be accelerated or even set in motion, by human intervention (man-induced subsidence).

Among the most common natural causes which lead to subsidence, we can enumerate:

1. Deep-seated tectonic movement, volcanic activity, earthquakes, and isostasy.

2. Compaction (i.e. the decrease in thickness) of recent, fine-grained deposits subjected to the loading of the overlying sediments (overburden), or by vibration during earthquakes.

3. Drying-up of lacustrine basins due to natural evolution of the environment, and oxidation of highly organic soils.

The most common man-made subsidence results from:

1. Removal of fluids from the subsoil, i.e.:

   (a) withdrawal of groundwater, thermal water and gas bearing water, causing a decline of the water head;

   (b) pumping of crude oil, natural gas, oil and associated gas, causing underground pressure depletion.

2. Compaction of fine sediments induced by:

   (a) application of water. Some unconsolidated dry deposits collapse when wetted: this process is referred to as hydrocompaction or shallow subsidence;

   (b) land drainage and reclamation and biochemical oxidation of peat and organic soils;

(c) loading by buildings or other engineering structures and vibration on sediments.

3. Mineral mining.

The largest and most remarkable instances of man-induced subsidence have been caused by the pumping of subsurface fluids. Such a phenomenon was first observed in Galveston Bay, Texas, in the early 1920s, where subsidence occurred above the Goose Creek oil field. The pumping of petroleum from the underlying strata caused the land to sink simultaneously, and cracks at the ground surface appeared quite suddenly.

But now pockets and regions of land sinking attributable to the same basic cause are a far more common phenomenon over the earth. In fact, in the last decades, with the growing need for water and energy to accommodate industrial, urban and agricultural developments, man has come to rely increasingly on underground resources, often extracting them imprudently.

It must, however, be mentioned that fluid exploitations will produce land subsidence only under certain geological conditions, in general, where the deposits involved are mostly composed of unconsolidated late Cenozoic and Neozoic sediments of high initial porosity. Almost all the subsiding areas where strata are tapped, are characterized by underlying, semi-confined or confined aquifers made up of sand/or gravel of high permeability and low compressibility, interbedded with layers of clay and/or silt of low vertical permeability and high compressibility (aquitards). The aquifers and aquitards are of variable thicknesses.

The Subsoil and Mechanism of Subsidence

Even though there are many differences between the extraction of water from that of other fluids, the principles involved in the mechanics of land subsidence are nonetheless the same. The variables of the system, among which are the size of the reservoirs, the lithologic nature of the deposits, their depth and physical characteristics, the effective tension and its increase and the time of subjection to the increase, determine the "nature" of the subsidence.

Since water is by far the most common fluid met with in the subsoil, the the most exploited, let us see what happens after tapping the aquifers.

To understand the mechanism of land subsidence better, it is essential to have some idea of the structure of the subsoil. The types of sediment common to the entire zones of subsidence are:

- *Sand and gravel.* A loose non-coherent material consisting of small rock and mineral particles, distinguishable by the naked eye. Gravels are different from sands, having larger particles. Layers of these materials are the source of productive aquifers, due to their high permeability. When subjected to loadings their behaviour is essentially elastic.

- *Silt.* Rock fragment, mineral, or detrital particles with little or no plasticity. The silts, that are not very permeable, are an intermediate aggregate between sands and clay, i.e. with a diameter smaller than fine sand and larger than coarse clay.

- *Clay.* An aggregate of microscopic particles which originated from the chemical degradation of rock components. It is formed primarily of silicon, aluminum, water, iron, alkalies, etc. It develops plasticity when a limited amount of water is present. The permeability of clay is very, very low.

- *Peat.* A dark brown or black aggregate of macroscopic fragments produced by the decomposition and disintegration of any vegetative organic matter (moss, trees, etc.). It is highly compressible.

The particles of all these materials have dimensions that vary from a pebble to a large molecule. In particular, coarse soils are composed of granules of about 0.06 mm in diameter, still visible with a magnifying glass; silt contains granules between 0.06 mm and 2μ ($1\mu = 0.001$ mm) that can only be observed with a microscope and clay is composed of granules smaller than 2μ. In the subsoil it is difficult to find an aggregate in a pure form; generally there are mixed types such as silty-sand, clayey-silt, sandy-clay, etc.

In subsidence the basic physical characteristics which the behaviour of the subsoil depends on are permeability and consolidation.

The *permeability* of a material is its capacity to transmit water (or other fluids) under pressure; it is dependent on the size and shape and interconnection of the spaces (pores) in the porous medium. The degree of permeability of a soil is defined in relation to the facility of water to flow through these pores. This is expressed by the permeability coefficient, commonly evaluated in the laboratory by observing the rate of movement of fluid through a determined sample of material. Indeed, the coefficient is higher for the coarse material and lower for fine-grained sediments.

Consolidation is the gradual reduction of the soil volume when underground equilibrium conditions are disturbed. Strictly speaking consolidation is the gradual reduction in water content of a soil, as a result of an increase in load, while compaction is the decrease in the volume as a result of the same cause. Compaction, as used by engineers, is synonymous with "one-dimensional consolidation." In a broad sense, the terms "consolidation" and "compaction" are used with the same meaning, and "compressibility" means only the aptitude of a soil to be deformed.

When a new pressure is exerted on layers, for example by the overloading of new sediments or any external load, the particles are pushed together, the water content of the sediment is squeezed out, the volume decreases and the deposit undergoes compaction. The same process occurs when the hydrostatic pressure of the water percolating in the pores of sediments is reduced after pumping begins.

To evaluate compaction, a laboratory test called the oedometric test is usually performed on undisturbed samples of representative fine-grained deposits. The coefficient of consolidation expresses the rate of consolidation under a load increase. In the process of compaction, part of the energy is spent in the breakdown of the "flow" structures of the particles and part is absorbed by the work of elastic deformation. This means that if the hydrostatic pressure is increased, one may observe that the water content and volume also begin to increase. In sand, where the flow structure is absent, the greatest part of the energy is spent in elastic deformation which is reversible; in clay, on the contrary, the greatest part of the energy is spent in the permanent breakdown of the flocculation structure, and the deformation is almost completely irreversible.

While the law of permeability of a porous medium had already been formulated in 1856, on the basis of the experiments by the French hydraulic engineer Henry Darcy, the "reaction" of an aquifer system to any, more or less rapid, perturbation could only be completely understood when Karl Terzaghi developed his theory of vertical consolidation in 1923, introducing the fundamental principle of "effective stress." This principle, valid for any depth, states that the total overburden load (geostatic pressure or total stress), σc, of a vertical column of unit cross section is sustained partly by the hydrostatic pressure (neutral stress), p, of the water in the pores of the porous medium, and partly by the intergranular pressure (effective stress), σz, that is by the forces which the grains exchange among themselves on contact. The formula is quite simple:

$$\sigma c = p + \sigma z$$

but the concept it expresses is of paramount importance. The total load per unit area, σc, is constant for each determined depth; when a variation in subsurface flow occurs, it is accompanied by a variation in p, then σz must vary. That is, if the pressure in a water-bearing stratum decreases, the intergranular stress must increase. Experience has demonstrated that while the variations of p have negligible effects on the deformation of the subsoil, an increase of σz causes the beds to compact.

From a practical point of view one can say: a pumping well produces a disturbance that propagates its effect, namely, the pressure head decline, in space and time, through the hydrogeological system (Figure 1 (a)). The reduction of the pore pressure at any point in the subsurface system increases the effective intergranular stress (Figure 1 (b)), under whose influence the formations compact—the amount of compaction being proportional to the compressibility of the compacting unit—and last step, the ground surface sinks taking the shape of a bowl centred above the point of maximum withdrawal (Figure 1 (c)).

This is valid for poorly consolidated soils; if on the contrary, the formation is well-consolidated, i.e. if the grains are strongly held together, it will retain its structure after the water has been withdrawn, without any subsidence.

What this means then is that because layers of sand and gravel (aquifers) compact quite elastically, their compaction is very negligible owing to their low compressibility. On the other hand, the clayey and silty layers (aquitards) that separate aquifers are highly compressible and will undergo significant compaction which is mostly non-recoverable.

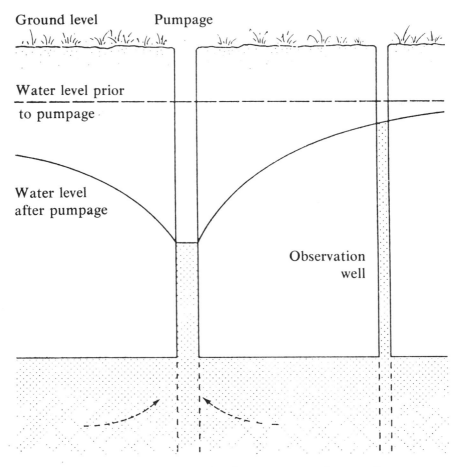

Figure 1(a). Water withdrawal from a pumping well creates a
disturbance in the pre-existing hydrodynamic equilibrium
and generates a cone of depression.

Field Measurements of Subsidence

As previously pointed out, land subsidence at the surface is the
additive result of the subsurface compaction of the various formations.

To measure the deformation of any individual clay layer,
compaction recorders (extensometers) are installed in wells at different
depths. Two types are generally used: pipe and anchored-cable both of
which are illustrated in Figure 2. For the operation of either type of

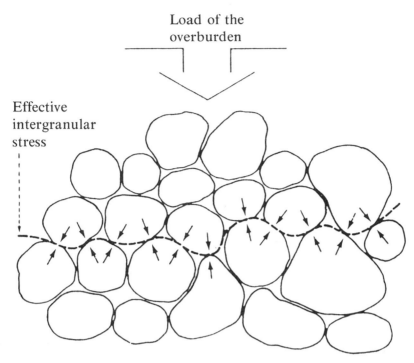

Figure 1 (b). The decrease of the water pressure produces an increase
of the effective intergranular stress under whose influence
soils compact.

equipment, the well should be drilled as nearly vertical as possible and,
for the anchor and cable installations the inside diameter of the well
casing should be at least 20 cm to decrease the cable-casing friction.

Even if subsidence processes are concealed below ground, it is
common practice to directly keep the ground surface elevation under
control by surveying a number of firmly anchored concrete posts (bench
marks). Bench marks are set up according to a network which covers
the area known as, or suspected of being, subsident and extends into a
broader regional network connected to reference bench marks assumed
to be stable.

In every country there exists a national levelling network but an
additional number of bench marks are established locally to provide a
denser grid over areas of special interest. Periodically surveyed by
precise levelling procedures, bench marks will show whether, where and

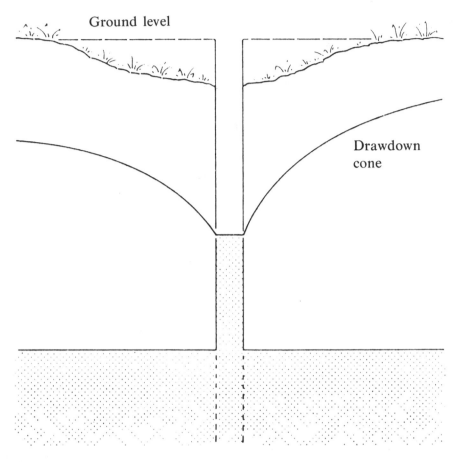

Figure 1 (c). The underground compaction induces a ground surface
settlement, which is proportional to the decrease in water
pressure and follows the shape of the drawdown cone.

how much ground surface lowering has occurred. Maps and/or profiles
of land subsidence are prepared from measured changes in the
elevation of bench marks (Figure 3).

Some Case Histories of Natural Subsidence

Ground surface displacements resulting from tectonic movement,
isostasy, and natural compaction involve almost the whole earth's crust.

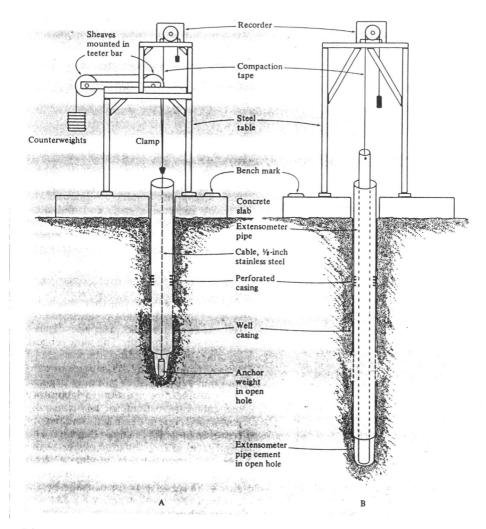

Figure 2. Recording extensometer installations. A. cable assembly; B. pipe assembly (after Poland, 1977).

Tectonic subsidence occurs on a very long-term scale and does not cause concern since it has the smallest impact on human activities. But tectonic activity may generate seismic and volcanic events responsible for both vertical and horizontal movements, even on a vast scale. In this connection it is worth mentioning that the 1959 Hegben earthquake in Montana caused an area of about 1,500 sq. km to subside asymmetrically with a maximum of 6.6 metres; the 1964 Alaska

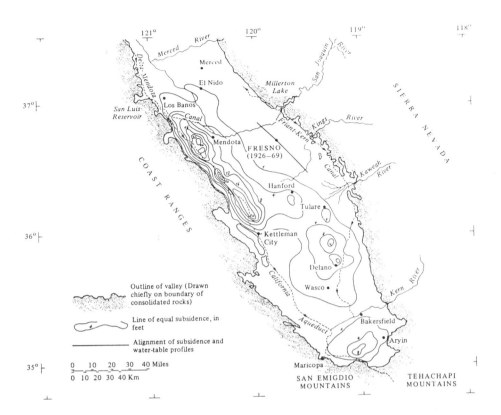

Figure 3. San Joaquin Valley, California: areal distribution of land
subsidence, 1926-70, due to groundwater withdrawal (after
J.F. Poland, Lofgren, Ireland and Pugh, 1975. "Land
Subsidence in the San Joaquin Valley as of 1972," U.S. Geol.
Survey, Prof. Paper 437-H).

earthquake provoked vast lowering of a regional area of 800 by 160 km,
and the vibrations then induced on the deposits led to a compaction
responsible for an additional notable subsidence.

Roman Ruins

A very interesting example of vertical downward movement, which
today has reversed its trend, is given by the Italian seismic-volcanic
area of Pozzuoli, close to Naples. Historically the ground of the "Campi
Flegrei" area was highest in the Roman times; nowadays the structures
of the ancient metropolis, including the entire port, lie submerged in

the Gulf of Pozzuoli (Figure 4). Worth mentioning are the ruins of the Roman Imperial Palace at Baia recently found underwater at a depth of 7 m; indeed, it is believed that the subsidence responsible for its disappearance was of about 14 m (Cotecchia, 1984).

The temple of Jupiter Serapis, at Pozzuoli, is the most singular monument of the region both for its geological as well as its archaeological interest. For 2,000 years it has represented the most significant available metric index for assessing the up and down land displacements that have occurred. In particular, the columns of the temple are marked by the burrows of litodomi, marine perforating mollusks which live at the surface of the water, indicators of the past levels of submergence.

The very, very long period characterized by a low irrelevant subsidence stopped in 1969. Since then an irregular upward movement has been observed, some with the alarming rates of 5 mm/day. A total ground raising of 2.60 m has been recorded from 1970 to 1983.

Surface loading over large areas of the earth is another very large-scale phenomenon leading to ground surface movements. For example, the crust moves under the weight of ice in an ice age, as a consequence of melting (uplift) or freezing of ice (downlift). This process, called isostasy, is of importance in regions of Scandinavia and the eastern North American continent.

Natural compaction of fine-grained deposits due to the loading of the overburden is accompanied by land subsidence. This type of subsidence chiefly occurs in Quaternary soils and it is most apparent where a great thickness of sediments accumulates rapidly; typical examples are the areas of river deltas. One can in particular mention the modern Mississippi River Delta where 400 to 500 million tons of sediments are deposited each year and the levee deposits on the lower delta have subsided more than 6 m.

Examples of Man-induced Subsidence

It is impossible in this article to list and analyze all the areas affected by manmade subsidence, but the case histories described here are notable for the magnitude of subsidence or the interest in their induced effects, or causes.

The most numerous and spectacular instances of man-made subsidence are those due to rash fluid exploitation.

Figure 4. The columns of the Temple of Jupiter Serapis at Pozzuoli on
which the burrows of litodomi clearly indicate the past levels
of submergence (picture courtesy of B. Liviera Zugiani).

California Agriculture

Numerous land sinkings have been recorded in California (United States) where vast amounts of water are withdrawn for irrigation, although also for domestic and industrial uses. Groundwater withdrawals in California are chiefly from intermountain basins in which the valley fill of late Tertiary and Quaternary age consists mainly of alluvial deposits, but also in places of lacustrine and shallow marine origin. In many of the basins, the aquifers being pumped are semiconfined or confined below depths ranging from 30 to 200 m, with much of the withdrawal coming from confined aquifer systems.

Water withdrawals have caused a piezo-metric decline in the aquifer of tens of metres, with recorded measurements of up to 153 m in the San Joaquin Valley where one of the greatest and most extensive man-induced subsidences in the world occurred with a magnitude of 9 m. Groundwater overdraft has prevailed in much of the valley since the 1930s. Subsidence apparently began concurrently, and became of widespread concern in the late 1940s.

Pumping extractions increased especially after the Second World War; during the 1950s an amount of more than one-quarter of all groundwater pumped for irrigation in the United States was used in the San Joaquin Valley alone. In the early 1960s pumping lifts frequently exceeded 150 m. The close correlation between water level decline, compaction of the aquifer systems and land subsidence became apparent.

Figure 3 has shown the curves of equal subsidence for 1926-70, but a more striking demonstration is visible on a utility pole showing the ground heights recorded in 1925, 1955 and 1977 (Figure 5). In fifty years, 20 billion m^3 of land have disappeared, corresponding to the volume of consolidation caused by the extraction of about 70 billion m^3 of groundwater. Since that period, subsidence has slowed in most of the San Joaquin Valley as a result of the drastic reduction of groundwater pumping with the large volume of surface water being substituted. As of 1976 artesian heads of the aquifers have recovered toward pre-subsidence levels and subsidence rates of the surface have decreased to near zero in much of the valley.

Mexico City: A Sinking Capital

Mexico City, Mexico, groundwater withdrawal has also produced 9 metres of land subsidence. But while in the San Joaquin Valley a large

Figure 5. San Joaquin Valley, California: land subsidence, 1925-77, shown through signs on a utility pole.

number of aquitards were subjected to compaction, in Mexico City most of the 9 m of compaction has occurred chiefly in the top 50 m below the land surface, especially in two very highly compressible silty-clay beds, 25-30 m and 5-10 m thick. This subsidence began in the last century, when deep wells were drilled all over the city to supply water for different uses.

In 1925 land surface sinking was confirmed through comparison of two precision levellings of 1877 and 1924, and in 1948 it was demonstrated that the subsidence of the city was due to groundwater exploitation. The rate of subsidence up to 1938 was about 4 cm/year; from 1938 to 1948 the yearly rate was about 15 cm and increased to 30 cm/year from 1948 to 1952. After 1952 the rate decreased gradually reaching between 1970 and 1973 a value equal to 5 cm/year. Today land subsidence is not a serious problem. But in 1959 land subsidence had already exceeded 4 m beneath all the old city and was as much as 7.5 m in the northeast part (reaching about 9 m late in the 1970s). Protrusion of well casings was a common occurrence in the subsiding area as a demonstration of the compaction of the sediments within the casing depth.

Figure 6 shows the protruding casing, in 1954, of a 100 m deep well drilled in 1923 that indicates a subsidence at least 5.45 m due to the compaction of the deposits above the depth of about 100 m.

The great and long continued settlement of Mexico City has caused many problems in water transport, drainage, in the construction of buildings and other engineering structures of the city. Pumping of underground water in the central part of the city has been prohibited since the 1970s and locally water injections have been carried out to improve the piezo-metric head.

Japan's Water for Industry

Japan offers other interesting examples of man-induced subsidence. Investigations and surveys have recognized 59 places affected by land subsidence by 1981, most of them concentrated in industrial regions on the coast. The total sinking areas covered 9,520 sq. km, accounting for about 12 percent of habitable land of the nation. According to many investigations the principal cause of subsidence in almost all the 59 places is the over-exploitation of groundwater from confined aquifers located in alluvial and shallow marine deposits.

Figure 6. Protrusion of a well casing in the northern part of Mexico City, Mexico (picture courtesy of R. Marsal).

Even though the groundwater is chiefly used for industrial purposes, large withdrawals are also made for domestic uses, fish farming, and irrigation. Among the subsiding areas, the well-known ones are those of Niigata, Chiba, Osaka, Taipai Basin with an overall subsidence (1.5 to 3 m), less than that of Tokyo (about 4.50 m).

Let us examine the latter case. The history of land subsidence has been described in detail for some areas of Tokyo for this century (Figure 7). In general the rate of land sinking has annually increased in Tokyo since 1950; by 1961 about 74 sq. km were subsiding (around) 10 to 15 cm/year. The maximum subsidence of 4.57 m was recorded in the period 1920-75 in the Koto ward of Tokyo, an area in the northeastern section of the city, where the groundwater head had dropped to about 60 m because of the intensive pumping from various aquifers. As a consequence of this subsidence the potential danger of tidal flood under a typhoon has been increasing year by year. Dikes had to be built along the edge of Tokyo Bay to prevent the city from flooding. Concurrently a series of restrictions in groundwater was taken. As a result of these legal interventions, the water levels recovered quickly all over the area, the subsidence first decreased and then stopped. A land rebound of a few centimetres was also measured at various places.

Venice and Its Lagoon

Another example of land subsidence due to groundwater withdrawals is that of Venice. The interest in this case is due not so much to the amount of subsidence, which is relatively small, but to the special prestige of the city of Venice which runs the risk of disappearing into the lagoon. We must in fact remember that Venice was built in the water and it is with respect to water that it must come to terms. The subsidence of Venice relative to the mean sea level has been quantified as 22 cm from the beginning of the century, most of which occurred in the twenty years from 1950-70. During this period in fact, the events of the "acqua alta" (high water) increased (Figure 8) and the problem aroused worldwide attention since the existence of the city and its historical monuments were threatened.[1]

For the same reason the subsidence of Ravenna, a coastal city south of Venice, has created a very great concern. Ravenna is known all over the world for the splendour and uniqueness of its mosaics, and for its monuments spanning the fifth to the fifteenth century.

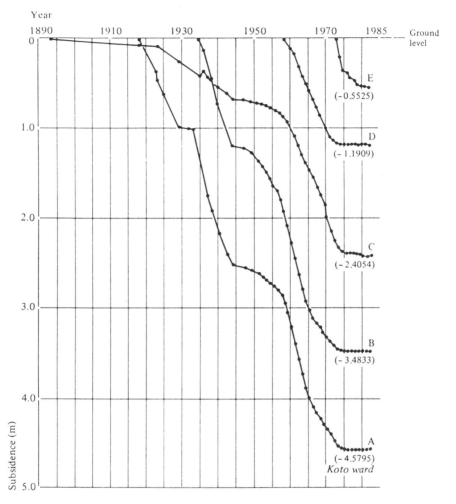

Figure 7. Total subsidence of several bench marks in the lowland of Tokyo since 1890 (updated after Y.I. Inaba et. al. Reviews of land subsidence researches in Tokyo. Proceedings of the First International Symposium on Land Subsidence, 1969, IAHS Publ. No. 89, Vol. 1, p. 87-98)

The subsidence, whose maximum has been of about 1.20 m, endangers the entire territory and influences the hydrologic balance of reclamation and the river network. As a consequence of land settlement, a regression of the shoreline, in some places even more than

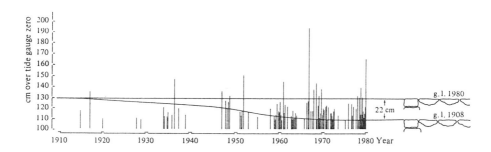

Figure 8. The "acqua alta" occurrences shown here as vertical lines and revealing an increase with time dependent on the loss in ground surface elevation (P. Gatto and L. Carbognin, "The Lagoon of Venice: Natural Environmental Trend and Man-induced Modification," Hydrological Sciences Bulletin, 1981, Vol. 26, No. 4).

130 m, has been observed, which in turn caused the destruction and submersion of the famous pine forest. The harbour installations sank below sea level (Figure 9), as well as building foundations in the historical centre where the existence of several important monuments is seriously jeopardized.

Asian Cities

Other cases of land subsidence due to groundwater withdrawals have been reported recently from the People's Republic of China. The most impressive among them refers to Shanghai which sank 2.63 m between 1921 and 1965, and to the Tianjin area, which is located in the northern China Plain, where a maximum cumulative amount of settlement equal to 2.15 m has been observed since 1950.

In Thailand, groundwater is pumped from unconsolidated deposits of sand, gravel and clay for the industrial and domestic needs of Bangkok. Starting in 1955, the water level declined by 50 m in 28 years, with as much as 88 cm of surface subsidence between 1978 and 1983 in the area east-southeast of Bangkok. Flooding of the city has become a problem.

Due to the relatively recent exploitation of geothermal fluids the consequence of subsidence has so far received only minor attention, although it may be of significant magnitude. Evidence of this is given in

Figure 9. The protective wall that was built to save the dockworks in Ravenna harbour is below sea level today.

New Zealand where the Wairakei field, the most extensively developed one, has experienced a ground surface settlement up to nearly 5 m from 1956 to 1974. Other areas indicate a much lower rate of subsidence, but demonstrate the need for further investigations in this field.

Pumping of gas-bearing water has also caused subsidence at different places. Two examples worth mentioning are those of Niigata, Japan, and the Po River Delta, Italy.

At Niigata a piezometric head decline of about 50 m in the period 1950-68 induced a subsidence up to 2.60 m. In the Po Delta area more than 3 m of land sinking was recorded between 1951 and 1965 following a piezometric decline also of 50 m. The two areas are very similar in their subsurface geology: the deposits involved in the process belong chiefly to the Pleistocene and consist of lagoonal and marine sediments. The main difference between the two cases is the thickness of the sediments subject to compaction, 0-1,000 m at Niigata and 100-600 m at the Po Delta. Since both zones are close to the sea, the consequences are quite the same: coastal facilities have been severely damaged; some river and road embankments disappeared; and farms and houses, perpetually flooded, have had to be abandoned.

Oil and Gas Withdrawal: Effects and Remedies

For subsidence due to oil and gas withdrawal, since the productive fields are generally considerably deeper than aquifers (they can reach a depth of 3,000 m), the surface effects are not always so apparent. In fact, among the thousands of oil fields existing in the world, the most serious effects of subsidence have been felt in the Los Angeles-Long Beach area of California. Above the extremely active Wilmington oil field the ground surface subsided about 9 m between 1926 and 1968 (Figure 10); the maximum annual rate of 71 cm was reached at the centre of the bowl in 1952. The geologic structure of this area is a broad, asymmetrical anticline broken by a series of transverse normal faults. The seven major producing zones range in age from Lower Pliocene to Upper Miocene, spanning a vertical section of about 1,500 m. In general most of the compaction took place in the oil zones between 600 and 1,200 m.

This case is particularly noteworthy for three reasons: (a) the vertical settlement of 9 m at the centre, one of the greatest subsidences to occur in the world; (b) many fields yielding oil from deposits of

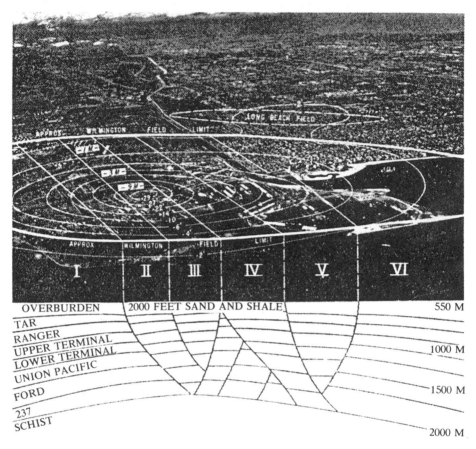

Figure 10. Subsidence and geologic cross-section, Wilmington Oil
Field. A close relationship exists between the shape and
location of the axis of the bowl of subsidence and that of the
underlying structure (after Allen, 1973).

similar age and from an equivalent depth range of approximately
similar lithology, and with comparable decrease in fluid pressure have
not experienced subsidence of more than a few feet; and (c) corrective
remedial action taken to stop subsidence.

A new process of salt-water injection was successfully used to
control the subsidence which even accomplished some elastic rebound
of land surface and raised the field's oil production.

Venezuela offers other troublesome instances of oil-produced
subsidence; worth mentioning is the 3.4 m of subsidence over the
Lagumillas field measured in the period 1926-54.

Considering gas production, there is evidence of several tens of centimetres of subsidence in the gas fields of Rio Vista and River Island, United States. For the gas extraction in Groningen, Netherlands, a few mm/year of land sinking are occurring today, but measurements and mathematical models have suggested the expectation of 1 m of subsidence up to the year 2056. This gas field is perhaps the largest in the world. It was discovered in 1959 and its large size of approximately 900 sq. km was completely identified in 1963. The sandstone reservoir is situated at a depth of nearly 2,900 m and has an average thickness of about 150 m.

Compaction: English Fens and Russian Plains

A peculiar process of compaction which occurs for reasons quite different to water exploitation is that called *hydrocompaction* as mentioned in the introduction. The soils subjected to this type of subsidence, namely loessial deposits, can support relatively large loads when they are dry, without compacting. When they are wet, the bond between individual grains is reduced, rapid compaction occurs, followed by a subsidence of the land surface. Hydrocompaction usually begins near the land surface taking place soon after the deposit becomes wet, then progresses downward with the advancing water front.

Reports of subsidence due to hydrocompaction refer principally to the United States, but in vast areas in western Europe and west-central Asia where loess deposits are present, subsidences due to application of water are not uncommon. Nearly 350 sq. km of farm land are irrigated in western and southern San Joaquin Valley with a resulting land settlement of nearly 3 m occurring. In several areas of the Ukraine, a region of the USSR, about 65 percent of which is covered with loess soils with a thickness from 20 to 40 m, subsidence may range from 1.0 to 1.5 m.

Subsidence due to hydrocompaction causes serious concern either in the design or maintenance of aqueducts, irrigation canals, buildings and other major engineering structures. Surface cracks, sunken ditches and other evidence of hydrocompaction are readily apparent even to the casual observer (Figure 11).

Compaction of recent deposits often occurs as one of the results of drainage and reclamation works, carried out on wetlands (e.g. swamp, mudflat, etc.) in order to transform them into more profitable areas.

Figure 11. Hydrocompaction. Subsidence and cracking along the unlined canal; Columbia Basin Project, Washington.

Generally the settlement rate is proportional to the drainage rate: the lower the water table, the greater the subsidence; but the amount of subsidence is always larger in the presence of peat and organic soils because they undergo irreversible oxidation from biochemical action on drying that reduces the volume. For example in the Fens of Cambridgeshire and Lincolnshire, United Kingdom, a ground surface settlement ranging between 5 and 10 m has been observed since 1800. The same process occurred in the reclaimed plains of the USSR and in the Florida Everglades in the United States. The latter represents the most extensive deposits of organic soils in the world (8,000 sq. km). About 1.6 m of subsidence has occurred, with different sinking patterns since 1913. A visual evidence of the ground surface settlement is given in Figure 12.

Figure 12. Example of subsidence in the Florida Everglades. When this
house was built (on piles established on the limestone
bedrock covered with peat), the original ground surface was
level with the porch floor; the steps were added (picture
courtesy of Dr. N.P. Prokopovich).

With regard to land subsidence in reclaimed areas, perhaps the
Netherland polders, in Europe, offer the best example, and in
particular the Yssel Lake (Figure 13) area. Here the recently reclaimed
"Flevoland" subsided within fifteen to twenty-five years after
reclamation, from a few centimetres in the shallow, sandy layer, to a
little over a metre in the deposits with a peat soil.[2]

In Israel the swamp area of about 4,000 ha reclaimed in the Hula
Valley in 1958 had experienced in 1980 a subsidence ranging from 8
cm/year in the high organic peat soil to 2.8 cm/year in the sedimentary
lake deposit soil.

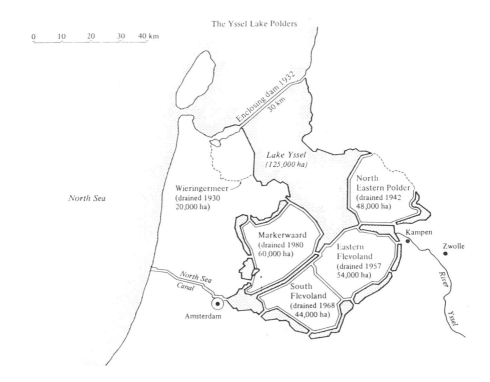

Figure 13. Map of the Netherlands and the Ijsselmeerpolders (F.C.
Zuidema, "The Transformation of the Hydrological Regime
of Marsh-Ridden Areas by Land Reclamation, and
Forecasting of its Influence on Hydrometeorological
Conditions with Reference to the Netherlands," Hydrology
of Marsh-Ridden Areas, Unesco-IAHS, 1972).

New York's Sinking Airport

Loading of the surface due to man-made structures has induced soil
compaction and therefore subsidence. Intensive urbanization has been
one of the biggest responsible factors of this in many areas. For
example the area of New York's La Guardia Airport had subsided by
artificial loading more than 2 m after twenty-five years of operation.

In addition, urbanization may induce further compaction by
vibration produced by heavy traffic, and a variety of man-made
sources.

Land subsidence can also result from the extraction of solids such as coal, mineral ores, salt and sulphur, either in the solid state or as a result of solution mining techniques.

The cavities produced by extraction will always cause stress and deformation in the adjacent soils. The resulting displacements at ground surface mostly depend on the geological and geotechnical conditions of the deposits, the amount of material removed and the size of the underground opening. The cavities formed in the subsoil often progress upwards through the soil overburden; when the underground opening is sufficiently close to the land surface a sudden collapse of the surface ("sinkhole") occurs. In regions underlain by limestone these events are a common occurrence.

One must remember at this point that in the Karst terrains sinkholes may result from natural causes. Nevertheless, land subsidence due to natural sinkholes generally develops in geologic time and it is not regarded as so serious a problem as subsidence resulting from man-induced sinkholes. The incidence of sinkhole development can be increased considerably when natural equilibrium conditions are changed by man's activities, in particular those that change groundwater levels or increase infiltration. These are widespread in the southeastern part of the United States, in particular in Georgia, Alabama and Florida. Their diameter ranges from 1 to 90 m, and their depth from 0.3 to 30 m. Figure 14 shows the largest collapse occurred in Alabama.

Coal mining operations have caused subsidence in Germany and in Great Britain, in Nigeria and other places in South Africa and in Australia. Two localities of instances of subsidence due to extraction of salt are the town of Tuzca, Yugoslavia, and the districts of Cheshire in England. However, in general, surface deformations caused by mining activities are confined to relatively small areas immediately overlying the mines and do not create great concern.

The Remedies

Land subsidence has always produced severe damage on the environment and particularly in coastal-plain regions, where land can sink below sea level. Disappearance of stretches of beach, increase in flooding, shore erosion, pollution of fresh water from salt water intrusion and spoiling of harbour efficiency are the quite common

Figure 14. A collapsing surface in Alabama, United States, caused this
sinkhole of 90 m diameter and 30 m deep.

detrimental effects. In many areas land subsidence has ruined
buildings, wrecked bridges, cracked city pavements, twisted railroad
tracks, etc. It is evident that all these devastating consequences
represent an incalculable cost for mankind.

What can be done to avoid or reverse subsidence? It is obvious that
subsidence due to natural causes is unavoidable and remedial measures
can only be taken against man-induced subsidence.

A number of countermeasures to prevent damages or to reverse
subsidence have been adopted. They can be summarized as
follows: (a) cessation or regulation of subsurface resource extractions,
legal action, or replacement with substitute supply; (b) construction of
dikes in areas susceptible to flooding; (c) repressuring by water
injection. This method, highly successfully applied in the Wilmingtron
oil field, cannot be adopted everywhere because it can produce very

serious problems which stem from the quality of water injected, especially in an aquifer system.

Since subsidence is a mostly irreversible occurrence, the environment will never recover fully its original condition.

Conclusion

In the past, man was the "victim" of subsidence because he lacked the knowledge to either predict or to control the phenomenon. Today, however, research on the causes of subsidence and the possibility of forecasting physical changes through mathematical models, should help planners to avoid, or at least minimize, the dangers when building urban and industrial complexes.

FOOTNOTES

1. For a more comprehensive treatment of the subject, see Augusto Ghetti and Michel Batisse, "The Overall Protection of Venice and its Lagoon," *Nature and Resources*, Vol. XIX, No. 4, October-December 1983.
2. See also A. Volker, "Polders, an Ancient Approach to Land Reclamation," *Nature and Resources*, Vol. XVIII, No. 4, October-December 1982.

TO DELVE MORE DEEPLY

1. Barry F. Beck, editor. *Sinkholes: Their Geology, Engineering and Environmental Impact.* Rotterdam: A.A. Balkema. 1984. Proceedings of the first multidisciplinary conference on sinkholes, Orlando, Florida, 15-17 October 1984.
2. Unesco. *The Guidebook to Studies of Land Subsidence Due to Groundwater Withdrawal.* Paris: Unesco. 1984.

PART II

Mountain Hazards

Five actors have parts to play in the drama of a volcanic crisis: the volcano itself, of course; teams of scientists; administrative authorities; the media (press, radio and television); and the inhabitants of the region affected. Examining the interactions among these actors throws light on such fundamental issues as the part scientists should play in the discussion of a society's values.

Chapter 6
The Five Components of Volcanic Risk

Denis Westercamp

Denis Westercamp studied at the University of Paris where he specialized in the geology of volcanism. He entered the Bureau of Geological and Mining Research in 1974 as a geological engineer and was assigned to Martinique where he has prepared new geological maps of Martinique and Guadeloupe. The crisis of La Soufrière of Guadeloupe in 1976 drew him into the work of volcanic assessment and hazard-zoning. He co-ordinated the programme of the French Geological Survey and of the Civil Security of Paris.

Geologists are now, after 250 years' study of the history of the earth, able to show that it is nothing but a long series of change and violence. What was true in the past will remain so in the future, and cataclysms will occur again and again. Of all the dangers that beset us, volcanic eruptions are perhaps the most spectacular and are most frequently accompanied by awesome and terrible effects. They are also the ones that leave most evidence in the form of different kinds of lava, since eruptions produce vast quantities of rock material. The study of this material allied with our ability to measure geological time by methods based on radioactivity makes it possible to check up on events which occurred thousands of years before the first written evidence left by man. This is crucial to the study of risk—the possibility of loss or damage to property or persons.

Several recent eruptions, particularly those of La Soufrière in Guadeloupe in 1976/77, the Soufrière volcano in St. Vincent in 1979 and Mount St. Helens in the United States in 1980, have given fresh impetus to research and thinking in the field of volcanic risk. Unesco has taken a leading part in this, organizing working groups and sponsoring publications on zoning of volcanic hazard and on the response that scientists and the civil authorities can and should make to an emergency. This article places these problems in a wide context that includes the media and the populations at risk.

A Short Story

It was Friday, 21 March 1987, and the head of the volcano surveillance observatory, Jean-Paul Diové, was again a worried man. He had just read the automatic instruments placed on the major thermal springs around the volcano to monitor their temperature, acidity, and chemical content. The changes since the previous week's readings were considerable. The temperature, for one, was climbing steadily at all the springs. The average reading was 65°C, a far cry from the 30-40°C level of the past two months, indeed of the long period since the volcano had last erupted 150 years ago. And if only that were all there was to worry about!

Other readings taken by the team—seismic activity and the tiny changes in the volcano's altitude and tilt—all showed the same accelerating climb. The eight seismometers installed when the crisis had begun, in addition to two normally in place, showed a tenfold rise in seismic activity directly below the cone at a depth of two to six kilometres. The volcano itself had risen around twenty centimetres in two months—a significant figure, since the instrument used was a laser gun accurate to within one centimetre.

"It looks more and more as if the volcano is waking up," he said, thinking aloud. "I'm going to call the regional defense committee together in the next day or so, and if the weather holds tomorrow, send a reconnaissance team up in a helicopter."

At that point, his thoughts were interrupted by a violent tremor that shook the observatory windows. When it ended a few seconds later, he dashed into the recording room where seismic information came in by radio from the ten field stations. One glance at the instruments confirmed that the source of the quake lay deep beneath the volcano.

The first phone call came barely a minute later. "There we go," he thought; "people looking for news. And I'll bet it's that old fox Hébrard wanting a story for tomorrow's first edition."

This short story, which is of course fictitious, is intended to show who the concerned "parties" are in a volcanic crisis. The first is the source of the crisis itself, the volcano; next are those who study it, the teams of scientists; then those who decide what action to take to reduce the danger, the administrative authorities; also those who divulge the information, the media; and finally, those who are exposed to the risk, the population who live near by. The behaviour of each of these parties and the relationships between them will determine the extent of the risk as well as the possibility of minimizing it. Each party in this "pentagon" of risk is shown in Figure 1.

The Volcano: Source of the Risk

In the most general terms, a volcano is a place where molten rocks containing gases, or gases alone, reach the surface. A volcano as such is not eternal. It is born one day and, a few months or a few hundred thousand years later, it dies. Apart from a few permanently active volcanoes, Erta-Ale in Afar, Ethiopia, or Etna in Sicily, for example, the period of quiescence is generally 10 to 100 times longer than the duration of an eruption. In other words, "living" volcanoes are normally quiescent, as may be seen from the fact that scarcely 10 of the

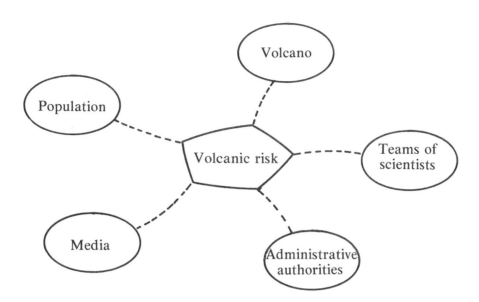

Figure 1. "Pentagon" of risk.

500 or so volcanoes in the world considered to be living erupt in any one year.

But how can a dormant volcano be distinguished from an extinct one? This question arose in tragic terms in Costa Rica where the Arenal, which had never erupted in human memory and was considered extinct, awoke violently in 1968, claiming almost eighty lives. There are volcanoes that have been producing fumaroles or hot springs for tens of thousands of years but are otherwise inactive; these are classified as active although they may simply be cooling down.

The only way to determine whether a volcano is extinct or dormant is to compare the length of its current dormant period with the length of other dormant periods that separated its eruptions in the recent past. A detailed geological survey backed up by a carbon-14 dating programme (especially for rarely active volcanoes) and a careful study of written evidence (particularly for frequently active volcanoes) enable us to determine a volcano's real cycle over a given period of time. Finally, a volcano will be considered as living if the time elapsed since its last eruption is within the range of previous periods of quiescence, and as extinct if its current quiescent phase is considerably longer than the previous ones. Doubt still remains, however, in a number of cases.

Who is at Risk?

Volcanoes are not distributed at random on the planet's surface but are concentrated chiefly at the edge of the tectonic plates (see map on page 23), in relatively narrow zones, running around the Pacific in the famous "fire belt," from the western Mediterranean to the Himalayas, etc. The imperilled regions approximate very closely to these zones.

While active volcanoes on the ocean bed threaten virtually no one, those located in overcrowded countries such as Japan or Java may, in the event of a cataclysmal eruption, imperil tens of millions of people.

And What is the Hazard?

Volcanic activity can be of the effusive type, typical of the mid-ocean islands such as Hawaii or Réunion, or an explosive type, predominantly confined to the island arcs (the Lesser Antilles, the Aleutians, etc.) and continental coastal ranges such as the Andes. Within each category, activity ranges widely, from minor overspills of lava lakes to vast discharges of successive flows for the effusive type, and from feeble explosions of overheated water (phreatic activity), such as geysers, to incredible cataclysms involving hundreds of cubic kilometres of mixed gas and pumice capable of destroying an area the size of France (500,000 square kilometres) in a matter of days. The earth has known several such eruptions during the last 100,000 years. They occur at intervals of around 10,000 years, which is by no means negligible if it is realized that no eruption within historical times has yet reached such dimensions.

Each volcanic phenomenon poses a different risk to living creatures, infrastructures, farmland, etc. Lava flows, for instance, generally advance slowly enough to enable the population to take refuge. Conversely, the area they cover is made unfit for any form of cultivation for a long period. Deposits of ash often affect vast regions. Although their immediate effect is to ruin crops, they are more of a nuisance than a real danger to man and they rapidly become extremely fertile soil.

The Teams of Scientists: Those Who Study the Hazard

In terms of volcanic activity alone, the risk depends on the frequency and intensity of the event. In periods of quiescence, an estimate of the next eruption is based on the written record of past eruptions or, in the case of prehistoric eruptions, on dates estimated using whatever absolute dating information is available, chiefly that obtained by the carbon-14 method. Here we touch upon the concepts of "living" and extinct volcanoes discussed above. This is the probabilistic aspect of risk evaluation.

The intensity of the event is estimated in two different and complementary ways. During a dormancy past events are investigated in respect of possible dangers: area of impact and frequency. This evaluation is the basis for the zoning of hazards and is known as "long-term forecasting." During actual volcanic activity signals such as tremors and changes in land contours or in springs are studied by the surveillance team in terms of past events. This is known as "short-term forecasting."

The importance of a volcano's past record in assessing its future activity has led to the axiom, "The past is the key to the future," emphasizing the uniqueness of each volcano. The way in which it will erupt depends essentially on the size, shape, depth, and groundwater permeability of its magmatic chamber. Magma from deep within the earth flows into this "pocket" located five to twenty kilometres below the volcano where it undergoes chemical transformations to become gas-enriched and hence potentially explosive.

Studying a Volcano's Future

A volcano's "future" may be studied in three different ways: first, by witnessing an eruption at first hand (studies of such events constitute handbooks of eruption phenomenology for all volcanologists); second, by critically analysing written descriptions of past eruptions (a famous description is the letter from Pliny the Younger to his friend Tacitus describing the eruption of Vesuvius in A.D. 79); and, finally, by studying the deposits of prehistoric eruptions.

There are severe limitations to this geological approach, of course. In 1979 the Soufrière volcano in St. Vincent erupted with extremely violent explosions in the enormous crater lake at its summit (phreato-magmatic phenomenon). Although the plume of ash reached a height of almost twenty kilometres, and the surface was ruined for tens of square kilometres around the crater, the total volume of volcanic material produced in the shape of ash or associated pyroclastic flows remained slight. This combination of intense explosions and a low volume of lava has been a feature of other eruptions, such as those of Mount Pelée in 1902 or Mount St. Helens in 1980, where savage directional explosions marking the start of the "climatic" phase left irregular deposits of roughly strews ashes at most a few tens of centimetres thick. In both cases these ash-falls were followed by pyroclastic flows that were large in volume but confined to certain valleys leading out from the volcano's summit. Almost the only cases in which no volcanic matter is deposited and in which the geologist is consequently helpless are those in which toxic gas is emitted quietly, as happened with the Dieng volcano in Java in 1979.

As recently as ten years ago, these ash-fall deposits were frequently neglected by geologists. Today, however, painstaking fieldwork can recognize as little as a few centimetres of deposit, usually where it has been preserved in such extreme climates as those of the tropics.

Zoning Probable Danger

Hazard zoning around a "living" volcano provides civil authorities with maps showing the probable extent of danger and nuisance resulting from its future volcanic activity. Such maps help them to take the necessary emergency action during crises and to direct socio-economic development during dormancy.

Zoning considers first past phenomena as evaluated by the geologist in mapping the strata of sediment. Account is then taken of the volcano's present structure—the depth of the valleys and the presence or absence of lateral features. The third factor in zoning is the influence of atmospheric conditions likely to prevail during an eruption. A study of current winds and rainfall indicates the zones that will be affected by the ashes first and the importance that should be attached to mudflows. And last, but only if geological knowledge is inadequate, the area affected by recorded phenomena in the case of other volcanoes may be used, though such a comparative procedure is hazardous in the extreme.

Surveillance of an Awakening Volcano

A volcano awakens when the vent joining its magmatic chamber to its crater is reactivated. The volcano moves out of the state of constant equilibrium that prevailed during its dormancy and into one of successive disequilibria that mark the various stages of the magma's ascent. The signs of this awakening are as follows:

- Old fissures in the vent are reopened and new ones appear, causing seismic shocks, especially if the magma is viscous.

- Changes occur in the structure's gravimetric and magnetic properties.

- An increase in the local heat-flow raises the temperature of phreatic aquifers. The temperature and flow of surface springs and fumaroles[1] increase.

- Magmatic gases escape through the walls of the vent, modifying the chemical composition of phreatic aquifers and subsequently of springs and fumaroles.

- The structure is raised and/or deformed to an extent depending on the volume, viscosity, and gas content of the rising column of magma.

These changes in the volcano as it comes to life and during its active phase are studied by a surveillance team, which uses techniques and equipment for recording in the field. The technical details of surveillance have been described in a book published by Unesco in 1972.[2]

In each case the basic principle is the same, and consists of comparing each new analytical finding with previous information and with data gathered during the dormant state of the volcano, referred to as "background noise."

Volcanoes are located in such geologically unstable areas that certain signals may reveal a major change in comparison with the background noise without relating to a rise of magma. An example is the superficial seismic crises occurring directly below the volcano resulting merely from the reactivation of fissures.

The fact that different causes may send similar signals to the surface means that several surveillance techniques must be used together since each technique has its own advantages and limits. For example, seismology can pinpoint the epicentre or exact origin of seismic phenomena and also follow their shifts and is thus better suited to predicting the site of the future crater and the time of eruption than to gauging the type of eruption. On the other hand, the geochemistry of fumarolic gases, by providing close contact with the ascending magma, gives information about the type of eruption. Comparison of findings from different methods allows the volcanologist to achieve a complete diagnosis.

Although the multidisciplinary approach is universally acknowledged to be the only realistic way of observing an active volcano, its practical implementation differs widely from country to country and from team to team. Current operational styles fall under one of two radically different options. In the first a volcano is monitored from a multidisciplinary observatory with a complete range of scientists and technical staff. This "stationary" approach is suited to permanently or semi-permanently active volcanoes such as Etna (the Catania observatory) or Mauna-Loa and Kilauea (the Hawaii observatory). It allows a team to carry out surveillance of volcanoes in populated regions that may come to life at any time. It enables the team to gain experience and to keep the resident staff and equipment up to date. Other teams from elsewhere are able to visit the stationary site to study and to test their own equipment. And last, it provides sound working conditions for studies on the phenomenology of volcanoes.

The second option consists of entrusting surveillance to an autonomous, multidisciplinary intervention team. During periods of quiescence, a small-scale warning system is installed permanently on the volcano, while the staff goes away to gain experience and submit its equipment to the test of the world's active volcanoes and other observatories as described above. If the warning system shows a change from background noise, the team immediately returns to set up all the equipment needed for complete surveillance. This "mobile" approach is well suited to living volcanoes with a 100-year cycle of eruption, the commonest kind (Mount Pelée or the Guadeloupe Soufrière in the French West Indies are examples). Regardless of its potential for eruption, this type of volcano does not warrant tying men and equipment down completely, perhaps for generations, in a field of operation that is unproductive from the surveillance viewpoint. Of course this implies that the volcano will come to life slowly enough for the surveillance team to take up its positions. The time-lapse corresponds exactly with the time the magma needs to ascend from the magmatic chamber and is hence directly proportional to the chamber's depth (several kilometres) and the speed with which the magma rises (a few metres per hour at the most). Thus the real problem is to be able to detect the activation of the volcano's system soon enough; the more sensitive and suitable the equipment, the sooner it will be detected. Since the initial form of surface activity is rarely the climax, there is time available to bring in a team. The one exception to the rule concerns volcanoes with a very large crater lake. These may reach the climax of their eruption very quickly, resulting in gigantic lahars or extremely violent phreato-magmatic explosions as in the case of the St. Vincent Soufrière is 1979. This simple, flexible, "mobile" approach demonstrated its effectiveness in the recent Mount St. Helens eruption.

The mobile approach requires attention to certain important preliminaries. First, the background noise must be determined; next the volcano's past record of eruption must be known; and, finally, the problem of keeping the alarm system operational must be solved. This is far from easy, especially in the tropics.

A World Campaign Against Volcanoes

Many volcanologists would like to see a world campaign against volcanoes, perhaps through an international body such as Unesco. This would require drawing up a list of qualified specialists. A jury would choose these specialists and for each a dossier would contain information about his field of technical competence, his experience, the technical resources he can muster, and how he can be contacted quickly in case of need. Such a catalogue of specialists, which any country could even now compile, should make it possible to put the ideal team together. This team would provide a wide variety of information recording and processing possibilities, the advisory services of research scientists, the services of geologists with knowledge of the volcano's record of eruption or with ability to evaluate quickly its usual forms of activity.

Caution in Comparing Volcanic Events

Comparison is among the standard procedures of scientific thought, but the complexity of volcanic phenomena prompts caution in its use as a forecasting technique. Since different underground processes can produce identical surface effects, it is pointless to draw comparisons on the basis of just one parameter. To illustrate, consider two seismic activities each liberating comparable amounts of energy, with one erupting cataclysmically, as did, for example, the 1956 eruption of the Bezymyanny in the USSR, while the other shows only a very minor phreatic eruption, as did the Guadeloupe Soufrière in 1976.

To take the argument further, we describe the chain of events in two recent explosions already referred to several times: the Guadeloupe Soufrière in 1976 and the Mount St. Helens eruption in 1980.

On 8 July 1976, following a year of unusual seismic activity, there was a phreatic explosion in the summit of La Soufrière. Similar explosions followed at a rate of around two per month until 1 March 1977, when all surface activity ceased. The seismic crisis developed independently during July and August. On 15 August the authorities evacuated the population of the south of Basse-Terre, some 73,000 persons, since a surveillance team feared a cataclysmic magmatic eruption—which in the event did not take place.

In mid-March of 1980, Mount St. Helens showed unusual seismic activity culminating in a phreatic explosion on 27 March. Similar explosions followed until 20 April, and began again on 10 May. This phase of activity led the authorities to evacuate the Mount St. Helens area at the end of March. In mid-April scientists noticed that the volcano's north face was rising several metres each day and was deforming. On 18 May, a particularly violent tremor caused the land and ice raised by the swelling of the north face to collapse. There was an immediate directional phreatic explosion of cataclysmic proportions, followed two hours later by a pumice eruption. Four hundred square kilometres were devastated by the blast of the explosion or covered in flows of debris and pumice. Activity still continues on a lesser scale.

Taking account of just one parameter—the phreatic start of the Mount St. Helens eruption—some officials of the French volcanological surveillance service were led to believe that the eruption of the Guadeloupe Soufrière in 1976 might easily have culminated in a cataclysmic magmatic eruption such as that of Mount St. Helens. This was used after the event to justify the evacuation decreed on 15 August. In actual fact, other parameters—the distortion of the volcano, the heat-flow as measured by infrared photometry—show fundamental differences between the two eruptions of a kind that should rule out all comparison.

Difficulty in Generalizing on Volcanic Phenomena

Generalization is also a cherished goal of scientific thought, but when dealing with active volcanoes this, too, is rarely justified and often unacceptable. Taking again the example of Mount St. Helens, following the cataclysmic explosion of 18 May, some scientists felt it safe to conclude that "until then a phreatic eruption was considered to be generally less dangerous than a magmatic eruption." Statements of this kind are meaningless unless applied to a clearly defined area: (i.e. unless the factors determining the nature—in this instance, paroxysmal—of the phreatic eruption have been recognized and stated), in this case, the collapse of part of the volcano's flank caused by a rising column of highly gaseous magma. The lack of such factors in the Guadeloupe Soufrière enables us, with hindsight of course, to conclude that the sequence observed in the Mount St. Helens eruption could not have happened there.

Scientists' Code of Ethics

The 1976 eruption of La Soufrière in Guadeloupe brought to light the unpreparedness of the society in coping with the problem of volcanic risk. Before discussing the attitudes of the press and the authorities, we must first analyze an issue that gave rise to the greatest controversy among the international scientific community—the deontological problem. [3]

There is a very French failing to which all of us are prone: we cannot acknowledge an error or admit that we were wrong. No French scientist, after the evacuation of 15 August in Guadeloupe, ventured such a critical self-appraisal as that undertaken by American scientists following the Mount St. Helens explosion of 18 May. And yet the American authorities by all the evidence managed their situation better than we did ours.

Let us take another example from the eruption of the Guadeloupe Soufrière in 1976. One of the elements that influenced the decision to evacuate the volcano's slopes on 15 August was the discovery of a large proportion of healthy volcanic glass—i.e. of new magma—in the "ashes" ejected during the phreatic explosions. As early as the month of September detailed laboratory analyses showed that the diagnosis was wrong, and that the "balls of new glass" were in fact only lumps of fumarole clay. The "ashes" in their entirety were merely tiny fragments of old volcanic material torn from within the volcano. Many French and foreign petrographers, including myself, were deceived to some extent. Yet none has publicly analyzed his error. What is more, some have tried to minimize this error, for example by publishing analyses of volcanic glass from La Soufrière that have no bearing on the problem. This behaviour has raised the question of the advisability of drawing up a professional code of ethics.

The debate was launched in the pages of the *Journal of Volcanology and Geothermal Research* which, from 1978 to 1980, published the views of researchers involved in the Soufrière "affair." Some argued that no code could stop volcanologists, influenced by their lack of experience, natural apprehensions, nervous fatigue, or even their thirst for publicity, from tending to over-react to risk situations. A code would not protect them from the demagogic prophesies of sensation-hungry newspapers, or from pressure on the part of administrative authorities with scant regard for collaboration. Nor would a code help to sharpen critical faculties or the ability to note and rectify inadequacies in the machinery of surveillance. Others, however, felt that a professional code would strengthen moral and intellectual attitudes underlying the realistic appraisal of risk, and would help scientists to distinguish clearly between fact and opinion, to recognize the limits to competence, to acknowledge a share of responsibility for the consequences of decisions, or to refuse to subordinate objectivity to political requirements, etc.

Scientific Information and the Public

In the field of communication, the first duty of the scientists is undoubtedly to speak in clear and understandable terms with a minimum of distortion. At the start of a crisis when the future is still unpredictable, scientists are strongly tempted to say nothing because the public often over-reacts to news of a potential hazard. Yet when the public realizes that news has been withheld, it talks of censorship and suspects subsequent news, possibly losing confidence in the scientists themselves. It denounces, rightly so, the "excessive kindness" that deprives it of information about a problem and thereby makes it difficult to make up its own mind about risk.

The media can either advise the public directly or leave this to the authorities. The first allows information to flow more quickly and more freely, but it assumes that the media will not indulge in sensationalism, that the authorities will renounce their absolute powers of decision and that the public will remain calm and will understand that differing views exist among scientists. Such direct transmission of information can only really be envisaged in a society that is well informed and mature in respect of volcanic risk.

The second approach cuts scientists off from the media and the public. They are less disturbed in their work, but they must accept state control and usurpation of the right to make decisions concerning risk. This raises questions about the part scientists should play in the discussion of a society's values. In this case, should the final decision in matters of safety rest with the state or with the citizen and voter? Such questions are, of course, political and go to the heart of democracy. In answering them, the scientist must decide whether he wishes to inform the public directly and as fully as possible or whether he prefers to isolate himself from the public.

The Population: Those Exposed to the Risk

The worldwide need for food is pushing man to inhabit and cultivate the flanks of volcanoes at whatever price. The more explosive and hence dangerous the volcano, the greater is the sediment of ashes that rapidly creates a fertile soil. Apart from the occasional permanently or semi-permanently active volcanoes, most living volcanoes are dormant. As time after an eruption passes, memories become blunted and awareness of the risk diminishes. In two or three generations the very fact that the volcano is living becomes unreal and abstract. Only lifelong education will keep the public aware of the risk. This calls for volcanology classes at school, newspaper articles, radio and television programmes, lectures, films and exhibitions, and the establishment of permanent museums. Authorities in the French West Indies have established these activities in towns threatened by the Guadeloupe Soufrière or Mount Pelée.

The better the public is informed, the greater will be its powers of initiative when risk occurs.

The Media: Those Who Divulge Information

The media have an important role to play in times of volcanic crisis, their first duty being objective reporting. They must avoid systematically emphasizing the dramatic or spectacular, reporting all shades of opinion that are part of assessing a crisis situation, and not enlarge upon reality.

This last point would seem self-evident, but in the 1976 eruption of the Guadeloupe Soufrière, a major Paris weekly showed no compunction in enlarging on the event by publishing photographs of casualties and damage. One photograph showed a child with a bandaged head allegedly burned by hot ashes, while another showed a car claimed to have been struck by a volcanic bomb. In view of what really happened (the explosion merely flung up blocks around the crater and ejected cold "ashes" downwind), these photographs could only be of a sick child in hospital and a road accident.

The dilemma is real. How can such unscrupulous media be given access to the source of information? Yet, conversely, if news is not forthcoming, will they not feel impelled to pick up every bit of gossip? Some French surveillance officials have suggested that media representatives should be brought together with government authorities and staff of surveillance teams to discuss public information. This suggestion lies between the total access offered during the Mount St. Helens eruption in 1980 and the rigid barrier between the media and the scientists that was maintained in St. Vincent during the 1979 eruption.

The Administrative Authorities: Those Who Reduce the Risk

On one point there is unanimity in the scientific community: administrative authorities are more competent than scientists to judge the full weight of socio-economic consequences ensuing from volcanic activity and to specify the required safety precautions. Therefore, responsibility for action to combat the danger must rest with these authorities even though in assessing that danger they are wholly dependent on the opinion of the scientists. In France, it is the public safety authorities who define the areas exposed to natural hazards, who organize relief, and who prepare the appropriate precautionary measures.

In defining endangered areas, officials must refer to soil-occupation maps and risk-zoning maps drawn up by geologists. Those areas exposed to major ash-falls should be used exclusively for agriculture, while heavy investment should be avoided in areas almost certain to be destroyed in the event of an eruption.

An adequate set of emergency relief plans would contain a complete list of manpower and equipment resources as well as infrastructure such as hospitals or emergency accommodation that can be made available in times of crisis. In the plan, the role of each infrastructure unit should be defined, access routes should be identified, and codes and radio frequencies should be assigned.

Direct Action Against Hazard

There is a limited range of volcanic phenomena—mud flows or lahars and lava flows where direct action against the hazard can be taken. To prevent lahars, tunnels can be dug to drain crater lakes or protective dykes can be built. Dykes can also divert lava flows towards uninhabited areas and lateral obstacles can be bombed to pierce them. Attempts have been made to slow down such flows by pouring water on them, although this is more a means of mobilizing citizens than effective action against the flow. To counteract explosive phenomena, underground shelters have been dug for scientific teams, houses have been hermetically sealed and gas-masks have been issued as a precaution against whirlwinds carrying fine toxic ash. In most cases, however, the only possible reaction is to flee. This may seem obvious and simple, but in practice it is usually highly complex and even debatable. We shall return to this after discussing the fundamental issue of risk-acceptance.

Accepting Risk—at What Level?

Risk is inherent in life, as we are reminded by the inevitability of death. No action is free of risk, whether it be the voluntary activity of driving a car or the necessity of coping with an unforeseeable event such as a volcanic eruption. And the greater the advantages to a society, the higher the price in terms of lives it is prepared or resigned to paying. To expect an absence of risk is, of course, absurd. In the case of car-driving, this would require a ban on driving at week-ends—a particularly dangerous period—or a speed restriction of thirty kilometres an hour, combined with draconian safety-rules for manufacturers, etc. In the case of volcanoes, every highly active volcano would have to be declared a permanently prohibited area, which would be an impossibility, in view of the risk of famine it would entail.

The level of acceptability of volcanic risk varies from country to country and from individual to individual and depends on a great number of factors. One of these is the intensity of the feared volcanic phenomenon. The more intense it is and the greater the numbers and areas threatened, the less acceptable the risk. At the upper limit of the unimaginable cataclysms, such as an eruption of several hundred cubic kilometres that can lay waste to an area half the size of France, there is no possible recourse. Evacuate an entire country? Millions and millions of people? And where to? It is simply too much to contemplate, and the only response is pure fatalism.

Acceptance may also depend on the ease of monitoring an eruptive process. This calls for trust by scientists in their surveillance equipment and hence in its ability to identify the meaningful signals of an impending crisis. It also calls for the population, administration, and media to place trust in the scientists themselves.

Acceptance of risk varies with the development level of the country concerned. An anecdote that I brought back from a recent mission to Guatemala illustrates this well. One evening we were watching the news on television, including details of the dreadful murders perpetrated by the counter-insurgency forces, when a message was flashed on the screen: "Zunil volcano erupted: no casualties so far." Such a presentation would be wholly inconceivable in a country like France; in Guatemala, it is a measure of a very high rate of risk acceptance.

The size of the endangered area's population and industry is a factor that bears on the level of risk considered acceptable. Indeed, this factor weighs heaviest in decision making by determining the degree to which advantages in running a risk—continuity of socio-economic activities, improvement and protection of personal property, etc.—outweigh the disruption caused by evacuation—the suspension of socio-economic activities, problems relating to refugees, greater unemployment and the flight from the land, etc.

The longer a risk takes to materialize, the greater the danger that it will be seen as unreal, even if its scientific probability remains the same or increases. Studies carried out by the Massachusetts Institute of Technology in the United States have shown that evacuations lasting longer than three weeks are unlikely to be tolerated if the expected event does not occur. Impatience mounts steadily along with the wish to go home and accept the risk.

Societies tend to compare a present risk with others whose acceptability threshold is already known. It would be useful to quantify risks by the same unit of measure, such as the fatal-accident frequency rate (the number of fatalities per 1,000 population for total working time of about 100 million hours) thereby making it possible to compare low-frequency natural hazards with the risks people choose to run in their everyday lives, such as by driving, smoking, etc. It should be observed that in the rich countries, the former are on average 100 times less acceptable than the latter.

An individual will accept risk at levels different from that of his society as a whole. His range of criteria may include: (a) the size and kind of his property, the risks against which he is insured, whether he owns or rents his home; (b) his personality (optimism or pessimism, individuality, attitude to death, or attachment to the soil); and (c) his own judgement of situation, which depends on the quality of information available, on his critical faculties, and on his level of knowledge.

In the final analysis, how should responsibilities be divided between the state and the citizen in reacting to risk? Since few countries have as yet studied volcanic risk in such depth, the following observations are purely illustrative of the complexity of this societal problem.

A society that favours free enterprise and guarantees the personal freedom of a citizen viewed as an adult might place its risk-acceptability threshold fairly high. In that case the citizen, well informed by competent media, would adopt his own threshold. If this were lower than that chosen by society and if he thus left the endangered area of his own free will, he could not ask the state to underwrite his status as a refugee until the event from which the danger stemmed had actually occurred. If his threshold were higher, he would free the state of all responsibility. Of course, were the risk to materialize, indemnities, insurances, and liabilities would take effect. Society takes a risk in order to reduce the risk!

Conversely, a state that assumes responsibility for all the individual's actions and places its risk-acceptability threshold very low loses on all counts. If the risk materializes, the citizen is indemnified; if it does not, he still receives assistance. The very high price this society would appear to place on the life of the citizens is belied by the loss of identity that inevitably results from the state's refusal to delegate any part of its powers. We are in a paternalistic or, worse, a totalitarian system.

Evacuation in the Face of Hazard

In March 1980, at the time of the phreatic explosion of Mount St. Helens, the American authorities decided to evacuate the surrounding area in view of the explosive nature of the volcano's previous magmatic eruption. This decision was taken without any proof that magma was ascending within the volcano's structure, and hence the evacuation could be termed preventive. As weeks went by, the prohibition caused growing resentment among the population of the evacuated area. More and more people started bypassing the safety barriers. When the volcano reached its climax on 19 May, only two of the eighty or so people killed belonged to the surveillance staff while the others were there in breach of the ban. In Guadeloupe, where the evacuation was also preventive, the will to go home was so strong after just two weeks that the area was officially reopened the same day. Had the feared event actually materialized six weeks later, thousands would have been lost. Excessive caution may salve the conscience of scientists and administrators but is indirectly open to strong criticism on those grounds.

In the case of Mount St. Helens, the deformation of the north flank of the volcano was observed some three weeks after the evacuation had been ordered. In view of the volcano's violent past, this evidence of rising some three weeks before the paroxysmal phase was late enough to spare the lives of dozens of hasty, rash people. Had the same attitude prevailed in Guadeloupe, an unnecessary and hideously expensive evacuation could have been avoided.

This is not just the wisdom of hindsight; we are now able to make an objective critique of past experience. When all is said and done, the attitude of scientists working on a volcano during a crisis will depend on their conviction that the surveillance mechanism can be relied on to detect the ascension of magma and perhaps its explosive potential. The equipment is now sufficiently sensitive to make this more than a "profession of faith." Some devices for measuring soil movements are sensitive to changes of a few centimetres, and the side of Mount St. Helens rose by almost 100 metres before the paroxysm of 19 May! It is a reasonable conviction that should lead to an order for protective action, the only kind that provides real safety.

Conclusion

Volcanic risk entails a surprising number of psychological and political ramifications apart from the event itself and its immediate impact on the environment. Admittedly, the definition of risk-acceptability threshold may appear contradictory, but this only demonstrates the extreme complexity of the issues and shows that volcanic risk has not yet been given sufficient thought by the four human components described in this article. Each of these must search their minds and speak out, even at the cost of reopening some of the wounds that the seismo-phreatic crisis of the Guadeloupe Soufrière has inevitably left in our society. It was to underscore this need that this article was written.

NOTES

1. A hole in a volcanic surface issuing gases at high temperature.
2. *The Surveillance and Prediction of Volcanic Activity: A Review of Methods and Techniques*, Paris, Unesco, 1972, 166 pp. (Earth Sciences, 8.)
3. The science of duty, ethics.

REFERENCES

Allard, P.; Sabroux, J. Un an après l'explosion du Mt. St. Helens [One Year After the Mount St. Helens Explosion]. *La Recherche*, No. 123, 1981, pp. 756-9.

Barberi, P.; Gasparini, P. Letter to the Editor. *Journal of Volcanology and Geothermal Research*, 1979, No. 6, pp. 1-2.

Bazelon, D. Risk and Responsibility. *Science*, Vol. 205, 1979, pp. 277-80.

Bodelle, J. L'éruption du Mt. St. Helens. Qüelles lecons en tirer [The Eruption of Mt. St. Helens. What Lessons Should be Drawn]. *Corpus géologique*, 1981.

Booth, B.; Fitch, F. *La terre en colère—les cataclysmes naturels* [The Earth in Anger—Natural Cataclysms]. Paris, Éditions du Seuil, 1979, 328 pp.

Brousse, R.; Moneyron, N.; Semet, M. Sur la présence de verres non altérés dans les projections de la Soufrière, Guadeloupe, durant la crise de 1976 [Concerning the Presence of Non-devitrified Glass in Matter Projected from La Soufrière, Guadeloupe, during the 1976 Crisis]. *Comptes rendus de l'Académie des Sciences*, Vol. 285, 1977, pp. 753-4.

Fiske, R. A Deontological Code for Volcanologists? A Response to D. Bostok's Editorial. *Journal of Volcanology and Geothermal Research*, No. 5, 1979, pp. 211-12.

———. Volcano Hazards: Lessons Learned in the Eastern Caribbean, *Earthquake Information Bulletin*, Vol. 12, No. 4, 1980, pp. 150-4.

Kerr, R. Mount St. Helens: An Unpredictable Foe. *Science*, Vol. 208, 1980, pp. 1446-8.

Kilburn, C. Volcanoes and the Fate of Forecasting. *New Scientist*, 16 November 1978, pp. 511-13.

Kletz, T. The Risk Equation: What Risks Should We Run? *New Scientist*, Vol. 74, 1977, pp. 320-2.

McBirney (alias Bostok), D. Editorial: A Deontological Code for Volcanologists? *Journal of Volcanology and Geothermal Research*, Vol. 4, 1978.

McGinty, L.; Atherley, G. Acceptability versus Democracy. *New Scientist*, Vol. 74, 1977, pp. 523-5.

Ministère de L'Équipement et Ministére de l'Intérieur. *Concerning the Participation of the Public Safety Services in the Preparation of Urban Development Plans*, 24 February 1976. (Circular No. 76-36.)

Ravetz, J. The Risk Equation: The Political Economy of Risk. *New Scientist*, 8 September 1977, pp. 598-9.

Semet, M.; Vincent, P. La difficile prévision volcanique [The Difficult Job of Volcanic Forecasting]. *Le Monde*, 6 August 1980, p. 10.

Sigvaldson, G. Reply to Editorial (D. McBirney: A Deontological Code for Volcanologists?). *Journal of Volcanology and Geothermal Research*, Vol. 4, 1978, XI-III.

Tazieff, H. La Soufrière, Volcanology and Forecasting. *Nature*, Vol. 269, 1977, pp. 96-7.

———. L'activité volcanique et la prévision des risques [Volcanic Activity and Risk Forecasting]. *'Martinique-Guadeloupe'*, *guide géologique régional*, Paris, Masson, 1980.

———. Letter to the Editor. *Journal of Volcanology and Geothermal Research*, Vol. 8, No. 1, 1980, pp. 3-6.

Tomblin, J. Deontological Code, Probabilistic Hazard Assessment or Russian Roulette? *Journal of Volcanology and Geothermal Research*, Vol. 5, 1979, pp. 213-15.

———. Learning to Live with a Volcano. *Caribbean Commercial and Industrial Report*, No. 3, 1979.

———. The Definition of Acceptable Risk. *Volcanic Emergencies*. Paris. Unesco. (In press.)

———. Communication between Scientists, Civil Authorities, News Media and the Public. *Volcanic Emergencies*. Paris, Unesco. (In press.)

Walker, G. Volcanic Hazards and the Prediction of Volcanic Eruptions. *Geological Society of London, Misc.*, Vol. 3, 1974, pp. 23-41.

Westercamp, D. Une méthode d'évaluation et de zonation des risques volcaniques a la Soufrière de Guadeloupe [A Method for Volcanic Risk Evaluation and Zoning at La Soufrière, Guadeloupe]. *Bull. Vokan*, 1980, p. 4342.

———. Le risque volcanique [Volcanic Risk]. In: J. Goguel (ed.), *Géologie de l'environnement*, pp. 45-66. Paris, Masson, 1980.

TO DELVE MORE DEEPLY

Evaluation of Risk and the Decision-making Process. A joint seminar by the United States National Academy of Sciences and the Mouvement Universel de la Responsabilité Scientifique (MURS), 173 boulevard St. Germain, 75272 Paris Cedex 06, Paris, December 1980.

The New Superstition

Paul Larson

When the world was young, man's ignorance of psychology was exceeded only by his ignorance of everything else. He knew nothing of the laws of physics, but he did have an intuitive understanding of the way humans think, feel, and behave. That's when he did a ridiculous thing; he applied what he knew about human psychology to inanimate objects.

When a volcano erupted, for instance, he figured it must be angry, because that's the way people act when they're angry. Based on this, the treatment for active volcanoes was clear—they must be placated with gifts and sacrifices. That's called superstition.

We've come a long way since then. We've learned that when things get hot, they expand and build up pressure. Our understanding of physical science has progressed far beyond our knowledge of human psychology. When people get angry, they still act like volcanoes. We understand why volcanoes erupt, but now we want to know the proper treatment for an angry man. You guessed it—the wisdom of our time is to apply the laws of volcanoes to human behavior.

We must not allow pressure to build up; we must blow off steam, express our anger. The repression of feelings is viewed as the root cause of mental illness. This treatment is applied to all emotions, desires, drives, urges, and itches.

The application of physical science to human nature is no less ridiculous than was the application of human nature to physical objects. It is the new superstition.

We live in a very superstitious age. We're told to assert ourselves to prevent stress. They say crying will prevent depression. We believe pornography will reduce the incidence of rape and mourning will preclude suicide. We've bought the idea that if our feelings are not fulfilled, an emotional pressure will build up within us until we explode into some form of mental illness.

But when desire is gratified, it grows stronger, not weaker. Appetites are enlarged by feeding, muscles by exercise, and skills by practice. In this respect, at least, people are different from volcanoes. Human habits are strengthened by repetition and weakened by abstinence.

Although some invoke this superstition to justify hedonism, others are true believers. Intelligent, well-meaning parents teach their children to drink alcohol to prevent alcoholism, relax sexual taboos to hedge against debauchery, and condone recreational drugs to ward off addiction.

They believe small doses will immunize them from the potential disaster of pent-up passion. Likewise, many parents fear they've driven their own children to drugs by being too repressive. While the freaky kids are getting high at parties, it's the guilt-ridden parents who are in psychotherapy. These are the people who used to lay sacrifices at the foot of angry mountains.

The repression of feelings will not make you sick; it will make you civilized. There are people who hardly ever throw temper tantrums, yet remain reasonably healthy. Whole societies have been stoic in the face of tragedy and suffered no diminution of their mental capacity.

People can control their emotions without developing nervous tics, neurotic fears, or heart conditions. The rise of civilization is the story of how man learned to repress his feelings.

I'll now reveal the secret to a happy life: do things that are good for you and stop doing things that are bad for you, regardless of how you "feel" about it. I'll confess, this is not original with me. But it's been forgotten by this superstitious generation.

Reprinted from the *Washington Post*, 17 August 1983, with the kind permission of the author, Paul Larson.

Haroun Tazieff first of all places the danger of loss of life from either volcanoes or earthquakes far behind that found in driving, smoking and drinking, and blames the mass media for this distortion of the public's view of things. As for the two violent forces of nature, he sees loss from earthquakes minimized through better design of earthquake-resistant buildings while the toll from volcanoes can be reduced through improved forecasting and public education.

Chapter 7
Seismic and Volcanic Hazards

Haroun Tazieff

Haroun Tazieff holds ministerial rank in the French Government, with the title, Secrétaire d'État auprès du Premier Ministre chargé de la prévention des risques naturels et technologiques majeurs (Secretary of State, Prime Minister's Office, for the Prevention of Major Natural and Technological Hazards). A French volcanologist of Polish and Russian origins, he holds degrees in agriculture and geology. He is best known for his technical advisory missions to volcanic sites in Alaska, the Antarctic, the Azores, Chile, Costa Rica, Ethiopia, Guadeloupe, Iceland, Indonesia, Iran, Italy, Japan, the New Hebrides, New Zealand, the Philippines and Yemen; he is also respected for his numerous scientific and popular books, films, and other audio-visual materials dealing with seismology and volcanoes.

Mass Media Distorts Relative Danger

Volcanoes kill fewer people than earthquakes, earthquakes kill fewer people than road accidents, and road accidents kill fewer people than wars! In the present century less than 100,000 casualties have been caused by volcanic eruptions, and earthquakes have been responsible for twenty-five times that number, whereas millions and millions of lives have been lost in car and motorcycle accidents, not to mention those tens of millions of individuals who have suffered serious, permanent injuries; there is really no comparison.

Yet volcanic and seismic catastrophes, less dangerous though they are, inspire far more terror, for three reasons: the spectacular aspect of natural disasters, their unpredictability (contrasting with the daily quote of road accidents), and the influence of the press and the mass media. If television were as willing to show the horrifying injuries inflicted every day by bad drivers as it is to feature the devastating effects of earthquakes, the accident statistics would certainly fall sharply (just as there would be a significant drop in the uncountable number of victims of alcohol or tobacco, if television were to bring home the ravages of those two scourges). But outspoken descriptions of the havoc wrought by volcanoes or earthquakes do not give offense to any financial or industrial lobby, whereas such descriptions would not be tolerated in the case of cars, alcohol, or tobacco.

Having made this point so as to cut the earthquake and volcano "ogres" down to size among the murderous enemies of mankind, we must admit, despite the above-mentioned averages for the casualties caused in a century or in a year, that they are very hungry monsters and sometimes devour an appallingly large number of victims: some volcanoes have claimed several tens of thousands of lives in a single eruption. But this is exceptional, and the two or three death-dealing eruptions that occur in an average year somewhere in the world claim only a few thousand. In fact, several years may go by without anyone at all being killed by a volcano. Earthquakes, however, take an annual toll of human lives and almost every year their victims are counted by thousands and even, as in 1928, 1950 or 1976, by hundreds of thousands.

Acceptance of Risk Widely Observed

On hearing of a catastrophe caused by an earthquake or a volcanic eruption, many people exclaim in bewilderment: "But how is it that people choose to stay in such places when they *know* that sooner or later an earthquake (or a volcanic eruption) is going to destroy their homes and even kill them? Worse still, if they happen to survive the disaster, how can they rebuild their homes on the same spot?"

For anyone with first-hand knowledge of these things, the answer is clear: first of all, people know from experience that the probability of a cataclysm occurring twice in the same part of the world during their lifetime is, if not nil, at least negligible; secondly, people are attached to their country, their region, and their village, both for sentimental and for economic reasons, and emigration means tearing up their roots even if their town has been completely destroyed; thirdly, unless they are willing to settle abroad, and then only in areas carefully selected for that purpose, they have little or nothing to gain by leaving their part of the country and might even feel less secure. We can point to the striking example of El Asnam which, though destroyed twice within a quarter of a century (1954 and 1980), is being rebuilt on the same site to everyone's astonishment. But since all the Mediterranean part of Algeria, as opposed to the Saharan, is doomed to suffer at any time from violent earthquakes, where could they build another town that would not be equally at risk? If a person having survived the El Asnam earthquake were to move to Algiers, Oran, or Annaba, he might well be killed by an earthquake occurring there a few years or a few decades later.

And so hundreds of millions of human beings are living with the danger of a catastrophic earthquake or volcanic eruption hanging over their heads, and they have no alternative, because even if they wanted to (which is usually far from being the case) they could not make new homes in regions free from such hazards: the earth is already overcrowded.

Earthquake-Resistant Buildings

Must they then resign themselves to the inevitable and simply hope that nothing will happen during their own lifetime or during that of their children? Not at all. It is possible, by applying the straightforward but strict rules for designing earthquake-resistant buildings, to reduce very substantially the scale of earthquake destruction and hence the number of casualties; it is also possible, by predicting violent eruptions, to prevent hecatombs of the type experienced at Pompeii or at Saint-Pierre in Martinique. The aim of predicting a disaster is to enable the threatened zone to be evacuated in time, but the prediction can only serve a practical purpose—though it may be of scientific interest—when it is sufficiently accurate as regards both time and place.

At present it is almost impossible to forecast precisely when and where a lethal and destructive earthquake will occur, and the magnificant success scored by the Chinese in 1975 when they accurately predicted the Haicheng earthquake is the one and only exception which proves the rule. On the other hand, wherever people are exposed to seismic hazards, it is easy to build structures that will not collapse upon their occupants, which would cost very little more than badly constructed ones.

Volcanic Activity Prediction

Contrary to what can be done in the case of earthquakes, it is all but impossible to build anything capable of withstanding fairly thick lava-flows, heavy showers of volcanic ash or the devastating blast-wave sometimes produced by an eruption; the only hope is to evacuate the area, but this is only economically feasible when the prediction is absolutely accurate. Fortunately, accuracy is possible, though not easy. Unlike earthquakes, which suddenly occur deep inside the earth's crust without any conspicuous, or at least unambiguous, sign appearing on the surface, volcanic eruptions, though likewise generated in the bowels of the earth, are nevertheless exclusively surface phenomena. This means that the magma cannot reach the surface without giving premonitory signs, and these signs are relatively easy to interpret.

An earthquake is a sudden shock coming at the end of a long preparatory period lasting several decades, during which there is a build-up of pressure originating in the depths of the earth, beyond the reach of investigation. The earthquake occurs at the moment when the accumulated strain exceeds the limit of the rock's resistance to stress. A volcanic eruption, on the other hand, matures as molten magma rises towards the surface, and physical and chemical changes gradually take place within the magmatic mass. The upward movement of the magma, as well as the physical and chemical reactions, can be easily detected. So long as volcanologists are competent enough to interpret their measurements correctly, they have no difficulty in predicting the time when the eruption will take place.

Unfortunately, however paradoxical it may seem, there is usually nothing to be gained from forecasting the eruption of a volcano (except where people live very close to the area concerned, as at Vulcano or on the slopes of a volcano such as Etna). There are two reasons for this.

The first is that an eruption hardly ever begins violently enough to endanger the local population, so that there is plenty of time, once the phenomenon has got under way, to decide whether or not evacuation is advisable.

The second reason is that scarcely three, four, or five eruptions out of a hundred take the form of really dangerous explosions. It would not be very sensible to evacuate a population when the risk is estimated at only 5 percent, and is not likely to rise—except in the few cases of volcanoes whose slopes are populated right up to the edge of the crater—before the end of the first harmless phase.

Public Education

What we must be able to do, on the other hand, is to predict whether or not there will be a dangerous explosion and, if so, what it will be like and when precisely it will happen: a few days after the beginning of the eruption or a few weeks or months later? The point is that, if there has to be an evacuation—an operation that is both very distressing and extremely costly for the community—it must be delayed as long as possible and people must be allowed to go back home as soon as possible after the cataclysm. An attempt at this kind of prediction can be successful provided that the way in which the eruption develops during its initial phase is intelligently observed and careful measurements are made of all measurable parameters; and also on condition that the volcanologist is capable of interpreting all data in terms of volcanic activity. This skill cannot always be taken for granted, nor is it always very easy to acquire, but it can quite often be successfully practised by experienced volcanologists.

Throughout the world, a few hundred million human beings live at the foot, or even on the very flanks, of dangerous volcanoes. A monitoring system should therefore be developed to reduce the number of victims to the minimum. But there would already be less loss of life and less destruction of property if these communities were taught what volcanoes are, what they risk in the event of an eruption, what protective action to take against the various types of hazard, and so forth. There could be no better way of disseminating such information than to use the prodigious facilities offered by radio and especially by television. A population that has been well educated in matters concerning volcanic hazards runs half the risk of a population left in the dark.

Since 1950 growing pressures on mid-latitude mountain areas—largely recreational demands in the developed world, fuel-wood and agricultural demands in the developing regions—are destroying long-standing balances and accelerating the incidence of landsliding, mud flows, avalanches, river erosion, etc. Work begun in Alpine regions of Switzerland, Austria, and the United States has evolved a new discipline—multiple hazards mapping. A United Nations University project in Nepal is extending this approach to developing countries.

Chapter 8
Mapping of Mountain Hazards

Jack D. Ives

Jack D. Ives is professor of Mountain Geoecology at the University of Colorado (United States) where he has also been Director of the University's Institute of Arctic and Alpine Research from 1967 to 1979. Prior to that he was Director of the Geographical Branch of the Canadian Federal Government in Ottawa. His interests in mountaineering and photography have drawn him into the International Mountain Society, of which he is currently President, into editing periodicals (Mountain Research and Development, Arctic and Alpine Research), *and into worldwide work for the United Nations University and Unesco's Man and the Biosphere Programme.*

Post-1950 Land Use Abuses Environment

The popular image of high mountains embraces ice and snow, great rock faces, raging torrents, inclement weather, and, at lower elevations, precariously placed villages and farmhouses, with fields clinging to steep slopes or overhanging deep gorges. To this could be added snow and ice avalanches, rock-falls, mud-flows, landslides and floods, amongst other catastrophic processes acting under the influence of gravity. Traditionally the world's mountain areas have been occupied by small groups of subsistence agriculturalists and pasturalists who, through generations of accumulated wisdom, have learned to minimize the catastrophic potential of their special environment. Through this process the relatively safe sites have become well recognized and occupied.

This view of high mountains is biased towards the Alps. With some modification it will fit the Caucasus, the Pyrenees, the Carpathians, the Rocky Mountains, and the North American coastal ranges. With further modification it can be applied to the Japanese Alps, the Southern Alps of New Zealand, and the southern Andes. In essence it encompasses the high mountains of mid-latitudes prior to about 1950. Since 1950 the traditional mid-latitude mountain areas have had to absorb a massive influx of new activities and large transient populations. This has been associated principally with the unprecedented development of two-season tourism and recreation, especially skiing, for the growing urban populations of the neighbouring lowlands. The enormous pressures generated by such growth in demand for recreation have all but submerged traditional land-use intelligence. Once hitherto marginal land has soared in value because of the demands for hotels, ski-resort infrastructure, and roads. In another mode of post-1950 land-use intensification, the construction of hydroelectric or irrigation reservoirs emerges as a new form of inexperienced mountain entrepreneuring. Construction occurs under such circumstances on sites previously avoided by the traditional subsistence mountain farmer. Control passes from the mountain village to large financial interests located far away from the development sites. The motif is one of short-term cash profit rather than long-term balance between subsistence livelihood and environment. While the Alps were the first mountains to experience these tremendous economic and social forces that in turn led to severe environmental impacts, the other mid-latitude mountain areas are now also being similarly threatened. One observer has commented on these disturbing changes as follows:

> An unmistakable increase in the number of disasters (floods, torrents, landslips, landslides and avalanches) occurring in the Alpine territories raises the question: What are the causes of this dangerous development? In former times, a balance existed between the vegetation, the water regime, and erosion, and man had no power to make drastic changes. With no modern techniques to help him, man had to trust to his instinct when siting his settlements and choosing his working methods. Our century, and especially the last decade, has seen the multiplication of anthropogenic components until they became practically dominant.[1]

The tropical mountain regions are also incurring progressive destabilization but the processes involved are, for the most part, very different. Here the pressures are also generated by large increases in population, but in this case the increases are mainly due to the natural growth of local populations rather than the influx of transient recreation seekers. Again 1950 is a convenient benchmark date, although in many tropical mountain areas pressures were building up during the preceding decades. Nevertheless, following the Second World War, the great expansion of health care and provision of medical facilities produced worldwide reduction in infant mortality and extended life spans. The mountain kingdom of Nepal serves as an effective example. Nepal first opened its borders to the outside world in 1950 and began its transformation from a closed feudal kingdom to a small mountain state increasingly tied to the world market and progressively dependent upon it. In this case a rapidly growing rural subsistence population covered its immediate needs by felling trees, both for cooking fuel and to make way for new agricultural terraces on steeper and steeper slopes. As the nearest trees were cut, the villager had to spend progressively more time carrying fuel from increasingly more distant sources.

When a family finds itself devoting more than two man-days per week to cutting and fetching wood-fuel, a critical limit is reached whereby animal manure, the principal and often the only form of fertilizer, is used more and more for fuel. This is the current condition of almost half the rural population of Nepal. As the agricultural terraced lands are deprived of manure, two additional developments become progressively more severe. First, crop yields are lowered, necessitating additional terracing of more marginal terrain on steeper slopes. Second, reduced soil fertility leads to a weakened soil structure and increased incidence of landsliding during the monsoon season.

A Serious Threat to World Stability

The somewhat simplified scenario outlined above represents a series of vicious circles one within another. Torrential rains during the monsoon induce mud-flows and debris-flows (locally referred to collectively as landslides). Such geomorphic processes are characteristic of steep mountain slopes, with or without human modification. However, the type of modification occurring in Nepal and many other tropical and subtropical mountain areas has led to a rapid acceleration in the incidence of landsliding. Basically, as deforestation continues, soil erosion accelerates. This is a chronic rather than a catastrophic situation since it can best be compared to a slowly spreading infection or disease. Nevertheless, the consequences of this process, while severe in the longer term for the mountain area itself, may have effects downstream of even greater magnitude. Thus significant changes in the mountain hydrological regime, with more rapid run-off during the rainy season and reduced flow during the dry season, lead to floods and siltation and to dry-season water shortage in the neighbouring lowlands.

Nepal has lost half its forest cover in the last thirty years. This situation characterizes much of the Himalaya. As a direct consequence, the Ganges delta is rapidly advancing into the Bay of Bengal and silt in suspension can be seen 500 kilometres south of the present coastline. The problem of the Himalaya/Indo-Gangetic Plain is of sufficient magnitude, with major international ramifications, that it can be described as one of the more serious threats to world stability over the next two decades. Yet this situation is not unique to the Himalaya. It embraces much of the Andes, the East African highlands, the mountains of Burma, Yunnan, Laos, and northern Thailand, and the high country of Papua New Guinea and Indonesia, amongst many other areas. Concern for this international problem has been expressed by many agencies and governments.

The United Nations University Mountain Hazards Mapping Project

The involvement of the United Nations University is by no means unique or original. What is new, however, is the approach that is being taken to mountain-hazard problem solving in tropical mountain countries. This approach stems from the realization that the overall problem of increasing economic, social, and environmental instability in mountain lands would be unmanageably large even if enormous financial resources and manpower were available. With the very modest resources of UNU's Programme on the Use and Management of Natural Resources, it was decided that the best approach was to develop, and apply on an experimental scale, the recently emerging methodology of natural hazards mapping.

As implied in the opening paragraphs, steep mountain slopes, by definition, are subject to downhill movement of material (snow, water, rock, soil, and vegetation, in various mixtures) under gravity. Mountain geomorphologists with an academic bent and engineers with a practical interest have involved themselves in the study of the effects of geomorphic processes and snow mechanics on mountain-slope stability for several decades. Furthermore, there have evolved numerous methods of identifying areas especially subject to mass movement. Perhaps the best known is the work of the Swiss Foundation for Snow and Avalanche Research from which has evolved the Swiss Avalanche Zoning Plan.[2] In Austria, H. Aulitzky has recommended and implemented combined mapping of avalanche paths and mountain torrents and has developed a traffic-light colour system (red, amber, and green) to designate areas subject to hazardous processes.[3] Many individuals and agencies throughout the world have tackled specific problems, whether they be landslides, mud-flows, floods, the dramatic interaction of volcanic eruption and mud-flow, coastal erosion, and so on.

Within mountain areas many forms of natural processes overlap both in time and space. An avalanche path may be a threat to life and property from flowing snow in winter and spring, while in summer and autumn the dominant processes could be mud-flow, mountain torrent, landslide, or rock-fall, and the flooding of the valley-bottom run-out area. This concern with multiple hazards has recently led to a geographic or regional approach to the delineation of areas subject to mass movement. Amongst others, two projects, one in the Bernese Oberland, the other in the Colorado Rockies, led to experimentation with the cartographic representation of all natural hazards within a single area. The Swiss approach resulted in the production of a very detailed and highly accurate series of multicoloured maps for the area around Grindelwald on a scale of 1:10,000.[4] In the Colorado Rockies the area to be covered was significantly greater and the available topographical base maps were at the reconnaissance scale of 1:24,000.[5] This resulted in the production of two series of maps in black and white (avalanches treated separately as one series). From these beginnings the two groups joined forces and developed a combined natural hazards map at 1:24,000 for a test area of the Colorado Front Range.[6]

Nepal Selected for Experiment

The brief foregoing description provides the setting for the United Nations University involvement in mountain-hazard mapping. Within the UNU programme on natural resources, concern over the use and management of these resources in mountain lands led to creation of a subproject to study highland-lowland interactive systems. One component of this became mountain-hazard mapping, with Nepal selected as a test area. This development depended upon the natural-hazard mapping collaboration between Berne University and the University of Colorado. It was deemed timely to attempt an adaptation of the natural-hazard mapping in the two mid-latitude high-mountain areas to a tropical or subtropical mountain area. Following an invitation from the Nepalese Government, Nepal was selected for the experiment in 1978. And it was quickly realized during a field reconnaissance in March-April 1979 that the term "natural hazard" should be replaced by "mountain hazard" taking cognizance of the overwhelming human modification of the Himalayan landscape.

The reconnaissance in the spring of 1979 led to the outline of a medium-term research project. The major component was the production of prototype mountain-hazard maps for three representative areas of Nepal: a high-altitude area extending above and below the upper timberline in Sagarmatha National Park of the Khumbu-Himal; a section of the Middle Mountains, extending along the Trisuli Highway between Kathmandu and Kakani; and a low-altitude transect across the Siwalik Range and out on to the Terai. This selection of three areas was also appropriate in providing a field base for possible future in-depth analysis of highland-lowland interactions. In addition, realization that human activities had almost totally modified some of these areas led to the incorporation of ethnographic studies as a means of determining the responses of the local people to landslide and other catastrophic processes as well as assessing their possible reaction to future land-use policy making.

For a variety of reasons the Middle Mountain area (Kathmandu-Kakani) was given first priority. The fieldwork was initiated in September 1979 and completed in April 1981. Much data analysis and report writing has been completed, two multicoloured maps have been printed (land use and geomorphology), and several technical papers are already in print.[7] The final mountain-hazard prototype map, on a scale of 1:10,000 actually materialized as two maps, a Base Map and a Mountain Hazards and Slope Stability.[8] Field work began in autumn 1982 in the Khumbu-Himal for the second phase of the project, and a final piece of work on the hard rock geology is currently in progress. For this area the mapping scale will be 1:50,000.

Mountain Research Benefits Development

Multiple-hazards mapping is still so recent an approach that effort to justify it is needed even in developed countries:

> Mountain hazards mapping is far from being a widely recognized component of either regional or site specific land-use planning. This may seem surprising in view of the series of spectacular disasters that have occurred in mountain areas in recent years. This may be because many of the large-scale mountain developments are very recent and because of the relatively new awareness that manipulation of one or a few components of a landscape affects all other components. This applies particularly to the mountains of the "Western World" where a major proportion of human impact is due to large-scale technological modification. It can also be applied to the mountains of the "Developing World" where population growth and deforestation resulting from the expansion of subsistence agriculture is the main driving force, although large-scale engineering works are by no means rare.[9]

Justification for mountain-hazard mapping in Nepal rests upon a number of assumptions. First, any land-use decision making, whether it relates to the relatively simple process of locating and designing a new highway or to the more complex process of design of an integrated regional plan, will depend for its effectiveness in large part on the type and reliability of available information. Thus a mountain-hazard map should be regarded as one component of the overall data bank to be used as a basis for decision making. In the case of the UNU project in Nepal, some additional and very useful components are being added:

studies of dynamic geomorphic processes and of human responses and perceptions. A second consideration is that the very attempt to produce a series of experimental prototype maps should lead to a much fuller understanding of landscape dynamics, including the human-natural interrelations, so that prediction of the possible effects of implementing a given policy should be that much more reliable. Additionally, the project, through its incorporation of young Nepalese scientists, is seeking to reduce Nepal's dependence on the contribution of "outside" scientists. Finally, should the experiment lead to production of a practical applied mapping methodology, with minimal modification it will be available for immediate transfer to other tropical mountain areas around the world.

Rate of Land Loss Alarming

But in terms of results gained from fieldwork in the Kathmandu-Kakani area, some provisional conclusions can be drawn. First, the studies of geomorphic processes have led to the realization that land is being lost much faster than the local people with their existing resources can reclaim. See Figure 1. It was calculated that the areal density of landslides is in excess of $2/km^2$, with an average expansion rate of 60 m^2/year. From this it can be estimated that the mean rate of land loss due to landsliding alone is 120 m^2/km^2/year. Furthermore, this figure should be doubled to take into account the inception of new landslides (estimate at 1 in 6 km^2). With a mean depth for landslides of 4 metres, an annual loss of 1,000 m^3/km^2 will result. This is an extremely high rate of loss for agricultural land, to which must be added losses from other forms of mass movement, soil erosion, and loss of soil fertility, which may appreciably exceed the losses due to landslides.

Even if the population of the Kathmandu-Kakani field area had already achieved a zero growth rate, the figures for the rate of land loss have serious implications for the near future. Given a continuation of the existing high population growth rate, the predictable outcome is mountain desertification, mass migration, and increased pressure on other lands. It can be argued, therefore, that a study such as the one described here, if given adequate publicity, could influence the decision making process before the drift to mountain desertification gets out of control.

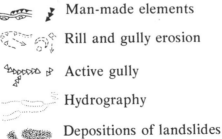 Man-made elements

Rill and gully erosion

Active gully

Hydrography

Depositions of landslides

Figure 1. Kathmandu-Kakani area: geomorphic damage.

Local Practices on Land Use

The ethnographic studies also led to some interesting conclusions. First, there is extensive local knowledge about mountain hazards and their control and mitigation derived from close, long-term observation and experience. This knowledge is interwoven with local occupancy and land-use practices. There are two local practices that at first glance appear to be contradictory, but in fact complement each other in face of the increasing pressures of slope instability and population growth. The first practice is to reclaim landslide areas by reterracing during subsequent dry seasons as labour becomes available. The second is to reduce the intensity of land use when hazard potential cannot be controlled. Thus, wet terrace slopes, the most productive and intensively utilized, are allowed to revert to dry terraces, dry terraces to rough pasture, and so on. Up-grading and recovery is then attempted when labour is available. Finally, reforestation is regarded as impractical because it limits essential crop production. This is the key indicator in terms of a mountain system moving from a stable to an unstable mode. Nevertheless a general confidence, even if qualified, is in order. Land-use planning and technical measures developed in mid-latitudes and modified for local use can facilitate conversion from the unstable to the stable mode based upon available knowledge, or relatively easily acquired knowledge, provided the political will can be generated. At least it is well known what types of information are needed and how they should be collected. But such an optimistic view becomes impaired when it moves from immediate focus on one, or a few, specific areas to the worldwide span. The situation in the Nepal Middle Mountains is not unique. Proof of this can be obtained from a quite casual inspection of the Himalaya westward and eastward from Kathmandu.

The Darjeeling floods of 1968 provide an example of the magnitude of problems associated with population growth, deforestation, and landsliding in the eastern Himalaya. Towards the end of the 1968 monsoon, heavy rains deluged Sikkim and West Bengal, and over a three-day period precipitation amounts varying between about 500 and 1,000 mm fell on the Himalaya foothills in the vicinity of Darjeeling. While this may have been a rare event (for instance, a 100-year event) and while such heavy rain would likely damage mountain slopes untouched by human activity, extensive deforestation and the presence of innumerable roads, jeep trails, and foot trails set the stage for a disaster. Some 20,000 landslides released during the third day of the rain storm; approximately 30,000 people lost their lives, and the sixty-kilometre mountain highway to Darjeeling was cut in ninety-two places. Many of the losses were incurred by the villages and farms on the plain where the mountain streams debouch from the Siwaliks. But the hard lesson to be learned is that unplanned use of mountain lands can lead to disaster. This disaster may occur suddenly and spectacularly as in the Darjeeling foothills in 1968, or as a creeping disease with a little more land lost per unit area per year than can be reclaimed. And the two are by no means mutually exclusive.

The Need for an International System of Mountain Hazards Mapping

One of the very real needs facing the mountain world at large is a substantial increase in accurate data on processes both human and natural. In addition much of the large volume of existing data is scattered, relatively inaccessible, or not available in suitable format. Synthesis of available data is urgently needed as well as identification of gaps in knowledge. The dangers of mountain deforestation, overgrazing, and soil erosion have been highlighted for a decade or more. Much of this has been based upon qualitative inspection of critical areas, hypothetical considerations, and emotion, all necessary as a vital first step. But precise calculations of soil losses under different cropping systems and on different slopes are a rarity. It is common to sound the alarm about the silting of reservoirs due to soil erosion in the neighbouring hills, but accurate measurements are required under a range of different natural and human-use systems, and a time perspective must be developed.

Mountain hazards individually, such as a single winter avalanche in the Alps or the initiation of a landslide in the Middle Mountains of the Himalaya, are insignificant compared with other struggles between humanity and nature. Also, individually these chronic disorders can be controlled or checked. Nineteenth-century deforestation and, after 1950, uncontrolled land use in the Alps led to the insertion of people and property in places subject to the ravages of mountain hazards. The Alpine countries have gone a long way towards controlling the situation. While the countries concerned had a much stronger economic base from which to respond than have developing countries in the tropics, it can be argued that the prime needs are development of awareness and creation of political will, as much within international aid agencies as within the countries themselves. In this sense the concept of highland-lowland interactions is potentially very important simply because the need to avert mountain instability is crucial for the well-being of the neighbouring lowlands. However, the efforts to control and check specific sites will be much more effective if the location and size, date of initiation and rate of growth are known. Governments as well as international and bilateral agencies have expended enormous sums of money on disaster relief, repair, succour to the destitute. Some proportion of such funds should be devoted to prediction and prevention and establishment of an international system of mountain-hazard mapping would seem one useful step.

NOTES

1. H. Aulitzky, *Endangered Alpine Regions and Disaster Prevention Measures*, Strasbourg, Council of Europe, 1974. (Nature and Environment Series, 6.)
2. H. Frutiger, "History and Actual State of Legislation of Avalanche Zoning in in Switzerland," *Journal of Glaciology*, Vol. 26, No. 94, 1980, pp. 313-24.
3. H. Aulitzky, "Berucksichtigung der Wildbach und Lawinen gefahrengebiete als Grundlage der Raumordnung von Gebirgslandern," *100 Jahre Hochschule fur Bodenkultur*, Vol. IV, No. 2, 1973, pp. 81-113.
4. H. Kienholz, "Kombinierte geomorphologische Gefahrenkarte, 1:10,000 von grindelwald," *Catena*, Vol. 3, No. 3/4 (parts A and B), 1977, pp. 265-94; "Maps of Geomorphology and Natural Hazards of Grindelwald, Scale 1:10,000," *Arctic and Alpine Research*, Vol. 10, No. 2, 1978, pp. 169-84.
5. J. Ives, A. Mears, P. Carrara and M. Bovis, "Natural Hazards in Mountain Colorado," *Annals of the Association of American Geographers*, Vol. 66, No. 1, 1976, pp. 129-44; J. Ives and M. Bovis, "Natural Hazards Maps for Land-use Planning, San Juan Mountain, Colorado, U.S.A.," *Arctic and Alpine Research*, op. cit., pp. 185-212; J. Ives and P. Krebs, "Natural Hazards Research and Land-use Planning Responses in Mountainous Terrain: The Town of Vail, Colorado Rocky Mountains, U.S.A.," *Arctic and Alpine Research*, op. cit., pp. 213-22.
6. H. Kienholz, "The Use of Aerial Photographs for Natural Hazard Mapping in Medium Scales for Planning Purpose on a Regional Level in Not Very Accessible Mountain Areas from Experience and Mapping Experiments in the Colorado Rocky Mountains," *Interpraevent*, 1979; V. Dow, H. Kienholz, M. Plam and J. Ives, "Mountain Hazards Mapping: The Development of a Prototype Combined Hazards Map, Monarch Lake Quadrangle, Colorado, U.S.A.," *Mountain Research and Development*, Vol. 1, No. 1, 1981, pp. 55-64.
7. N. Caine and P. Mool, "Channel Geometry and Flow Estimates for Two Small Maountain Streams in the Middle Hills, Nepal," *Mountain Research and Development*, Vol. 1, No. 3/4, 1981; J. Ives and B. Messerli, "Mountain Hazard Mapping in Nepal: Introduction to an Applied Mountain Research Project," *Mountain Research and Development*, op. cit.
8. Kienholz, H., Schneider, G., Bichsel, M., Grunder, M., and Mool, P. *Mountain Research and Development*, Vol. 4, No. 3, 1984, pp. 247-266.
9. Dow et al., op. cit., p. 56.

AUTHOR'S ACKNOWLEDGEMENTS

The UNU/Nepal Mountain Hazards Mapping Project is the result of collaboration amongst several institutions and many individuals. Unesco's Man and the Biosphere (MAB) Programme has provided much conceptual input and has actually combined with UNU and His Majesty's Government of Nepal to make this a collaborative project. The authors of all the papers cited here have made significant contributions together with The Honourable Dr. Ratna S.J.B. Rana, Drs. C.L. Shrestha and K.K. Shrestha, Miss Sumitra Manandhar, Mr. Pradeep Mool and Rabindra Tamrakar, all of Kathmandu. Dr. Kirsten Johnson, Messrs. Heini Hafner and Guy Schneider and Miss Ann Olson have made valuable contributions to the fieldwork. Dr. Hans Kienholz bore the brunt of the responsibility for the fieldwork as well as providing the framework for the mountain hazards mapping. Berne University (Switzerland); Clark University of Worcester, Massachusetts, and the University of Colorado at Boulder (United States); and Tribhuvan University, Kathmandu, and the staffs of many departments of His Majesty's Government of Nepal provided vital assistance. Finally, Professor Dr. Walther Manshard, former vice-rector, Mr. Lee MacDonald, Programme Officer, UNU, and Dr. Gisbert Glaser, Unesco MAB, were indispensable to the initiation and progress of the project. To these and many more, acknowledgements and thanks are due, and not least to the patient, kindly, and helpful people of the Kathmandu-Kakani field area.

Avalanches today represent a greater potential hazard because of the influx of skiers into mountain resorts in winter. A determined effort must be made to understand the causes of avalanches and to predict them in good time so as to prevent the occurrence of catastrophes. At present the forecasting of avalanche risk depends primarily on a better understanding of snow as a material and of the way it changes and evolves each season between falling and melting.

Chapter 9
What Triggers an Avalanche?

Dominique Marbouty

The author, a graduate of the École Polytechnique in Paris, is head of the Snow Study Centre at the National Meteorological Service in Grenoble, France. This article is reproduced (with minor modifications) from La Recherche, *May 1981, with the kind permission of the editor and author.*

Avalanches have occurred ever since mountains and snow have existed. History tells us that they afflicted Hannibal's army during his famous crossing of the Alps. They have always been an impressive sight for the rare spectators who happen to have witnessed the sudden disruption of the peace of the mountains by a mass of snow hurtling down the slopes. Until quite recently, however, only the inhabitants of high mountain regions were obliged to take a close interest in them. They accumulated a store of empirical knowledge based on observation of the valleys where they were a regular occurrence and of the weather conditions conducive to them.

The first representatives of technological civilization to come face to face with the phenomenon were the builders of roads, railways, and houses. More recently, fresh impetus has been given to the scientific study of avalanches by the influx of tourists into mountain resorts. There is a need for more scientific information concerning avalanches. A map must be prepared of all the places where avalanches have been known to occur, drawing on people's remembrances, records and aerial photography. Estimates are needed of the risks involved in building in a particular area. On a more theoretical level, researchers must try to construct models for the flow of a mass of snow after the avalanche has begun. This should, among other things, make it possible to estimate as accurately as possible the strength and extent of the protection required in danger zones where buildings already exist or where building will prove unavoidable. In this article, we shall be concerned primarily with the bearing this knowledge has on the forecasting of avalanches.

What Makes Snow "fracture"?

One of the first ideas that springs to mind is that an avalanche is triggered by a mechanical phenomenon, which must therefore be examined and reproduced in model form. Major research is in fact in progress to identify the laws governing the process of deformation and fracture of a mass of snow under certain strains. There is still a long way to go, however. Researchers agree in assigning snow to the category of "visco-elastic" bodies but they are not yet in agreement over the particular model to apply. They know that density, elasticity, and viscosity are essential for determining the behaviour of snow, but that these are not sufficient to give a complete picture. In addition, the models are still very simple (a cross-section of a mass of snow on an inclined plane), whereas a realistic simulation would have to take into account the three physical dimensions and time as well, since snow is an evolving material.[1] Any mechanical approach is rendered extremely complex by the fact that there are a number of different types of snow with very varying mechanical properties which change with time.

What exactly is snow anyway? It is ice crystals of very variable form in equilibrium with air saturated in water vapour and, in some cases, with liquid water. Depending on their form, their relative density and the presence or absence of water, the mechanical properties of the crystals are entirely different. The density of snow varies from a possible minimum of 20 kg/m³ in the case of very light freshly fallen snow, to 600 kg/m³ (more than half the density of water) in the case of old, closely packed snow.

Important Changes over Time

The picture may be complicated still further by the fact that several layers of snow with different properties may be rapidly superimposed in the same spot and, in particular, by the fact that a given type of snow evolves in time. The form and density of the grains vary in accordance with the thermodynamic changes that the snow undergoes (the melting process being the most obvious). By altering the mechanical properties of a given layer of snow in the course of the season, these changes play, as we shall see, a very important role in triggering avalanches. In simplified terms, snow may be considered as a body in equilibrium on an inclined plane. It may begin to slide if the forces pulling it downwards (the weight of the snow) become too strong. But equilibrium may also be disturbed if the reaction forces holding it in place (the cohesiveness of the snow and friction against the slope) tend to weaken.

For the time being, distinguishing between the different types of snow and knowledge of their development play a more important part in our understanding of snow and in the practical activity of forecasting than the mechanical understanding of what occurs within a mass of snow. Just as there are several different kinds of snow, there are also several kinds of avalanche corresponding systematically to the various stages in the life of snow: avalanches of fresh snow, slab avalanches (with wind crusts constituting a special case), and avalanches of melting snow.

Avalanches of Fresh Snow

Avalanches may range from a small, inoffensive flow to a huge, destructive and lethal mass consisting of up to 100 million cubic metres of moving snow with a pressure of impact that may be anything up to 100 tons per square metre. The most dangerous and proportionately most frequent avalanches (roughly 80 percent of the total) are those of fresh snow which occur, as their name indicates, during or shortly after a snowfall. They are particularly spectacular if they set in motion a large mass of powdery snow, that is, very recent snow that has not yet become compact and cold (below $0°C$ there is no liquid water between the crystals to add weight to the snow). Once set in motion, this snow mixes with the air and flows like a heavy gas. It may reach a very high speed—up to 300 km/h according to Soviet publications—and it accumulates considerable energy as it pushes the air along in front of it, creating a kind of shock wave (see Figure 1, avalanche drawing). The aerosol thus formed suffocates anyone who comes in its way, fills the whole atmosphere, and spreads into houses.

The triggering mechanism in the case of avalanches of fresh snow is relatively simple. As the crystals interlock with one another, the snow can adhere to slopes that are quite steep, a phenomenon that snow scientists call cohesion by contact. However, the resulting equilibrium is very unstable. The slightest disturbance or even the additional weight of a further snowfall can set off a slide. As the accumulation of snow is the decisive factor, forecasters are very much concerned with the depth of fallen snow, especially when it has been snowing heavily for several days running, and they would like to be able to predict it. This is why the strictly meteorological problem of forecasting the amount of precipitation is the subject of a great deal of research at the moment.[2]

When the Wind Blows

There is a special danger if there is a wind blowing. An average snowfall of, say, fifty centimetres may cover practically no ground at all in some places and create snowdrifts over a metre thick in others, thereby enhancing the risk of avalanche. Accurate measurements of such transport, having regard to snowfall and wind, would therefore be of great value to the forecaster.

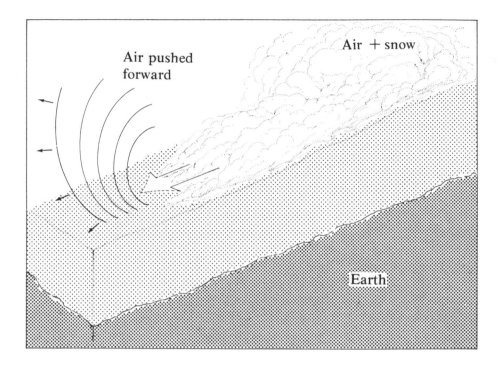

Figure 1. Avalanches of powdery snow (fresh, light and dry snow) may
be very spectacular and dangerous if a large mass of snow is
involved. Avalanches of fresh snow, caused by the weight of
the snow, do not all occur immediately after the fall.

Forecasters should also be sure of the mechanics of snow transport
before they can predict its volume accurately, but this is not the case.
There are two schools of thought. One, the Russian school (Duynin),
assumes that particles move chiefly by saltation; in other words, by
leaps within a layer of ten centimetres above the ground through the
impetus of wind-shear. Another, the Australian school (Radok),
considers that snow is transported principally by means of turbulent
diffusion, the particles remaining suspended in the air.[3] To settle the
question, therefore, measurements need to be taken at different
heights. The studies already carries out in the polar regions have been
repeated in the United States and Switzerland. At a given site, the
question that must be answered by architects, safety experts, or
hydrologists (snow being a water reserve) is where the transported snow
is going to be deposited. As a rule, it is deposited on the lee side of any

obstacles. But in the mountains the prevailing wind may be diverted by an infinite number of factors.

Delayed Avalanches

An avalanche of fresh snow is not finished when the first slide has occurred. A further part of the avalanche occurs in the days following, even if the temperature has not been high enough to start a thaw. The cause of this strange delay is now well known. It is one of the three major transformations to which snow is subject, namely isothermal metamorphism. When snow first falls, it is made up of a large variety of crystals. Some days later, only fragments of the initial forms remain and these are smooth and rounded as though they had melted. Still later, only small round grains a few tenths of a millimetre in diameter remain, the "fine grains" (see Figure 2). What has happened? On the one hand, the snow has been subjected to mechanical forces. As it is gradually buried, the snow has to support the weight of the upper layers, which leads to destruction of the crystals. This process is accelerated if the precipitation is accompanied by wind which breaks the crystals in transporting them and reduces them to fragments. It may also be accelerated by artificial compaction (compression of snow on ski slopes). Nevertheless, such mechanical action does not fully account for the smooth and rounded shape of the crystal fragments or the subsequent formation of fine grains. An additional thermodynamic mechanism also comes into play. It is based, as are all processes occurring in dry snow, on pressure disequilibria in satured vapour.4

Figure 2. Some avalanches occur only several days after a snowfall when the cohesion of snow crystals due to contact no longer exists because the crystals themselves have been gradually transformed into recognizable particles, and then into fine grains.

The mechanical consequences of this transformation account for the delay in some avalanches of fresh snow. Initially, the crystals of fresh snow are interlocked, thus causing the mass of snow to cohere by contact. However, as the isothermal metamorphism proceeds, this cohesion vanishes and, at a certain point, snow lying on a slope will enter into a phase of disequilibrium. The duration of the metamorphosis will depend largely on the temperature.

Thermodynamic Mechanism

In snow, the gaseous phase is continuous (the pressures therefore tend towards equilibrium) and it is saturated in water vapour so as to be in equilibrium with the solid phase (any change of pressure leads to water condensation or sublimation). But the pressure of saturated water vapour at a given point depends on the radius of curvature of the ice-gas interface of which it is a decreasing function. There is therefore disequilibrium between areas with a low radius of curvature (points) and areas with a high radius of curvature (planes). A transfer occurs between these two areas. The points will be sublimated and the vapour thus released will be transported towards the plane surfaces where it will condense. This is what causes the rounding of the crystals. In practice, this theory has not provided an adequate explanation for the process as a whole. Several authors have tried to quantify the transformation described. Using a very simplified model, Perla* calculated that a particle of one micron disappears in one hour, while a particle of a hundred microns takes a whole year. This process thus seems to be an effective way of eliminating very fine dendrites and irregularities but it does not explain the whole metamorphosis. Theory also shows that the pressure of saturated vapour at a given point depends not only on the radius of curvature but also on temperature, of which it is an increasing function. Consequently, differences in temperature between different points of the crystal or of the layer may likewise result in transfers from "warm" to "cold" areas. The process dependent on the radii of curvature predominates at the outset but temperature irregularities very rapidly take over the principal role in metamorphism.[†]

* R. Perla, "Temperature Gradient and Equitemperature Metamorphism of Dry Snow," *Report of the Second International Meeting on Snow and Avalanches*, Grenoble, ANENA, 1978.
† S. Colbeck, "Thermodynamics of Snow Metamorphism due to Variations in Curvature," *Report of the Workshop "Snow in Motion*," Fort Collins, 1979; *Journal of Glaciology*, Vol. 26, No. 94, pp. 291-301.

If it is close to zero, a few days will be enough. If it is very cold, on the other hand, the process is much slower and may take several weeks.

The practical implications are in any case important. It should be stressed that the process of isothermal metamorphism is inexorable. Sooner or later after a snowfall, a certain number of slopes will be ripe for an avalanche. If the temperature rises, the transformation will be rapid and the necessary dislodgements will occur within a short time. On the other hand, if the snowfall is followed by a cold period, the metamorphosis will be impeded so that the danger remains latent.

Sintering and Slab Avalanches

Concurrently with isothermal metamorphism, another phenomenon begins to develop with the rounding of the grains. This is known as sintering. By causing the grains to adhere to one another, it leads to renewed cohesion in the snow that has not been carried away. It thus completes the transformation from light, fresh snow to a much more compact and rigid mass which, pending a thaw, is no longer in danger of moving, except in the form of a slab avalanche.

The sintering process accounts for the formation of wind crusts. These hard slabs of snow are formed when snow is deposited on leeward slopes. The transport of snow by the wind fractures the crystals, making them much smaller than before and thus promoting fast and firm cohesion once the snow is redeposited. The influence of the temperature is small, and the theory occasionally heard that crusts do not form when it is very cold is unfounded.

Slab avalanches are due to the fact that highly cohesive snow (wind crust or sintered snow in general) behaves as a solid attached to the slope with varying degrees of firmness by its upper, lateral, and lower bonds. There is a risk of slab avalanche when the lower bond is inadequate, that is to say, when the crust rests on an unstable sublayer. This sublayer may consist of frozen snow, graupel, or simply fine grains that are less effectively welded together than those forming the crust. It may also consist of depth hoar or surface hoar created by two very interesting phenomena that we shall be considering below.

In the case of wind crust, it may happen that there is no lower bond at all if the snow deposited by the wind forms a very hard layer that does not follow the contours of the compacted lower layers and thus leaves a space. A slab will then be set in motion if another bond

The Sintering Process

The sintering process can be demonstrated very easily by placing two small spheres of ice together. After a few hours, a solid bond forms between them. This phenomenon is also known in the field of powder metallurgy. It is due to the fact that the free energy of two grains in tangential contact is not minimal and can be reduced by a transfer of material towards the point of contact. This transfer may be effected by several different mechanisms. In the case of snow, the mechanism is similar to the one we have just mentioned in connection with isothermal metamorphism. The pressure of saturated vapour also depends on the radius of curvature where concave surfaces are concerned (negative curvature), since they have an even lower saturated vapour pressure than flat surfaces. Hence, there are appreciable differences in saturated vapour pressure between the surfaces with a very small negative radius of curvature, represented by the points of contact, and the immediately adjacent convex surfaces. Thus, bonds or bridges are formed between the crystals. It has been possible to study the impact of different parameters, in particular the average size of grains, on the effectiveness of this sintering process.* Thus in 1977, Delsol, using a very simplified model (two grains, isothermal environment), calculated that it required only a few minutes for grains of 0.1 mm to reach the same state of cohesion, while those of 1 mm needed several hours and grains of 10 mm (which exist only in theory) would require several years. Temperature, on the other hand, is of only secondary importance and provided that it is below the freezing-point, does not affect size.†

* P. Hobbs and B. Mason, "The Sintering and Adhesion of Ice," *Philosophical Magazine,* Vol. 9, 1964, p. 181.
† F. Delsol, *Premier rapport sur l'étude des plaques de neige,* Grenoble ANENA/DSC, 1977.

weakens and breaks or through intervention by an outside agent (increase in weight due to a fresh fall of snow, a passing skier, etc.). The configuration of the terrain then plays a major role, and fractures usually occur on convex surfaces where snow is subject to traction (to which, unlike compression, it has very little resistance). R. Perla, a Canadian researcher to whom we owe a large number of practical observations, found on the basis of 190 case studies that fractures occur on slopes of between 25 and 55 degrees. These slabs are very dangerous for skiers because they are extremely difficult to locate and their degree of instability is hard to assess because it depends on conditions inside the snow.[5] Slabs are at present the subject of numerous studies, especially in the United States. These studies are aiming, first of all, to reproduce accurately the release mechanism, because it is not yet known for sure whether it is caused by shearing or traction. Naturally, it is hoped to formulate decisive and quantifiable criteria of stability.[6]

Depth Hoar

Among the phenomena that lead to the creation of an unstable sublayer, that of depth hoar has been very widely studied during the past few years. The studies carried out have highlighted the importance of a phenomenon of which one is not always aware because the hoar is not visible beneath the snow. They have also enabled the parameters on which it depends to be quantified, which is of considerable value to forecasters. The hoar takes the form of large hollow crystals (the density of the snow cover does not change) which look somewhat like coarse salt and are often shaped like striated pyramids. They are very fragile and their tendency to crumble under the weight of the upper layers is what creates the risk of avalanche. It often takes them one or more weeks to develop, but the process is irreversible and is due to another type of snow metamorphism, known as "gradient metamorphism."

Depth hoar is all the more dangerous because once it develops it may persist throughout the winter, forming an unstable foundation for the mass of snow above. The size of the crystals makes them insensitive to the isothermal process. They can undergo no further change until fusion takes place in the spring.

Gradient Metamorphism

It is quite common to find a negative temperature gradient in snow, since it is an effective thermal insulator (because of the air it encloses) and as energy is generated by the underlying soil (a geothermal flow of 5 watts per square metre), the base of the cover hardly ever falls below 0°C provided there is a sufficient depth (over 50 cm). The surface of the snow, on the other hand, by coming into equilibrium with the surrounding air, can become extremely cold. Such conditions are especially prevalent at the beginning of winter. Differences in temperature between adjacent points will again lead to saturated-vapour pressure differences and transfers of material from grain to grain. In contrast to isothermal metamorphism, the direction of temperature variations is in this case well defined. The upper portion of each grain is sublimated and condensation occurs on the lower portion of the colder grains above, or rather on a few grains only, since the grains decrease in number and the large crystals become more numerous. What causes some crystals to grow and not others is still unknown. This type of transformation has been studied in detail by the Japanese Akitaya and by Delsol.* It was long considered to be the result of a convection mechanism within the layer but it is now known that the dominant factor is transfer from grain to grain (vapour-phase diffusion).

Incidentally, an inverse (downward) metamorphosis has been produced by changing the direction of the gradient, a result which would have been impossible in the case of convection because "warmer" water vapour is supposed to rise. The form and size of the resulting crystals depend on the temperature. The closer one gets to 0° C, or ground level, the larger the crystals are. Many models have been made of this phenomenon and they have made it possible to simulate the growth of the crystals very successfully. These studies have led to the discovery of certain thresholds of great practical importance. It is known, for instance, that this metamorphism only occurs if the gradient is greater than about 0.25° C per cm—hence the importance of the temperature profiles obtained weekly by means of snow cross-sections. Recently, it has been shown that a low-temperature gradient (less than 0.2° C per cm) actually increases the cohesion of the snow by speeding up the sintering process. It is also known that metamorphism only occurs when the snow density is less than 350 kg per m3. This is one reason for the regular measurement of density and for the consolidation of ski slopes by compressing the snow as soon as it falls, starting with the very first snowfall.†

* E. Akitaya, "Studies on Depth Hoar," *Contr. Inst. Low Temp. Sci.*, Series A26, 1974, p. 1; F. Delsol, D. Marbouty, E. Pahaut and B. Pougatch, *Étude de la métamorphose de gradient par simulation en chambre froide,* Établissement d'Études et de Recherches Météorologiques, 1978. (Technical Note, No. 7.)

† D. Marbouty, "An Experimental Study of Temperature Gradient Metamorphism," *Snow in Motion*, op. cit.; D. Marbouty and A. Martin, "Étude du frittage en présence d'un faible gradient de témperature," *Report of the Sixteenth Congress of Alpine Meteorology*, Aix-les-Bains, Société Météorologique de France, 1980.

Surface Hoar

A further example of the complex way that snow evolves during the winter is a second type of hoar known as surface hoar, which may also form an unstable sublayer for subsequent precipitation. Its formation during cold clear nights is due to the fact that in the field of thermal radiation, which is to say long wavelengths from 10 to 15μ, snow is a blackbody, which always seems somewhat surprising. This means that within that particular range of wavelengths it absorbs all the radiation it receives and at the same time emits maximum radiation (an emissivity value of 0.97 is generally accepted, although measurements carried out by Dunckle in the United States yielded a value of 0.85 for very cold snow.)[7]

On some clear nights, when the clouds do not reflect emitted radiation towards the earth, this loss of energy is so great that the surface of the snow cools by more than ten degrees and also has such a powerful cooling effect on the air closest to it that the water vapour in it condenses into vertical crystals, forming surface hoar. Once broken and flattened by the next snowfall, these crystals create a sliding surface. The fact that snow is a blackbody that absorbs thermal radiation also explains why it melts in the vicinity of houses and trees which emit this type of radiation. This brings us to the last type of snow metamorphism, melting, which is the main cause of spring avalanches.

Melting Snow

It might almost be said that the sun melts snow in the spring but not in the winter. The albedo of snow, which is the proportion of solar radiation that it reflects, is a function which decreases with time. Fresh snow, for instance, has an albedo that is very close to unity, which means that it reflects almost the whole of incident solar radiation. Old snow, on the other hand, especially after it has begun to melt, may have an albedo of less than 0.5. A fine winter's day has no melting effect on cold, fresh snow. In spring, however, a day's sunshine has a considerable effect on snow that has reached a later stage of development, all the more so as the incidence of radiation is much better.

A great deal of research is being carried out on the whole subject of the interaction between radiation and snow, since the radiative properties of snow depend on a variety of factors such as thickness, crystallization, temperature, etc. The most urgent need at the moment is for accurate measurements (albedo, coefficient of attenuation) based on the different types of snow, so as to adjust existing models accordingly. Radiation is, in fact, the principal source of heat in the case of snow and hence the mean thermal cause of melting. Relatively speaking, snow does not receive a great deal of heat by means of conduction or convection, except when there is a very strong foehn (warm wind). For that matter, the idea that rain causes a thaw is generally misguided. To prove the contrary, one need only consider that the latent heat for the melting of ice is 80 calories/gramme, whereas a gramme of water contributes only one calorie for each degree above freezing point. It is true, however, that rain is an important source of liquid water in snow and that this plays a part in the melting process by causing a pronounced change in thermodynamic interaction.

Water and the Melting Process

This transformation results in very rounded, smooth, and fairly large convex crystals (about 1 mm) occurring in clusters. The grains are round and are better known as spring snow or corn snow. Alternating cycles of freezing and melting are often the cause of the transformation. The thaw melts the smallest crystals first. The water thus released tends to flow into the interstices between the large crystals which have only melted at the surface, linking them by capillary action. On refreezing, a large polygranular crystal is obtained, but other phenomena are also involved. If there is a high water content (>14 percent of the volume of the pores), the small grains with a lower melting temperature melt to form large ones.[8]

It has also been shown that in the case of increased water content, the high pressure (caused by the weight of the snow) at the point of contact between grains sintered or welded by refreezing (bridges) lowers the melting temperature at that point. This is Le Chatelier's law: any increase in pressure causes a shift in equilibrium leading to a decrease in volume. Hence, the ice will melt more quickly in the places where the grains are interconnected. Layers of snow that are highly saturated with water will therefore tend to lose their cohesiveness and form sliding surfaces with a high avalanche risk. The danger is enhanced by the fact that water tends to seep down through the snow and accumulate above the waterproof layers such as refrozen crusts or the ground beneath. Loss of cohesiveness therefore begins at the base of a layer. It would be extremely useful to be able to measure water content accurately and stimulate the highly varied movements of water inside snow. As far as the measurement of water content is concerned, the most important procedures are gamma-radiation measurement by remote sensing and, above all, microware measurement. Microwaves in fact behave differently in the case of water and in the case of ice. According to research conducted by A.T.C. Chang, microwaves are capable of indicating temperature profiles, mean crystal size, water content, height, water equivalent, etc.[9]

Avalanches due to thaw can involve enormous masses of snow if melting has begun throughout the whole cover. They move slowly (30 km/h) but with great force. They are capable of crushing everything in their way (trees, houses, etc.) but fortunately their behaviour is predictable. They occur when the melting process is well advanced. The energy transmitted to the snow depends on the surrounding air and especially, as we have seen, on solar radiation. These avalanches therefore occur for the most part in spring (more intense and longer-lasting radiation, lower snow albedo) and generally in the afternoon (the energy stores in the cover reaches a maximum at about 5 p.m.). They may therefore be avoided by waiting for the refreezing period before going out on the slopes. In addition, avalanches of this kind usually follow known and well-inventoried courses because they are basically dependent on topography and occur regularly each year as a result of the snow that has accumulated at high altitudes during the winter. Thus, paradoxically, although these avalanches involve the greatest masses of snow, they are less dangerous than the others.

Forecasting

Having considered the three major types of avalanche, we may now ask whether anything further can be done to improve forecasting techniques. We have already mentioned the major research in progress on the forecasting of precipitation, snow transport and water content. As we have seen, the difficulties involved in the mechanical approach will not be easy to surmount in the short term. However, mention should be made of an attempt to devise a model based on determinist principles for forecasting avalanches in an area in Colorado with five adjacent valleys. Although the results of these forecasts are rather disappointing, it is none the less a very interesting experiment, being the first attempt at simultaneous simulation of all the processes affecting snow, i.e., metamorphism, transport and mechanics.[10]

In another direction, considerable effort is being devoted at present to the development of statistical models based on past data with a view to predicting a possible avalanche rate under specific conditions: snow, weather, etc.[11] At this juncture, the results they provide are correct but obvious and the forecasts are no more accurate than those obtained in other ways. They run up against three main problems.

On the one hand, no satisfactory method has yet been found of introducing structural and stratigraphical parameters into these models. On the other hand, avalanche observation records are very incomplete and very limited. One particular couloir may, for instance, be closely observed but not the adjacent ones. A more comprehensive experiment, in so far as it takes account of the whole range of factors involved in avalanche activity, is under way at La Plagne in the French Alps.

Finally, from the purely statistical point of view, the forecasting of a rare event is a difficult task and tends, in particular, to lead to numerous false alarms. Measurements that will indicate avalanche probability in a specific location are also being sought. In this connection, the American, W. Saint Lawrence, has shown that because of microscopic fractures in the crystals, snow emits supersonic signals which enable its state of stress to be determined.[12] The emission of seismic signals, however, seems to be more promising, both for preventive purposes (warning signals) and in order to monitor avalanche activity (seismic signature of avalanches). The first results in this field were obtained in Bonneval-sur-Arc, and a study is now in progress in La Plagne.[13]

Extremely wide-ranging studies are therefore required to improve our knowledge of snow and avalanches. These studies have other applications too, especially in hydrology for the management of water resources in the form of snow. The most rapid advances in the near future will probably come from improvements in measurement procedures and the development of local statistical models. However, the forecasting of avalanches will remain rough and ready for some time to come because of the perennial difficulty of effectively simulating the behaviour of snow on a slope and the limitations imposed by the resolution of observation systems.

NOTES

1. J. Desrues, F. Darve, E. Flavigny, J.-P. Navarre and A. Taillefer, "An Incremental Formulation of Constitutive Equations for Deposited Snow," *Journal of Glaciology*, No. 92, 1980, p. 289.
2. J.-P. Navarre, G. Gallet and R. Clement, *Détermination de la répartition des précipitations sur les Alpes francaises*, Établissement d'Études et de Recherches Météorologiques, 1980. (Technical Note, No. 68.)
3. U. Radok, *Deposition and Erosion of Snow by the Wind*, Cold Regions Research and Engineering Laboratory, 1968. (Research Report, No. 230.)
4. h. Bader et al., "Schnee und seine Metamorphose [Snow Metamorphism]," *Beitrage zur Geologie der Schweiz, Geotechnische Serie Hydrologie*, No. 3, 1939; P.V. Hobbs, *Ice Physics*, Oxford, Clarendon Press, 1974.
5. R. Perla, in *Canadian Geotechnical Journal*, Vol. 14, 1977, p. 206.
6. D.M. MacClung, "Discussion of Deformation Movements in relation to Snow Slab Release," *Report of the Banff Symposium*, 1976; R.L. Brown and T.E. Lang, "On the Fracture Properties of Snow," *Report of the Grindelwald Symposium*, 1974.
7. R.V. Dunckle, J.T. Gier and J.T. Bevans, "Emissivity of Ice, Snow and Frozen Ground," *Refrigerating Engineering*, Vol. 65, No. 4, 1957, p. 33.
8. S.C. Colbeck, "Theory of Metamorphism of Wet Snow," *Cold Regions Research and Engineering Laboratory Report*, No. 313, 1975.
9. A.T.C. Chang, *Estimation of Snow Temperature and Mean Crystal Radius from Remote, Multispectral, Passive Microwave Measurements*, 1978 (NASA NTIS N78-26677/2ST). A prototype has been developed at the ENSERG (École Nationale d'Électronique et de Radio-Électricité de Grenoble).
10. A. Judson, C.F. Leaf and G.E. Brink, "A Process-oriented Model for Simulating Avalanche Danger," *Snow in Motion*, op. cit.
11. P. Bois, C. Obled and W. Good, "Multivariate Data Analysis as a Tool for Day-by-day Avalanche Forecast," *Report of the Grindelwald Symposium*, 1974; G. der Megreditchian, "Approche statistique de l'évaluation du risque de'avalanche," *Neige et avalanche*, No. 11, 1975.
12. W. Saint Lawrence and C.C. Bradley, "The Deformation of Snow in Terms of a Structural Mechanism," *Report of the Grindelwald Symposium*, 1974.
13. G. Bonnet, "Detection d'avalanche par méthode séismique," *Neige et avalanche*, No. 24, 1980.

TO DELVE MORE DEEPLY

Colbeck, S. (Ed.). *Dynamics of Snow and Ice Masses*. New York, Academic Press, 1980.
Hobbs, P. *Physics of Ice*. Oxford, Clarendon Press, 1974.
Perla, R.; Martinelli, M. *Avalanche Handbook*. United States Department of Agriculture/Forest Service, 1976.
Revue de l'ANENA (Neige et avalanche), 36 avenue Félix-Viallet, 38000 Grenoble.
Rey, L. *La neige, ses métamorphoses, les avalanches*. Distributed by ANENA.

Snow and Avalanche Study Centres

The first snow and avalanche study centre was established about fifty years ago on the Weissfluhjock in Davos, Switzerland. Outside France, the main laboratories are in the United States, which has a large research centre run by the armed forces (the CRREL: Cold Regions Research and Engineering Laboratory) in Hanover, New Hampshire; another run by the Department of Agriculture in Fort Collins, Colorado, and a large number of university teams in the Rocky Mountain states. Mention should also be made of the Sapporo Institute in Japan. Research is also being conducted in the Soviet Union but we know very little about it. In France, the laboratories working on snow research are located in Grenoble. Chief of these are the National Meteorological Snow Study Centre and the Centre Technique du Génie Rural des Eaux et Forêts, but there is also the Nuclear Study Centre, the Mechanical Institute, and the Glaciology Laboratory.

PART III

Water Hazards

Local floods are a perennial problem in the United States, and throughout the twentieth century the hazards of floods and ways of reducing those hazards have been studied and put into practice by American scientists and engineers. Hence, assessment of the risks raised by floods has by now become in many respects a simpler matter than assessing the risks of newer hazards, such as those presented by toxic substances, nuclear wastes, and food additives. This relative simplicity, however, can be helpful in illuminating certain methodological difficulties and ethical questions inherent in the process of arriving at decisions on how to deal with any risk.

Chapter 10
Assessment of Flood Risk

Gilbert F. White

Gilbert F. White is Professor of Geography and Director of the Institute of Behavioral Science at the University of Colorado. As a teacher and research scientist, he has received the Distinguished Service Award of the Association of American Geographers and the Daly Medal of the American Geographical Society. He has served as a member of the (U.S.) President's Water Resources Policy Commission and of the National Academy of Sciences Committee on Water and is chairman of the Academy's Commission on Natural Resources. His wide international experience includes service on the UN Panel on Integrated River Development. Author of over 100 papers and articles, he has edited books on flood hazards and on man-made lakes.

This paper was first presented at a seminar on Risk Assessment and Decision Processes (Paris, December 1980), organized jointly by the Mouvement Universel de la Responsabilite Scientifique (MURS) and the U.S. National Academy of Sciences. The French language version appears in *Recherche-Invention-Innovation*, No. 154, (1982), pp. 50-53. This previously unpublished English-language version of the text is published here with the kind permission of the author, the French periodical, and the National Academy of Sciences.

The natural hazard whose risk has commanded systematic and explicit public assessment over the longest period of time in the United States is flooding from inland rivers. Its mode of risk estimation and benefit-cost analysis took shape early in the 20th century, received initial legislative approval in 1936, and was applied subsequently in a variety of construction and resource development fields. That experience suggests a few analytical and evaluative issues that have wider relevance in assessing public policy.

The problems of assessing flood risk are in many respects simpler than those of most other risks such as toxic substances, nuclear waste and food additives. However, their very simplicity may help emphasize certain difficulties and ethical dimensions that are inherent in the general process of arriving at decisions about environmental risk. Within the framework suggested in the SCOPE* investigation of environmental risk assessment[1], floods may be viewed as readily identified, estimated with considerable accuracy, evaluated with great difficulty, and rarely interpreted with precision.

This brief outline of the experience with assessment of flood risk begins with definition of elementary concepts in the field, reviews the major periods in national policy in coping with the flood hazard, and appraises a few of the lessons learned. It does not pretend to cover all facets of flood risk estimation in the historical context; it is highly selective in discussion of both method and problem, drawing attention to those lessons most likely to be pertinent to the study of other risks; and it runs all the hazards of simplification. It uses the findings of a very large literature, only a few of which are referenced.

Elementary Concepts

Any unregulated stream has peaks in its hydrograph that cause overbank flow with a magnitude and recurrence interval that can be estimated with degrees of accuracy dependent upon the quality of streamflow records and of method. These overbank flows inundate zones that can be specified, and cause damages and other environmental effects that can be estimated with calculated probability. The damages sometimes can reach catastrophic proportions in the sense that they cause severe social dislocations. Whatever their magnitude, the losses may be computed for each of a variety of

* Scientific Committee on Problems of the Environment of the International Council of Scientific Unions (ICSU)

adjustments which individuals or social groups can make to them, using a benefit-cost framework. Decisions as to what to do, if anything, about floods in a given river in the United States since the turn of the century typically take into account the results of that general mode of analysis. Let us now define each of these terms as follows:

- *Flood hydrograph*: the volume of stream discharge over a period of time, usually a year and usually measured in cubic feet per second or cubic meters per second.

- *Stage-discharge*: the relation between the volume of discharge and the water level, or stage, in a given reach of a stream. This is a function of stream channel cross-section and velocity.

- *Overbank flow:* the stage at which the flow overtops the natural or artificial banks of the stream.

- *Flood magnitude*: the maximum stage attained at a peak in the flood hydrograph.

- *Recurrence interval*: the calculated percent probability that a flood of given magnitude will recur. This may be drawn from historical record and from statistical extrapolations.

- *Flood risk zone*: an area in the floodplain with uniform range of recurrence interval for a given magnitude of overbank flow.

- *Flood damage*: any loss to individuals or society caused by overbank flow. It may be distributed along a continuum from loss of life to increment in tax burden.

- *Adjustment to flood*: any action taken by an individual or society to cope with flood events. These may lead to loss or to benefit, and usually involves some cost. A conventional classification of adjustments is as follows:

Distribute the Loss

Loss bearing
Public relief
Insurance

Modify the Human Response

Land use pattern
Warning system
Emergency evacuation
Building design

Modify the Event

Weather modification
Land cover change
Flood control

— Channel improvement
— Levee
— Detention or storage dam

There always is some form of land use, ranging from preservation of a floodplain for open space wilderness purposes to highly intensive urban use. Basically, every flood hazard involves resource use and risk that there will be damage from overbank flow: without resource use there is no exposure of people or property to possible damage. Likewise, every conscious adjustment to flood hazard involves some effect on the future flow of benefits and costs, although occasionally the adjustment yields none of its anticipated benefits.

- *Benefit-cost analysis*: the calculation of the future flow of benefits and costs for a given adjustment in a specified flood risk zone. This, of course, requires a recurrence interval, a magnitude, and use of a discount rate and time horizon for the estimated benefits and costs.

Evolution of Public Approaches to Flood Risk

In the United States the individual property manager—owner or tenant—commonly has a wide range of options as to which combination of adjustments is adopted subject to the constraints or incentives imposed by the economic and political system and by public policy. That policy moved through five major periods during the 20th century.

Prior to 1936

Individuals were at liberty to deal with flood risk as they might choose, subject to the following:

- Any adjustment proven to cause damage to others, as in the case of diversion of water from a farmer's field to a neighboring field, was liable to recovery of damages by legal, tort action.

- State laws permitted landowners to join together in local or basin-wide districts for the purpose of reducing overbank flow by construction and maintenance of engineering works. The feasibility of the district organization and the assessment of costs for the construction and maintenance of the improvement was determined upon the basis of rough benefit-cost calculations using crude estimates of magnitude, recurrence interval, benefits from protection (often measured by projected changes in land values), and costs of construction and maintenance. By 1917 virtually all of the alluvial valley of the Mississippi River and much of the agricultural floodplain elsewhere, including the towns of the Miami valley in Ohio, were covered by such districts.

- Beginning in 1917 the technical difficulties of curbing the flows of the Mississippi River and the Sacramento River were so massive that the federal government through its Corps of Engineers intervened to care for regulation of the main channel. In the wake of the great flood of 1927 which destroyed many of the levees along the lower Mississippi River, the federal government gave relief to flood sufferers, assumed responsibility for flood control along the alluvial valley, and began studies of possible flood control in conjunction with navigation, irrigation, and hydroelectric power development in numerous other areas.

1936-1957

The Ohio Valley floods of 1936 and 1937 induced a new federal policy under which the Soil Conservation Service and Forest Service assumed responsibility for land improvement measures in the upper drainage areas, and the Corps of Engineers was responsible for engineering works along stream channels. The criterion for determining economic feasibility was that the estimated benefits to whomsoever they might accrue from proposed flood loss reduction works should exceed the estimated costs. This was the beginning of construction programs on all major streams of the nation costing in excess of $15 billion. Initially, local and state interests were to contribute the costs of lands, damages, and rights of way. In 1938 the complexities of obtaining local and state contributions led to a policy of building dams and reservoirs at 100 percent Federal cost.

1957-1967

After the national flood control policy and programs had been in operation about twenty years, a series of studies and activities reflected a mounting feeling that all was not well with the engineering program. These included a variety of measures. Systematic assistance from the Tennessee Valley Authority (TVA) to communities in that valley in planning land use and non-structural measures to cope with flood losses recognized that engineering works alone would not curb encroachment of property owners on to vulnerable zones. In the same vein, the Corps of Engineers began issuance of a series of floodplain information studies to help residents to take other steps to reduce losses. A national flood insurance program was introduced but aborted because of a policy of proposing to treat all property without distinction among risk zones and river basins.

1967-1974

By the mid-1960s a reassessment of the situation revealed that national flood losses were continuing to rise along with flood protection expenditures, that demands upon federal and state agencies for relief in the wake of flood disaster were mounting, and that information activities alone were insufficient to stem the continued uneconomic invasion of floodplains. A federal task force[2] recommended a wider range of actions to inform and assist floodplain users to reduce loss potential: these included improved warnings, an Executive Order to federal agencies to exercise caution in making further encroachments, improved technical advice to individuals and local agencies, and the establishment of a national flood insurance program in which coverage was conditional upon community enactment of land use regulation measures which would guide further invasion and prohibit reduction in channel capacity and in which new buildings were covered at actuarial rates while existing buildings were covered at subsidized rates. The insurance program began in 1968. Coastal flooding from storm surge was included in the program. It was recognized that some floodplain use and resultant damages would be warranted by social and economic benefits to be gained.

1974-1980

Following the catastrophic Agnes floods of 1972, with their damages of greater than $3 billion and more than 200 deaths, the Congress and public agencies stepped up the policies outlined in the mid-1960s.[3] Public assistance was reduced. Federal mortgage aid became contingent upon purchasing insurance. Aid in reconstruction was linked to enactment of community mitigation measures. Funds were made available on a small scale to relocate these buildings in highly vulnerable areas. Assistance was given to each state to establish coordinating offices to provide technical assistance to communities and individuals planning floodplain land use. In 1980, insurance was written on 1.7 million buildings with an insured value of $78 billion. There is hope but not assurance that uneconomic invasion of vulnerable areas at public expense will be stemmed.

Analytical and Evaluative Issues

Out of this long and shifting series of attempts to assess and cope with flood risk, a few observations may be drawn which have broader applicability.

Estimation of Probability

Notwithstanding the slow accumulation of historical records of discharge and magnitude and the refinement of methods of hydrologic analysis, the engineering fraternity has had great difficulty in arriving at concensus as to estimates of recurrence intervals: one federal agency may differ from another, for example, by estimates of 0.5 percent, 1.0 percent, and 2.0 percent for the same flood magnitude. Precision in estimating probability is hard to attain even with relatively solid and verifiable data bases.

Changes in Stage-Discharge and Precipitation-Discharge Relations

These occurred for three major reasons: (a) channel cross-sections were diminished by filling and building construction; (b) upstream urban development changed hydrologic conditions so that magnitude and recurrence interval were increased, thereby shifting risk zones; and (c) reservoir control works reduced the flushing action of streams, promoting channel filling and increasing the magnitude of a given discharge. Thus, unanticipated alterations in the hydrologic system made the previous risk estimates unduly low.

Delineation of risk zones

Because of errors in topographic or aerial survey and of the coarse grain of elevation determinations, there was much ambiguity as to precisely where the limits of risk zones were located in the field. This was exacerbated by frequent misinterpretation of scientific probability: a 2.0 percent flood was perceived as occurring every 50 years. While communities could agree that building design or land use should be regulated uniformly in a given risk zone, it was difficult to determine the proper classification of individual structures. Exceptions were easy to make and inaccurate decisions were made by planners and insurance agents as to location.

The 100-Year Limit of Acceptable Risk

In a somewhat arbitrary fashion it was decided early in the flood insurance program that the 1.0 percent flood, more popularly the "100-year flood" would delimit the upper part of the floodplain below which community land use regulation would be required. Property owners above that line inferred incorrectly in many instances that they were safe from all floods: in fact, they would be reached by a 0.9 percent flood. Likewise, persons located behind a levee designed to withstand 0.5 percent floods were surprised when a 0.4 percent flood overtopped the levee. By establishing a numerical definition of acceptable risk, individuals were either encouraged or not dissuaded from assuming slightly smaller risks.

Risk to Life vs. Property Damage

Public justification for expenditures for flood control works often was based during the 1930s and 1940s on their promise to prevent loss of life. More careful analysis suggests that loss of life from floods with gentle peaks occurred from people venturing into high waters rather than from inundation. The fatalities from being carried away by floods occurred in sharp-peaked floods, and these floods rarely are susceptible to being controlled by engineering devices. Building large works accordingly would have little effect upon danger to life except insofar as dams would be vulnerable to failure.

Recognition of Alternative Responses

For a long time the estimation of risk viewed the alternatives solely as loss bearing vs. presumably complete protection. If an individual or community could not obtain protection it was expected to bear the losses or seek public assistance. By doing so, the analyst neglected to call attention to the possibility of adopting other adjustments such as warning systems, flood proofing of buildings, and land-use management. Formal risk assessment locked society into a narrow range of action by defining desirable alternatives. Other courses of action thereby were discouraged, and the freedom of individuals to cope with risk in other fashions, sometimes displayed before 1936, was inhibited.

Measurement of Benefits and Costs

These estimates inevitably were fraught with the difficulties of attaching quantitative values to non-market phenomena, such as esthetic satisfaction or family attachment to a place. Some attempts to arrive at comparable numbers for various costs and benefits were crude, and others refined. The tendency, as with much benefit-cost analysis, was to estimate what could be quantified and to neglect the others: it was like the nocturnal drunkard looking for his lost car keys under the street light not because they had been dropped there but because it was easier to see the pavement. As a result, the risk assessments rarely recognized that the cure might cause larger social damages than the original condition.

Political manipulation

The large latitude provided in estimating the flood risk invited political manipulation. In beginning an assessment, a design engineer was tempted to ask the responsible supervising officer what benefit-cost ratio was desired so that coefficients and time horizons could be selected to assure that end. Excesses in that direction were especially acceptable where the individuals or communities affected had no financial responsibility for the choice of construction works. Recent proposals for revised public policy emphasize the importance of local financial contributions as a means of avoiding actions the local groups feel to be based on exaggerated risks or benefits.

Public Responsibility for Individual Risk

From the beginning there was ambiguity as to the suitable responsibility of a public agency to regulate an individual's right to undergo hazard. So long as state and local agencies served only to facilitate private investment to reduce risk from floods, the decision as to how much risk to bear was largely in the hands of property owners who would expect to pay the cost of remedial action. As public commitment centered upon the provision, often entirely at federal expense, of one engineering means of reducing risk estimated on a social evaluative scale in contrast to the scale of individual property owners, those individuals were encouraged to leave risk assessment to others and to narrow their range of choice. The counterproductive aspects of that policy led in time to a widening of the policy to support larger exercise of responsibility at the local and individual levels.

NOTES

1. R.W. Kates, *Risk Assessment of Environmental Hazards*, SCOPE 8, Chicester: John Wiley & Sons, 1978.
2. U.S. Task Force on Federal Flood Control Policy, *A Unified National Program for Managing Flood Losses*, House of Representatives, House Document 465, 1966.

3. U.S. Water Resources Council, *A Unified National Program for Flood Plain Management*, Washington: WRC, 1979.

TO DELVE MORE DEEPLY

Gilbert F. White, et al., *Flood Hazard in the United States: A Research Assessment*, Boulder: University of Colorado, 1975.

As far back as 1480 B.C. history records destruction by tsunami—huge ocean waves—with loss of life and property. Today population pressures on coastal areas bring more and more communities and installations under this threat. Tsunami warning systems employing advanced technological instrumentation require public education and confidence in government agencies for effectiveness.

Chapter 11
The Effects of Tsunami on Society

George Pararas-Carayannis

George Pararas-Carayannis is director of the International Tsunami Information Center (ITIC) established by Unesco's Intergovernmental Oceanographic Commission (IOC). Before joining ITIC in 1967, Dr. Pararas-Carayannis served as a research oceanographer for the United States Army Coastal Engineering Research Center and as director of the World Data Center—T Tsunami. Holding a doctorate in marine science from the University of Delaware, he is the author of numerous scientific and technical articles, monographs and institutional reports on oceanography and geophysics. He was born in Athens, Greece, in 1936.

Introduction

The tsunami is a series of ocean waves of very great length and period generated by impulsive disturbances of the earth's crust. Large earthquakes with epicentres under or near the ocean and with a net vertical displacement of the ocean floor are the cause of the most catastrophic tsunami. Volcanic eruptions and submarine landslides are also responsible for tsunami generation but their effects are usually localized.

Although infrequent, tsunami are among the most terrifying and complex physical phenomena and have been responsible for great loss of life and extensive destruction to property. Because of their destructiveness, tsunami have important impact on the human, social, and economic sectors of our societies. Historical records show that enormous destruction of coastal communities throughout the world has taken place and that the socio-economic impact of tsunami in the past has been enormous. In the Pacific Ocean where the majority of these waves have been generated, the historical record shows tremendous destruction with extensive loss of life and property. In Japan, which has one of the most populated coastal regions in the world and a long history of earthquake activity, tsunami have destroyed entire coastal populations. There is also a history of tsunami destruction in Alaska, in the Hawaiian Islands, and in South America, although records for these areas are not extensive. The last major Pacific-wide tsunami occurred in 1960. Others have also occurred but their effects were localized.

津 波 pronounced "tsunami," is the Japanese term usually incorrectly translated as "tidal wave." Because specific terms do not exist in most languages to describe the exact nature of the marine phenomenon involved, the term "tsunami" has been adopted universally by oceanographers. The word "tsunami" can be either singular or plural.—Ed.

We have witnessed in the last twenty years rapid growth and development of the coastal areas in most of the developing or developed Pacific nations. This is the result of a population explosion and of technological and economic developments that have made the use of the coastal zone more necessary than before. Fortunately, tsunami are not frequent events and therefore their effects have not been felt recently in all developing areas of the Pacific. History, however, has proved that although infrequent, destructive tsunami indeed do occur.

A major Pacific-wide tsunami is likely to occur in the near future. Among the countries bordering on the Pacific, a number are not prepared for such an event while others have let their guard down. The social and economic impact of future tsunami, therefore, cannot be overlooked. The purpose of this paper is to provide an overview of the social and economic impact of past, recent, and future tsunami, to examine tsunami hazard management, and to indicate the need for future planning, at least for the Pacific Ocean where tsunami frequency is high.

Historical Record of Destructive Tsunami

The impact of tsunami on human society can be traced back in written history to 1480 B.C., in the eastern Mediterranean, when the Minoan civilization was wiped out by such waves. Japanese records documenting such catastrophes extend back to A.D. 684.[1] North and South American records have dated such events back to 1788 for Alaska and 1562 for Chile. Records of Hawaiian tsunami go back to 1821.

While most of the destructive tsunami have occurred in the Pacific Ocean, devastating tsunami have also occurred in the Atlantic and Indian Oceans, as well as the Mediterranean Sea. A large tsunami accompanied the earthquakes of Lisbon in 1755, that of the Mona Passage off Puerto Rico in 1918, and at the Grand Banks of Canada in 1929.

Most of the people in the Pacific countries live on or quite near the coast since the interior is often mountainous and most of the good flatland is in the form of coastal plains. Many of these countries have populations with a natural maritime orientation. For many of these countries, foreign trade is a necessity and some maintain large fleets of ships and have major port facilities. Many of the Pacific island countries and those with extensive continental coastlines depend also on transport by small coastal ships necessitating many small ports to facilitate inter-island and coastal trade as well. Countries like Japan, for example, maintain many ports and have extensive shipbuilding facilities, electric plants, refineries, and other important structures. Similarly, many of the other developing and developed countries of the Pacific have harbours as bases for their large fishing industries. Peru, for example, at the port of Callao near Lima, maintains a large fleet for anchovy fishing. Callao is located near a strong seismic and potentially tsunamigenic region. Finally, when we also note that a number of coastal sites throughout the Pacific have begun aquacultural industries and canneries, we can only conclude that this combination of factors makes these developed and developing Pacific islands and continental Pacific nations socially and economically vulnerable to the threat of tsunami. The extensive coastal boundaries, the number of islands, the long coastlines of Pacific countries containing a number of vulnerable engineering structures, the numerous large ports, the productive fishing and aquacultural industries, and the great density of population in coastal areas can only place these countries in a very vulnerable position.

The Vulnerability of Japan

For Japan, to give an example, where all the above-mentioned factors of vulnerability are present, the social and economic impact of a tsunami can be truly devastating. Along the Sanriku coast or in the Tohoku district of northern Honshu there are many flatlands with coastal embayments where large fishing and aquaculture industries have been established. Throughout history, entire settlements in such areas have been struck and destroyed by tsunami, often requiring their rebuilding and relocation. The record reads as follows: a total of 65 destructive tsunami struck Japan between A.D. 684 and 1960. As early as 18 July 869 the Sanriku coast was hit by a tsunami resulting in loss of 1,000 lives and the destruction of hundreds of villages. On 3 August 1361, a tsunami destroyed 1,700 houses in this same area. On 20 September 1498 1,000 houses were washed away and 500 deaths resulted from a tsunami which struck the Kii peninsula. Kyushu was struck by a destructive tsunami in September 1596. Great loss of life occurred on 31 January 1596 from a tsunami on the island of Shikoku, affecting also a number of regions in Honshu. In recent times, the great Meiji Sanriku tsunami of 15 June 1896 resulted in 27,122 deaths, thousands of injuries, and the loss of thousands of homes. On 3 March 1933 a tsunami in the Sanriku area reached a height of about thirty metres and killed over 3,000 people, injured hundreds more, and destroyed approximately 9,000 homes and 8,000 boats. In December 1944, a tsunami in central Honshu caused almost 1,000 deaths and the destruction of over 3,000 houses. The Nankaido tsunami, on 21 December 1946, resulted in 1,500 deaths and the destruction of 1,151 houses. [2]

Tsunami Strikes in Pacific

Tsunami have struck the Hawaiian islands repeatedly, causing great loss of life and immense damage to property. Most noteworthy of the recent Hawaiian tsunami is that of 1 April 1946 which inundated and destroyed the city of Hilo, killing 159 people. Other recent tsunami that have hit Hawaii are those of 1952, 1957, 1960, 1964 and 1975. [3]

The most destructive Pacific-wide tsunami in recent times was that of May 1960, killing over 1,000 people in Chile, Hawaii, the Philippines, Okinawa and Japan, and causing tremendous loss of life and destruction to property.

More recently, on 16 August 1976, a large earthquake in the Moro Gulf in the Philippines generated a destructive local tsunami which killed over 8,000 persons, leaving 10,000 injured and 90,000 more homeless. [4] On 12 December 1979, another earthquake centred on the state of Narino in the southwest corner of Colombia generated a tsunami that completely destroyed several fishing villages, taking the lives of hundreds of people and creating economic chaos in an already economically depressed region of that country. [5]

Tsunami destruction has not been confined to Japan or to the Pacific Ocean. Destructive tsunami have occurred also in the Atlantic and Indian Oceans and in the Caribbean and Mediterranean seas. As mentioned earlier, the violent eruption and explosion of the volcano of Santorini in the fifteenth century B.C. generated a tremendous tsunami which destroyed most of the coastal Minoan settlements on the Aegean sea islands, acting as the catalyst for the decline of the advanced Minoan civilization. [6] Many more destructive tsunami have occurred in the Eastern Mediterranean since then.

In the region of the Indian Ocean, the violent explosion of the volcanic island of Krakatoa in August 1883 generated a thirty-metre-high tsunami wave that killed 36,500 people in Java and Sumatra. As recently as four years ago, a large earthquake in the Lesser Sunda Islands, Indonesia, on 19 August 1977 generated a destructive tsunami which killed hundreds of people on Lombok and Sumbawa islands along the eastern side of the Indian Ocean.[7]

The Atlantic Region

Historical records also document considerable loss of life and destruction of property on the western shores of the North and South Atlantic, the coastal waters of northwestern Europe,[8] and in the seismically active regions around the eastern Caribbean. Most noteworthy of the Atlantic tsunami was that associated with the Lisbon earthquake of 1 November 1755 which struck not only Portugal but Spain, Madeira, the Azores, France, the British Isles, and the islands of the West Indies. Tsunami have been reported frequently from southern Ireland, Wales, and England, as well as from the northern regions of the Iberian peninsula. One of the most destructive of the tsunami in the Caribbean sea was the tsunami at Port Royal, Jamaica, on 7 June 1692 which, in combination with the earthquake, took 3,000 lives. Other destructive events were the tsunami of 3 June 1770 and that of 7 May 1842 on the island of Hispaniola, the tsunami in the Virgin Islands on 28 December 1867, the tsunami in Jamaica on 14 January 1907, and the tsunami of 11 October 1918 in Puerto Rico.[9]

The above is simply a brief overview of some large historical tsunamis. It is very difficult to comment specifically on the impact each event has had on each stricken area. However, it can be clearly concluded that natural catastrophes, such as tsunami, have far more important and long-term social and economic impacts than any historical or statistical record can show. Furthermore, the historical record does not prepare us for the potential damage that can now be caused by tsunami in the coastal areas of many developing or developed coastal countries where development has taken place in the last twenty years. Future tsunami will have a much more severe social and economic impact in these areas than that of past events. It is therefore important that these areas begin now to plan and prepare for such future events.

Planning for the Tsunami Hazard

There is very little that can be done to prevent the occurrence of natural hazards. Floods, droughts, earthquakes, hurricanes, volcanic eruptions, and tsunami cannot be prevented. But humankind, being as adaptable as it is, has learned to live with all these hazards. In the past, we have taken a passive approach to hazards, justifying them as acts of God or nature about which we could do very little. But while these natural disasters cannot be prevented, their results, such as loss of life and property, can be reduced by proper planning. To plan for the tsunami hazard, however, we must have a good understanding not only of the physical nature of the phenomenon and its manifestation in each geographical locality, but also of that area's combined physical, social, and cultural factors. Some of these areas are more vulnerable to tsunami than others. Because tsunami frequency in the Pacific Ocean is high, most efforts in hazard management have concentrated in this area of the world. No matter how remote, the likelihood of a tsunami should be considered in developing coastal zone management and land use. While some degree of risk is acceptable, government agencies should promote new development and population growth in areas of greater safety and less potential risk. These agencies should formulate land-use regulations for a given coastal area with the tsunami risk potential in mind, particularly if such an area is known to have sustained damage in the past.

International Protective and Preventive Measures Established

Present protective measures involve primarily the use of tsunami warning systems employing advanced technological instrumentation for data collection and for warning communications. Countries like Japan, the Soviet Union, Canada, and the United States have developed sophisticated warning systems and have accepted the responsibility to share warning information with other countries of the Pacific.

In 1965, Unesco's Intergovernmental Oceanographic Commission (UNESCO/IOC) accepted the United States' offer to expand its existing tsunami centre in Honolulu to become the Pacific Tsunami Warning Center (PTWC). Also established was an International Co-ordination Group (ICG/ITSU) and the International Tsunami Information Center (ITIC) to review the activities of the International Tsunami Warning

System for the Pacific (ITWS). The Pacific Tsunami Warning System has become the nucleus of a truly international system. Twenty-two nations are now members of ICG/ITSU: Canada, Chile, China, Colombia, Cook Islands, Ecuador, Fiji, France, Guatemala, Indonesia, Japan, Republic of Korea, Mexico, New Zealand, Peru, Philippines, Singapore, Thailand, the United Kingdom (Hong Kong), the United States, the Soviet Union, and Western Samoa. Several non-member nations and territories maintain stations for the ITWS, and tide observers are also located on a number of Pacific Islands. The present system makes use of twenty-four seismic stations, fifty-three tide stations, and fifty-two dissemination points scattered throughout the Pacific Basin under the varying control of the member states. PTWC in Honolulu, operated by the United States National Weather Service, is the operational centre for the system. The objectives of the ITWS are to detect and locate major earthquakes in the Pacific region, determine whether they have generated tsunami, and provide timely and effective information and warnings to the population of the Pacific region in order to minimize the effect of the hazards on life and property.

Functioning of the Warning System

Functioning of the system begins with the detection by any participating seismic observatory of an earthquake of sufficient size to trigger the alarm attached to the seismograph at that station. Earthquakes of 6.5 or greater on the Richter scale are investigated. **PTWC collects the data and, when sufficient data have been received,** locates the earthquake and computes its magnitude. When reports from tide stations show that a tsunami poses a threat to the population in part or all of the Pacific, a warning is transmitted to the dissemination agencies for relaying to the public. The agencies then implement predetermined plans to evacuate people from endangered areas. If the tide station reports indicate that a negligible or no tsunami has been generated, PTWC issues a cancellation. In addition to the International Tsunami Warning System, a number of Regional Warning Systems have been established to warn the population in areas where tsunami frequency is high and where immediate response is necessary. Such regional tsunami warning systems have been established in the Soviet Union, Japan, Alaska and Hawaii. Vast areas exist, however, where tsunami cannot be adequately detected or monitored in time and the populations warned to prevent extensive loss of life.

Because of the rarity of large destructive tsunami, it is difficult to institute successful tsunami-prediction schemes for warning the public. However, we can make people aware of the potential hazard. Tsunami warnings are issued to the public for the purpose of convincing people to evacuate endangered areas. Ample time must be allowed for evacuation, which is a rather difficult procedure. Often the public does not understand the meaning of the warning signals and is not aware of the locations of endangered areas. Most people are reluctant to evacuate their homes and businesses, and their response to warnings in general may not be very good, particularly if a number of false alarms have been issued.

Hazard Perception by the Public

Tsunami hazard perception by the people of a coastal area is based on education and confidence in government agencies responsible for tsunami prediction. Overwarning, based on inadequate knowledge of the phenomenon or inadequate data on which to base the prediction, often leads to false alarms and lack of compliance with warning and evacuation attempts. Such false alarms result in a loss of faith in the capability of the system and result in reluctance to take action in subsequent tsunami events. Even if a tsunami prediction is based on valid information and data, warning and evacuation may not be sufficient to minimize the impact of tsunami on coastal populations. Hazard perception by the public is based on a technical understanding of the phenomenon, at least at the basic level, and a behavioral response stemming from understanding of the phenomenon and confidence of the public in the authorities. Fortunately, forecasting of tsunami in recent years has been quite good and the image of the tsunami warning system and its credibility has improved considerably. Forecasting, however, is not an exact science as the phenomenon itself is very complex and data on which the forecast is based may often be inadequate for certain areas.

Awareness through Public Education

A heightened community awareness of the potential threat of tsunami can be achieved through a public education programme. Civil defense authorities in each country can initiate such a public education programme consisting of seminars and workshops for responsible government officials, can publish informational booklets on the hazards of tsunami, and can co-ordinate with the communications media on the announcement of tsunami information. Other government agencies can take action also to mitigate future losses from tsunami. For example, government agencies can develop sound coastal management policies, which include zoning and planning for tsunami-prone coastal areas. Scientific organizations can undertake research and engineering studies in developing evacuation zones or engineering guidelines for building coastal structures. Audio-visual materials can be prepared for educating children in schools and the public in general. Brochures and pamphlets can be printed describing the tsunami warning system and what the public can do in time of tsunami warning. Internally, government agencies can streamline and co-ordinate their operating procedures and communications so they can perform efficiently when the tsunami threat arises. Procedures related to tsunami warnings should be reviewed frequently to define and determine better respective responsibilities between the different government agencies at all levels.

Conclusion and Recommendations

In spite of our technological improvements of the last two decades, we are still unable to provide timely warnings to many areas of the Pacific and none to other parts of the world. Improvements are necessary in communications to ensure that warning information is prompt and accurate. An increased degree of automation is necessary in handling and interpreting the basic data. Research is needed, for example, in the development of instrumentation such as deep-ocean sensors, which could be useful in early tsunami detection. Research is needed also in the real-time interpretation of seismic source parameters, which in turn may help in tsunami evaluation. Apparently more research is needed in improving our understanding of a tsunami interacting with the coast.

Research can also lead to improvement of warning systems, to better land-use management of tsunami-prone coastal areas, and to development of important engineering guidelines of critical coastal structures.

In conclusion, the long-term objective should be for each country susceptible to the tsunami hazard to build its technical and scientific infrastructures to meet the hazards of a disastrous event. The immediate objectives of each country should be to assess this hazard in terms of potential needs and available resources. Preparedness requires several capabilities, such as rapid identification of imminent tsunami, effective national and regional warning systems to alert coastal population and industries, and civil defense and community preparedness to respond to tsunami warnings.

Finally, appropriate improvements in warning capability in the form of improved instrumentation for tsunami monitoring and for communications should be developed, both for effective warning and for increased knowledge as an aid to long-term protection.

NOTES

1. K. Ida, D. Cox and G. Pararas-Carayannis, *Preliminary Catalogue of Tsunamis Occuring in the Pacific Ocean*, Honolulu, Hawaii Institute of Geophysics, University of Hawaii, 1967. (Data Report No. 5.)
2. Ibid.
3. G. Pararas-Carayannis, *Catalogue of Tsunamis in Hawaii*, Boulder, Colorado, World Data Center-A for Solid Earth Geophysics, 1977.
4. ITIC, *Tsunami Report*, N. 1976-26, 1978.
5. G. Pararas-Carayannis, "Earthquake and Tsunami of 12 December 1979 in Colombia," *Tsunami Newsletter*, Vol. 13, No. 1, 1980, pp. 1-9.
6. G. Pararas-Carayannis, "The International Tsunami Warning System," *Sea Frontiers*, Vol. 23, No. 1, 1977, pp. 20-7.
7. ITIC, *Tsunami Report*, No. 1977-12, 1978.
8. W. Berninghausen, "Tsunamis and Seismic Seiches reported from the Eastern Atlantic South of the Bay of Biscay," *Bulletin of the Seismological Society of America*, Vol. 54, No. 1, 1964, pp. 439-42.
9. *Tsunamis and Seismic Seiches Reported from the Western North and South Atlantic and the Coastal Waters of Northwestern Europe*, Washington, D.C., Naval Oceanographic Office, 1968.

To save lives and reduce property damage, the National Weather Service (NWS) provides flood forecasts and warnings serving 3,000 flood-prone areas. A comprehensive plan for improving this large-scale service has been formulated by the NWS Office of Hydrology based on several systems-economic studies. The one described highlights: (1) the concept of a flood forecast-response system which captures interactions among hydrologic, organizational, behavioral, and economic factors; (2) the concept of performance measures which capture the interplay between the quality of forecasts and the quality of floodplain dwellers' response, and (3) the economic value of flood forecasts and the benefits to be derived by the general public from the planned improvements.

Chapter 12
Toward Improving Flood Forecast-Response Systems

Roman Krzysztofowicz and Donald Davis

Dr. Donald R. Davis is a Professor of Hydrology and Water Resources at the University of Arizona doing research on the impact of uncertainty on water resources policy and management.

Roman Krzysztofowicz began his career at the Institute for Meteorology and Water Resources in Cracow, Poland, and has since held faculty posts at the University of Arizona, Massachusetts Institute of Technology, and the University of Virginia. He is a recipient of the White House sponsored Presidential Young Investigator Award.

Reprinted from *Interfaces* 14, No. 3 (May-June 1984) with permission of the Institute of Management Sciences and the authors.

National Weather Service (NWS) is a major component of the National Oceanic and Atmospheric Administration (NOAA), U.S. Department of Commerce. One of the principal missions of NWS is to save lives and reduce property damage. The social significance and economic efficiency of this mission have grown in the last decade because of several factors: the number of feasible (from engineering or environmental viewpoints) sites for new flood control reservoirs has shrunk; the costs of structural protection measures such as dams, levees, and diversion channels have been rapidly escalating; the potential for flood damage has increased because of the continued development of floodplains for urban, commercial, and industrial uses. At the same time, an opportunity for marked improvement of flood forecasting capabilities has been created by rapid advances in hydrology, data processing, and telecommunication.

There are about 20,000 flood-prone areas in the United States. NWS prepares flood warnings directly for 3,000 designated forecast points, 1,000 in headwater areas and 2,000 along main stem rivers. Planning and investment decisions about developing and improving this large-scale service should be preceded by systems analyses at the microeconomic level. Such an approach is imperative because of gross dissimilarities among the 3,000 flood-prone areas. The dissimilarities result from the multiplicity and complexity of factors which govern the real-time flood forecast-response (FFR) process; these factors are hydrologic, organizational, behavioral, and economic.

In order to better understand interactions among these factors and to obtain a comprehensive knowledge base for planning improvements of the hydrologic forecast service, NWS Office of Hydrology sponsored several systems-economic studies. We describe one of them. Its objective was twofold: (1) to formulate a methodology for evaluating the performance of flood forecasts as a means of reducing property damage, and (2) to carry out a number of case studies that would supply representative and generalizable information about the performance characteristics of FFR systems.

Economics of Weather Forecasts

The results of our study (Krzysztofowicz and Davis 1983) provided one of many inputs to a "Program Development Plan for Improving Hydrologic Services" formulated by the NWS Office of Hydrology

(NWS 1982). The plan is comprehensive, based on a systems approach and a long-term (20 years) planning horizon. It identifies deficiencies in the current hydrologic forecast service and recommends an eight-year improvement program beginning in 1985. The potential economic benefits are estimated at $2.6 billion per year (at the 1982 price level), almost 120 times the total cost of the improvements.

If the benefit/cost ratio of 120 appears surprisingly high in comparison with those for other public programs, it is perhaps because our intuitive judgments have notoriously undervalued weather and climate information which we, as the general public, are accustomed to receiving at no cost. Decision analyses such as the one we describe and those of Day and Lee [1976], Chatterton et al. [1979], Suchman et al. [1979], Alexandridis and Krzysztofowicz [1982], Katz et al. [1982], Morzuch and Willis [1982], and Tice and Clouser [1982] are, therefore, indispensable in shaping an objective basis for budgeting the development and improvement of weather forecast services for the general public. The evidence accumulated from these analyses, although still sparse, is consistent: Hydrologic and meteorologic forecasts, when used optimally [Krzysztofowicz 1983], provide one of the most cost-effective pieces of information to those who must make weather-sensitive decisions.

Systems-Economic Viewpoint

The methodology for evaluating the performance of flood forecasts as a means of reducing property damage is founded on two premises: (1) The hydrologic forecast service should be considered part of the total FFR system; (2) A flood forecast is of value only if it induces a response from a floodplain dweller which leads to an effective reduction of his loss.

FFR System

An FFR system can be conceptualized as a cascade coupling of five components whose functions are as follows:

(1) The *data collection network* records hydrometeorologic data in the field and sends them to a river forecast center where they are transformed into an input to a hydrologic forecasting procedure.

(2) The *forecasting procedure* includes all hydrologic models (for example, models which transform rainfall into runoff) and any subjective procedures employed by the forecaster in computing the flood forecast. Such a forecast indicates the magnitude of the flood crest and the time of arrival of the crest at a specific forecast point on the river. The forecasting usually starts before the flood begins. Updated forecasts are issued sequentially as new hydrometeorologic data are received until the crest passes. The lead time of the first forecast varies from just a few hours for fast-rising rain-floods in headwater areas to several days for slowly-rising floods on main stem rivers. (The lead time is the time between the issuance of the forecast and the occurrence of the flood crest.)

(3) The *dissemination channels* are radio, TV, telephone, and the various public and private organizations who after receiving a flood forecast from the river forecast center disseminate flood warnings to potential users.

(4) The *decision procedure* includes all formal decision methods as well as unaided decision processes by which recipients of flood warnings (henceforth called decision makers, abbreviated DMs) plan their responses. DMs are floodplain dwellers, or managers of commercial or industrial establishments. Their decisions concern the degree of response, the type of protective action to be taken, and the way of allocating resources to various protective activities.

(5) The *set of protective actions* typically includes evacuating the contents of a structure, flood proofing a structure temporarily, or shutting down a facility. The DM can undertake these actions in response to a flood warning in order to reduce his potential loss. The loss is the sum of the cost of response and the flood damage sustained.

Why a Systems Approach

An accurate forecast is valueless if it is not received by the DM in time to take protective action. It is also valueless if those who receive the forecast in time do not understand that they must take action. Conversely, an alert community with an effective disaster preparedness program is severely handicapped if it is provided with inaccurate or tardy flood forecasts. To capture the essence of this interplay between the performance of the forecast system and the performance of the response system was the foremost requirement in developing the model. Fundamental policy questions would be best answered if we could display a vector of three elements reflecting the performance of (1) the forecast system, (2) the response system, and (3) the total system.

The immediate implication of the systems viewpoint was that the methodology had to encompass all stages of the information flow, beginning from the data measurement and forecast preparation by the river forecast center, through warning dissemination by the mass media, to decision making and action implementation by DMs. Most important, human response behavior ought to be considered in the methodology and, therefore, had to be modeled along with the flood and forecast processes which affect it.

We took a systems viewpoint even though NWS has no direct control over the response system. NWS realized, however, that it can influence the degree of response and the type of protective action in a number of ways; for instance, it can promote the use of the NWS dissemination systems, or it can help tailor local warning systems to the communities' particular flood problems. How much influence such a tailoring of the forecast system would have on the performance of the response system was a question of great interest.

Structure of the Methodology

The methodology, whose structure is depicted in Figure 1, is built from two elements: (1) a comprehensive mathematical model of the FFR process and (2) an evaluation model.

The FFR model is for a system in which the forecast component provides flood forecasts for a single point on a river, and the response component is a single DM. The FFR model incorporates three sub-models: (1) a stochastic model of the flood forecast process, (2) a behavioral model of human response to flood warnings, and (3) a model of economic losses and physical constraints on preventive action. **These models are briefly described in the Appendices to this chapter.**

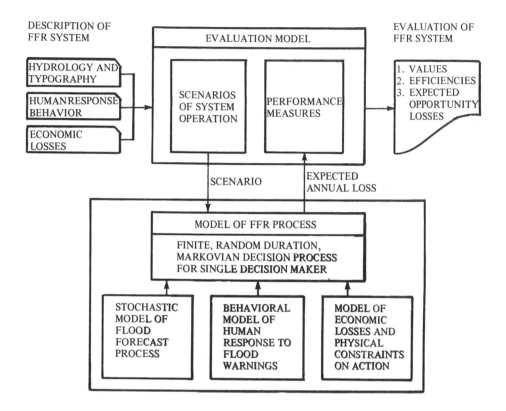

Figure 1. Informational structure of a methodology for evaluation of a flood-forecast response system.

The evaluation model provides the performance measures and expresses them in terms of the outputs of the FFR model. It also contains rules for aggregating the expected annual losses of all DMs located along a reach of river and responding to flood forecasts issued for the same forecast point. There are about 3,000 such FFR systems in the U.S.; a typical example is a community.

Evaluation Model

The key concept of our evaluation model is the distinction between normative operation of the system and actual operation. (Classical decision theory deals only with the former.) The performance of a system is determined by evaluating the actual operation relative to normative operation. Thus, two modes of operation are considered for each system component: a perfect and the actual forecast system, and an optimal and the actual response system. Thereby three scenarios of the FFR system are established as shown in Figure 2; also shown are the submodels needed for evaluating each scenario.

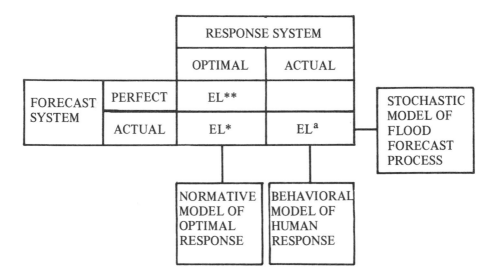

Figure 2. Scenarios, expected annual losses (EL), and submodels for evaluation of a flood forecast-response system.

Scenario 1: An "ideal" FFR system is composed of (1) a perfect forecast system which predicts the actual flood crest without any error and with an "infinite" lead time so that any feasible short-term protective action decided by the DM can be implemented, and (2) an optimal response system in which the DM selects the degree of response which minimizes his loss (the cost of response plus the flood damage sustained). Let the expected annual loss under this scenario be EL* * . The expectation is taken to account for the natural uncertainty: the magnitude of the actual flood crest given that a flood occurs and the number of floods per year.

Scenario 2: An FFR system is composed of (1) the actual forecast system which, most likely, provides a sequence of inaccurate forecasts of the flood crest with a relatively short lead time, and (2) an optimal response system, in which the DM makes a sequence of decisions in accordance with an adaptive response strategy which is an optimal solution to the Markovian decision process (see Appendix I). The uncertainty to be accounted for is the uncertainty in the sequence of the forecasted flood crest values and lead times. The optimal strategy minimizes the expected loss for each particular flood. Let the expected annual loss under this scenario be EL* .

Scenario 3: An FFR system is composed of (1) the actual forecast system and (2) the actual response system. The DM makes a sequence of decisions, each arrived at by subjective processing of information. The subjective decisions are, most likely, nonoptimal. Thus, if we were to describe mathematically the DM's decision behavior by a response strategy, this strategy (called here the actual strategy) would, most likely, differ from the optimal strategy. Let the expected annual loss under this scenario be EL^a. (For a description of the human response model see Appendix II.)

The scenarios form the basis for defining three measures of system performance: values, efficiencies, and expected opportunity losses. These measures are described below and illustrated in Table 1 for an FFR system in Milton, a small community of 840 DMs located on the West Branch of the Susquehanna River in northeastern Pennsylvania. One DM is assumed for each household, commercial, or industrial establishment. On the average, a major flood occurs at Milton every two years, and four forecasts are issued at six-hour intervals before the arrival of the flood crest.

Values: As a reference value for comparing various expected annual losses, we take EL^0—the expected annual loss with "no response" from the DM. This mode of decision behavior does not require the forecast system. Since there is also no cost of response, EL^0 represents the expected annual damage without the FFR system. The value of an FFR system is equal to the expected annual reduction of EL^0 due to the use of the system.

The value vector has three components:

- the *potential value*, $PV = EL^0 - EL*$ * ;

- the *optimal value*, $OV = EL^0 - EL^*$; and

- the *actual value*, $AV = EL^0 - EL^a$.

The following holds: $AV \leqslant OV \leqslant PV$.

The results are displayed in Table 1, Case 1. The actual value, $AV = \$126,000$, represents the annual benefit produced by the FFR system. If every DM in Milton were making an optimal response, then the annual benefit would be $OV = \$374,000$. If the forecasts were perfect, and every DM were responding to these forecasts in accordance with his optimal strategy, then the annual benefit would be $PV = \$1,827,000$. Clearly then, PV is the upper bound on the benefit that one may expect from an FFR system in Milton. Being considerably higher than AV and OV, PV indicates the potential of system improvements.

Performance Measure		Actual Parameters	Processing Time Shortened by 2 hrs.	Decision Constraint Released
		1	2	3
VALUES [10^3 $]				
Potential value	PV	1,827	1,827	1,827
Optimal value	OV	374	474	1,506
Actual value	AV	126	210	1,289
EFFICIENCIES				
Forecast efficiency	FE	0.205	0.260	0.825
Response efficiency	RE	0.336	0.441	0.855
Total efficiency	TE	0.069	0.115	0.705
EXPECTED OPPORTUNITY LOSSES [10^3 $]				
Forecast system	FOL	1,453	1,353	321
Response system	ROL	248	264	217
Total system	TOL	1,701	1,617	538

Maximum possible damage = 48,600 [10^3 $]
Number of decision makers = 840

Table 1. Evaluation of a flood forecast-response system in Milton, Pennsylvania

Efficiencies: For comparative analyses and discussions, we found it very convenient and meaningful to represent the performance of an FFR system in terms of efficiencies rather than values. The efficiency vector has three components:

- the *forecast efficiency*, FE = OV/PV;

- the *response efficiency*, RE = AV/OV; and

- the *total efficiency*, TE = AV/PV.

The following holds: TE = FE • RE, and FE, RE, TE ⩽ 1.

The forecast efficiency, FE, is a measure of how well the forecast system meets the needs of the response system. The response efficiency, RE, is a measure of how well the response system is utilizing the forecasts it obtains. As the results displayed in Table 1, Case 1, indicate, in Milton the response system is more efficient than the forecast system: RE > FE. The total efficiency TE is a measure of how close the performance of the actual FFR system is to the performance of an "ideal" FFR system. TE = 0.069 may seem rather low.

Expected Opportunity Losses: An opportunity loss occurs whenever forecasts are not perfect, or the response is not optimal, or both. The difference between the potential value, PV, and the optimal value, OV, is the expected opportunity loss due to imperfect forecasts. It will be referred to as the *forecast expected opportunity loss*, FOL = PV — OV. By analogy, we define the *response expected opportunity loss*, which is due to nonoptimal response, as ROL = OV — AV, and the *total expected opportunity loss* as TOL = PV — AV.

A perfect forecast system for Milton would be worth FOL = \$1,453,000 annually, while a disaster preparedness program which would develop an optimal response strategy for every DM in Milton and assure the use of this strategy would bring an annual benefit of ROL = \$248,000. The total expected opportunity loss TOL = FOL + ROL. By definition, the expected opportunity loss constitutes the upper bound on the value of partial improvements. The exact benefit resulting from a partial improvement can be evaluated as well, and we demonstrate such an analysis below.

Diversity of Alternatives

A comprehensive systems approach helps to identify and analyze in a methodical fashion alternative improvements in FFR systems. The alternatives are indeed extremely numerous and diverse. They include *technological* improvements such as automating the hydrometric network and installing a rainfall radar, *hydrologic* such as increasing the accuracy of rainfall-runoff models, *organizational* such as installing additional communication channels to reduce the dissemination time of forecasts, and *behavioral* such as educating the public about the flood hazard, the meaning of flood warnings, and the best ways of responding to them.

A conclusion reached in the "Program Development Plan" [NWS 1982] is that one of the most urgent improvements needed in the forecasting service is to increase the forecast lead times. The nationwide benefit from improving forecast lead times is estimated at $100,000,000 per year.

Using the Milton case study as an example, we will describe the decision analyses that identified the short lead time as the "bottle neck" in the performance of the system and provided estimates of the expected benefits from various improvements.

Benefits from Increased Lead Time

In Milton, the lead time of the first forecast for a flood event varies from one to 50 hours with an average of 20 hours. The average processing time (the time needed for data collection and forecast **preparation) is 3.2 hours. If an automated raingauge network were** installed and its observations used instead of manually collected raingauge measurements, it would offer the following advantages: the errors of the rainfall-runoff transformation would be reduced and the processing time considerably shortened. Since forecasts would be issued faster, the effective lead time would be longer. Consequently, the DMs would have more time to implement protective actions, and reduce their flood losses.

The effect of reducing the processing time by two hours is shown in Table 1, Case 2. We observe the following:

(1) Both efficiencies FE and RE go up. The increase of FE is obvious; the increase of RE indicates that even if the DMs do not account for the longer forecast lead time and continue to use the same response strategy, they still are able to benefit from the modification. By how much?

(2) The economic value of a modification is equal to the difference between AV prior to making the modification and AV after

making the modification. Thus, the additional two hours of lead time are worth $210,000 — $126,000 = $84,000 annually.

(3) The expected opportunity losses change too. FOL is decreased by $1,453,000 — $1,353,000 = $100,000; this is obvious for the improved forecast system is "closer" to the perfect system; hence the value of the perfect system relative to the actual system should decrease. On the other hand, ROL is increased by $264,000 — $248,000 = $16,000, thereby implying that with the improved forecast system the value of an optimal response is higher. In other words, when the quality of the forecasts improves then the upper bound on the economically justified expenditure for improving the response system increases.

(4) The sum of the changes in FOL and ROL ($100,000 — $16,000 = $84,000) is equal to the change in TOL ($1,701,000 — $1,617,000 = $84,000) which is also equal to the actual value of the modification. These changes admit the following interpretation. If the actual response system were optimal and if it adapted optimally to the modification of the forecast system, then the modification would be worth $100,000 annually. But because the response system behaves in a suboptimal manner, an opportunity loss of $16,000 is incurred. Hence, the actual worth of the modification is $84,000 annually.

Potential Benefits from Joint Improvements

A short lead time of a forecast is detrimental to the performance of an FFR system because the rate at which protective action can be implemented is constrained. Physical resources may be limited (for example, means of transportation for evacuation), manpower may be limited, and so forth. Such constraints are a characteristic of the protective action. A typical constraint for evacuation of an industrial establishment is shown in Figure 3; dd(t) is the maximum degree of response which can be implemented in the time interval of t hours. For instance, it takes about 20 hours to avert 60 percent of the maximum preventable damage, which for industrial establishments varies from 40 percent to 70 percent of the maximum possible damage.

If the forecast lead time were very long, say 120 hours, the decision constraint would be inactive. Thus, one way to determine the maximum

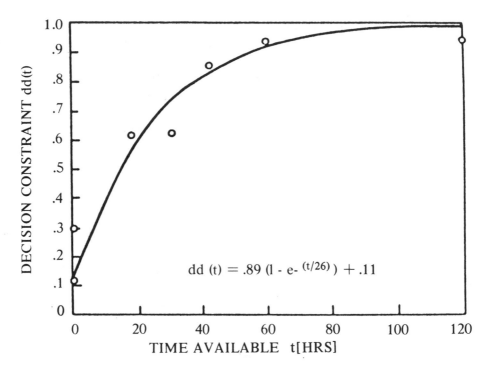

Figure 3. Decision constraint function for evacuation of an industrial establishment. $dd(t)$ is expressed as a fraction of the maximum damage that can be prevented by short-term protective action.

potential benefit from increased lead times is to release the decision constraint. This was done for Milton, and the results are shown in Table 1, Case 3. The conclusions follow:

(1) The very large increase of the total efficiency TE points out unequivocally the severe effect of the short lead time or, equivalently, of the decision constraint.

(2) The maximum potential benefit from longer lead times, assuming the actual (nonoptimal) response, is $1,289,000 — $126,000 = $1,163,000 annually.

(3) Both the forecast efficiency FE and the response efficiency RE markedly increased.

In view of the fact that it is infeasible to provide flood forecasts with the lead time of 120 hours or to completely eliminate the decision constraint, this result suggests that perhaps the best approach to closing the gap between the actual and potential system performance is through a cooperative effort of NWS and local authorities. To wit, NWS should focus on providing longer forecast lead times, while the local authorities should try to partially release the decision constraint by, for example, increasing community preparedness for floods, improving organization of or securing more adequate equipment for the civil defense units which support the evacuation. As the numbers in Table 1 indicate, the potential economic benefits from such a joint improvement of both forecast and response systems in Milton is very high.

Impact of Human Response Behavior

No technological, hydrologic, or organizational modification of an FFR system is economically efficient unless response behavior of DMs transforms it into better action. We illustrate this fact for an industrial DM in Milton who planned to improve his preparedness for floods and thereby to reduce the time T needed to achieve the maximum response. We analyzed his plan by varying T from its nominal value of 120 hours to zero hours (instant response feasible). The total efficiency function TE(T) was computed for two response strategies: (1) actual (human factors) strategy, (2) optimal strategy.

The two response strategies have different characteristics. The optimal strategy is based on expected loss. The human factors strategy is based on expected probability of loss because field surveys indicate that people move to action only if warnings and losses are perceived to be quite certain. Expected loss is a better discriminator between high and low floods than is the expected probability of loss. Also, early warnings tend to underestimate the crest of high floods, causing relatively little change in the prior probability. This is consistent with observations that people do not readily evacuate on the basis of first warnings. As a result, the human factors strategy is less anticipatory and, therefore, less effective in coping with the forecast uncertainty and the decision constraint than the optimal strategy. This is reflected in the total efficiency functions graphed in Figure 4.

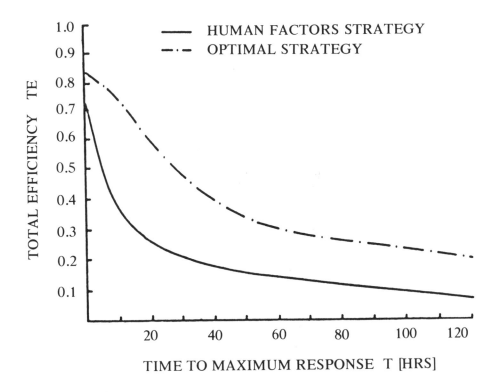

Figure 4. Effect of the decision constraint on total efficiency of two response strategies for an industrial decision maker in Milton, Pennsylvania.

The total efficiency function of the optimal strategy provides an upper bound on TE(T) attainable by any other strategy. The suboptimality of the human factors strategy is apparent. For example, TE of the optimal strategy under the actual system conditions (T = 120 hours) is 0.20. In order to achieve the same TE using the human factors strategy, T would have to be reduced to 30 hours! Conclusion: Perhaps instead of investing solely in an organizational solution that would shorten the time needed to achieve maximum response, or waiting for NWS to implement a technological solution that would increase the forecast lead time, a more cost-effective alternative for this exemplary DM would be to also invest in a behavioral solution: the development of an analytic model that would help him to better use the forecasts and to make an optimal instead of a suboptimal (heuristic) response.

Dissimilarities Among FFR Systems

The dissimilarities among FFR systems are crucial. Not only do they call for systems analyses at the microeconomic level, but they also imply that in all likelihood the most cost-effective improvements will vary from one FFR system to another.

Figure 5 gives but one example of dissimilarities among FFR systems in three communities: Milton on the Susquehanna River, Pennsylvania; Victoria on the Guadalupe River, Texas; and Columbus on the Tombigbee River, Mississippi. The three communities have quite different topographic, hydrologic, economic, and social characteristics. The totality of these differences is mirrored in the sensitivity of the forecast efficiency FE to the time T needed to achieve the maximum response. A typical house in each community was chosen as the response system, and T was varied from the nominal value of 24 hours to zero hours. The results poignantly illustrate that while the Victoria and Columbus FFR systems are only slightly sensitive to the decision constraint, the Milton FFR system is extremely sensitive.

In light of the Milton example, it should be apparent that there is no single improvement alternative that would be optimal nationwide. For that reason the "Program Development Plan" prepared by the NWS Office of Hydrology sets forth several improvement goals designed specifically for different situations. Only if budgeted and achieved as a "package" will these goals assure the most cost-effective improvement of our nation's 3,000 flood forecast-response systems.

Summary

We hope to have made a case for the following propositions:

(1) The concept of a flood forecast-response system, which captures interactions among complex hydrologic, organizational, behavioral, and economic factors, provides a logical and mathematical framework for analyzing system improvements.

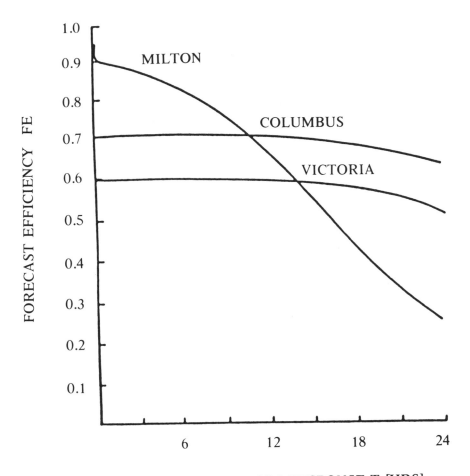

TIME TO MAXIMUM RESPONSE T [HRS]

MILTON   : 2-story house, 6 ft above flood stage
VICTORIA : 1-story house, 11 ft above flood stage
COLUMBUS: 1-story house, 10 ft above flood stage

Figure 5. Effect of the decision constraint on forecast efficiency for
three residential decision makers.

(2) The performance measures for forecast-response systems, which
capture the interplay between the quality of forecasts and the
quality of response, provide a comprehensive, "big picture" of

the system's economic performance and also indicate the system's potential for improvements.

(3) The economic value of flood forecasts and the benefits to be derived by the general public from the planned improvements of hydrologic forecasting by the National Weather Service are substantial and can be estimated quantitatively.

(4) The systems approach (supported by techniques from operations research, constructs from statistical decision theory, and empirical evidence from economics and cognitive psychology) can contribute a conceptual framework and knowledge base useful for long-term planning in a public sector.

Appendix I. Model of the FFR Process

The model of the FFR process is formulated for a single DM. The sequence of forecasts of the flood crest and the actual river stages are described by means of a Markov chain. The DM's response to the sequence of forecasts is formulated as a finite, random duration, Markovian decision process. At each decision time, k, the state of the process is a fourtuple (a, i, h, w)

where
  a - the degree of response already achieved (due to the decisions already made and implemented by the DM),
  i - the current flood level,
  h - the forecasted flood crest,
  w - binary random variable indicating whether or not more forecasts will be issued.

The decision to be made, d, is the desired degress of response defined as the ratio: (damage the DM wants to prevent)/(maximum preventable damage). Thus $0 \leqslant d \leqslant 1$, where $d = 0$ indicates no response and $d = 1$ indicates full response. The law of motion for the process is a two-branch Markov chain. Given the k-th forecast message (i,h), the first branch states the probability of transition to a $(k +\text{-}1)$—th forecast message, while the second branch states the probability of transition to the actual flood crest, in which case no more forecasts are issued and the process terminates. The branches are determined by the probability function of the binary variate w.

The loss function for the process represents the cost of implementing a given degree of response and the damage caused by the flood crest when it eventually arrives. The decision behavior of the DM is described by a response strategy, S. This strategy relates the degree of response d at the time k to the degree of response already achieved a and to the information contained in the forecast message, namely i and h. Thus, $d = S(a,i,h,k)$. Minimization of the expected loss throughout the whole flood process (with the aid of a dynamic programming algorithm) yields an optimal response strategy, $S*$. In reality, the DM may not behave optimally. His actual response is, therefore, described by an actual strategy, S^a. It is obtained via a behavioral model of human response to flood warnings.

The actual strategy, S^a, needs to be determined whenever the methodology is used as an evaluation tool or as a planning aid. Whenever the methodology is used as a normative decision aid, then it is the optimal strategy, $S*$, which is sought. $S*$ can be viewed as an "emergency plan," which assists the DM in deciding "what to do if." It can be computed in advance and, most important, it accounts for the randomness of the flood process and the uncertainty in the forecasts (i.e., errors in the forecasted magnitude and timing of the flood crest).

Details of the above concepts, theory, and case studies are reported in Krzysztofowicz and Davis [1983].

Appendix II: Human Response Model

The purpose of the behavioral model of human response to flood warnings is to simulate the actual response strategy, Sa. This strategy is meant to mimic the actual response behavior of the DM or to predict such behavior under future system conditions. It is a Bayesian learning model of a sort often found to apply to sequential changes in response tendency with intermittent reinforcement. The model is built of mathematical representations of four interconnected cognitive elements of response: (1) uncertainty about flooding and loss prior to a flood, (2) sequential inference based on warnings during a flood, (3) response strategy, and (4) learning after a flood.

The model assumes that the DM begins to respond when he is sufficiently sure that a flood will reach his property. His degree of certainty that this will happen is represented by a subjective probability, the value of which depends on his past experience with floods and losses and on the warnings he receives. When his subjective probability exceeds a threshold, he takes a characteristic course of action that will result in savings should he be flooded. The amount of savings he can accomplish is limited by the time available to him, and he stops his protective action if the flood reaches his property, or if the crest occurs below it. Following a flood event, the DM learns from that experience and revises his subjective probability of a flood and loss toward an objective (historical) value, to an extent dependent on his willingness to learn. Between floods and losses the probability decays exponentially toward zero to mimic the effect of forgetting.

Details of the model, behavioral evidence supporting its assumptions, and the method of its calibration are described by Ferrell and Krzysztofowicz [1983].

REFERENCES

Alexandridis, M. and Krzysztofowicz, R. 1982, *Value of Categorical and Probabilistic Temperature Forecasts for Scheduling of Power Generation, Report No. 282*, Ralph M. Parsons Laboratory, Massachusetts Institute of Technology, Cambridge, Massachusetts.

Chatterton, J.B.; Pirt, J.; and Wood, T.R. 1979, "The benefits of flood forecasting," *Journal Institution of Water Engineers and Scientists*, Vol. 33, No. 3, pp. 237-252.

Day, H.J. and Lee, K.K. 1976, "Flood damage reduction potential of river forecast," *Journal of Water Resources Planning and Management Division*, Vol. 102, No. WR1, pp. 77-78.

Ferrell, W.R. and Krzysztofowicz, R. 1983, "A model of human response to flood warnings for system evaluation," *Water Resources Research*, Vol. 19, No. 6, pp. 1467-1475.

Katz, R.W.; Murphy, A.H.; and Winkler, R.L. 1982, "Assessing the value of frost forecasts to orchardists: A dynamic decision making approach," *Journal of Applied Meteorology*, Vol. 21, No. 4, pp. 518-531.

Krzysztofowicz, R. 1983, "Why should a forecaster and a decision maker use Bayes theorem," *Water Resources Research*, Vol. 19, No. 2, pp. 327-336.

Krzysztofowicz, R. and Davis, D.R. 1983, "A methodology for evaluation of flood forecast-response systems, Part 1: analyses and concepts, Part 2: theory, Part 3: case studies," *Water Resources Research*, Vol. 19, No. 6, pp. 1423-1454.

Morzuch, B.J. and Willis, C.E. 1982, "Value of weather information in cranberry marketing decisions," *Journal of Applied Meteorology*, Vol. 21, No. 4, pp. 499-504.

NWS (National Weather Service), National Oceanic and Atmospheric Administration, US Department of Commerce 1982, *Program Development Plan for Improving Hydrologic Services*, Silver Spring, Maryland.

Suchman, D.; Auvine, B.A.; and Hinton, B.H. 1979, "Some economic effects of private meteorological forecasting," *Bulletin of the American Meteorological Society*, Vol. 60, No. 10, pp. 1148-1156.

Tice, T.F. and Clouser, R.L. 1982, "Determination of the value of weather information to individual corn producers," *Journal of Applied Meteorology*, Vol. 21, No. 4, pp. 447-452.

PART IV

Hazards of Climate

Whether in terms of lives lost or economic resources destroyed, the tropical cyclone is the major cause of natural disasters. The World Meteorological Organization (WMO) is assisting the fifty most-affected countries worldwide to improve their capability in predicting storm tracks and to organize national warning services.

Chapter 13
The Social and Economic Impact of Tropical Cyclones

Peter Rogers

Peter Rogers is Special Projects Officer at the World Meteorological Organization's headquarters in Geneva. After service with the British Meteorological Office, he joined WMO in 1956 and has been closely associated with the development and implementation of the Tropical Cyclone Programme (TCP) since its inception in 1971. From 1974 to 1976 he was seconded to the Economic and Social Commission for Asia and the Pacific in Bangkok to promote the work of the joint WMO/ESCAP Typhoon Committee and the Panel on Tropical Cyclones.

Measuring the extent of a disaster by loss of life, the tropical cyclone is the major cause of natural disasters. It is often called the greatest storm on earth. The worst earthquake during the ten-year period 1966-75 took a tragic total of 54,000 lives, but the toll of the cyclone that struck Bangladesh in November 1970, between 200,000 and 400,000 lives, is almost unimaginable. In the long catalogue of meteorological disasters befalling mankind, the cyclone has been responsible for 80 percent of all lives lost. A page out of this catalogue appears in Table 1.

Natural disaster type	1966	1967	1968	1969	1970	1971	1972	1973	1974	1975	Total
Earthquake	2,948	451	10,721	3,322	55,380	1,244	11,493	97	1,024	2,365	89,145
Tsunami	3	0	392	0	0	1	0	0	0	2	398
Cyclone/storm surge[1]	0	0	1,000	800	400,694	–	–	–	–	–	402,494
Volcanic eruption	247	0	78	5	0	30	0	0	0	0	360
Landslide[2]	–	–	–	–	–	414	572	128	1,128	84	2,326
Avalanche[2]	–	–	–	–	–	23	75	20	18	33	169
Total	3,198	451	12,191	4,127	456,074	1,712	12,140	245	2,170	2,584	494,892

1. Reporting ceased 1970.
2. Reporting started 1971.

Source: Unesco, Annual Summary of Information on Natural Disasters, No. 10, 1975.

Table 1. Loss of life due to natural disaster during the period 1966-75

What is a Tropical Cyclone?

Tropical storms are severe cyclonic disturbances of the atmosphere that form in low latitudes: between 5° and 30° in both northern and southern hemispheres. (They can exist as fully fledged storms far to the north or south of 30°.) The storms develop over the warm waters of the tropical oceans where water temperature is 27°C or higher and where atmospheric pressure is relatively low. The main areas where they originate as well as the main tracks they normally follow are shown in Figure 1.

These storms are cyclonic spirals, the winds forming a vortex which, as a result of the earth's rotation, turns clockwise in the southern and counter-clockwise in the northern hemisphere. The vortex of air spirals inwards towards the centre where the pressure is at a minimum. This area, known as the eye of the storm, contains only light winds or may even be calm.

Around the eye explosive cloud growth takes place as warm, moist tropical air escapes upwards to heights of 12,000 metres or more. This

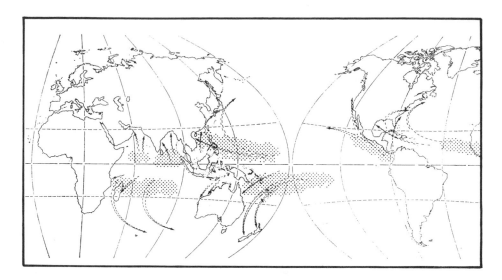

Figure 1. Main areas of origin and main tracks of tropical cyclones.

is the region of maximum winds which may exceed 270 km per hour. If the winds in such a cyclonic spiral exceed 120 km per hour the storm is called a "hurricane" in the western Atlantic, a "typhoon" in the western Pacific, or sometimes just a "cyclone" in the Indian Ocean.

From the mass of clouds around the eye, rainfall can be exceedingly heavy, amounting to 150-250 mm during the passage of a fully developed cyclone over coastal regions, and as much as 1,000 mm is possible.

One further characteristic of a cyclonic storm is its association with a strong reduction in atmospheric pressure. This reduction, as much as 60 to 100 millibars, causes a rise in water level known as the "storm surge."[1] When low pressure combines with the wind, drawing sea-water inland (as the cyclone approaches land), waves and tide may bring about a rise in water level of as much as fourteen metres.

The wind, rain, and water effects of a cyclonic storm may be felt over as much as 500 km away from the eye, diminishing progressively from the centre. I. Sinnamon has described the destructiveness of these multiple effects of a cyclone:

> The losses of life and property on tropical islands and in the coastal areas of continents are caused by the direct and indirect effects of the high winds and

excessive rains. The high winds may cause buildings to be severely damaged or even to collapse. In addition, there may be short circuits in the electrical system which may start fires. The action of the wind plus the low atmospheric pressure may result in storm waves and widespread inundation of low-lying land in poorly protected coastal areas. The heavy rainfall may cause landslides and rapid and extensive rise of the water levels of rivers.[2]

Economic Impact of Destructive Forces

As tragic as the high death tolls may be, they are not the only negative consequences of tropical cyclones. This loss of life cannot be separated from the tremendous economic impact of the destructive forces of these gigantic storms. It has been estimated that in an average year, eighty to a hundred tropical cyclones form over the world's oceans. They do not all cause disasters, but those that do, in addition to killing 20,000 people, also diminish the economic resources of the countries affected by $6,000-7,000 million.

Evidently there are wide variations from year to year and from place to place, and major catastrophes such as the Bangladesh cyclone can tragically distort any average figure. The twentieth-century hurricane damage in the United States alone has exceeded $12,000 million. There, the annual cost of hurricane damage, which was $13 million between 1915 and 1924, jumped to $295 million for the period 1959-68. Today, a single severe storm can cost over $3,000 million. In 1979, Hurricanes David and Frederick took heavy tolls of life and property in the Caribbean and the southern United States. David destroyed the banana crop in Dominica, thereby depriving the island of 85 percent of its annual income in a matter of hours. In the United States, Frederick killed "only" five people, but caused damage estimated at $2,000 million.

If we look at the typhoon areas of the Pacific and the tropical cyclone regions of the Bay of Bengal and the Arabian Sea, we find that the average annual cost of damage, which was $500 million in the period 1952-63, reached nearly $3,000 million for each of the years 1965-78. Over the whole of that fourteen-year period, it totaled $36,000 million.

Experience shows that the destruction caused by a single severe storm can, in developing countries, completely negate any real economic growth for several succeeding years. At the same time, such storms also have beneficial effects, the rainfall they bring being vital to crop production and in replenishing the water resources essential to many human activities. In the face of these facts, it is clear that measures to protect human life and reduce economic losses should receive high priority. What can be done to this end and how does it work in practice?

Early-warning Systems Protect Populations

Of the fifty countries threatened by tropical cyclones (see Figure 1), the Philippines is at the top of the list. There no less than nineteen tropical cyclones may affect its 7,000 islands in an average year. The first requirement is evidently for an efficient forecasting and early-warning system which will enable the population to escape from threatened areas or to take refuge in safe places, as well as to protect their property. This responsibility falls upon the national meteorological and hydrological services which must predict the time and area of impact and the expected dangers in terms of high winds and flooding.

In most countries, a similar system has been developed over many years, making use not only of more conventional sources of data collection, but also of the advanced technology now available. In general, this system is based upon the global and regional requirements for the World Weather Watch and Operational Hydrology Programmes of the World Meteorological Organization (WMO). Other national activities may also be set up to assist in the more accurate prediction and warning of tropical cyclones—a considerable input in itself. The aim is usually to provide twelve daylight hours' warning to the population and it may be said without fear of contradiction that this system works with a high degree of efficiency in most tropical cyclone areas.

Satellite Tracking

Earth-orbiting satellites and, more especially, geostationary satellites, have largely relieved the meteorologist of the difficult problem of detecting the formation of a cyclone over distant ocean waters from which he has little other information. However, cyclone tracks are notoriously erratic and in a twenty-four-hour forecast, an error of only 10 degrees in predicting the track results in the cyclone striking the coast more than 185 km from the expected spot. Surveillance by satellite and finally by storm-warning radar when the cyclone is within 300-400 km can ensure that its path into the coast is closely monitored. This in turn enables the forecast to be constantly updated and refined in the hours leading up to landfall. This efficiency of existing warning systems should not, however, be a cause for complacency. Disasters still occur with distressing regularity. One of the major purposes of the WMO Tropical Cyclone Programme (TCP) is to improve the ability of member states, individually and collectively, to meet the challenge posed by tropical cyclones.

The second requirement in a tropical-cyclone warning service is, in some respects, more complex. It concerns what happens when the population has been warned. What should the individual do? How can he ensure the safety of his family and minimize the risk of destruction of those possessions on which his livelihood may depend?

Co-ordinating Forecasting and Preparedness

A whole series of measures are necessary, based upon a sound national plan to cope with extreme conditions. A prime need is that each individual should understand the dangers and be able to respond in a way that will limit their impact. Thus, local arrangements must provide for everyone to be warned, for the availability of shelters and evacuation plans, and, when the cyclone has struck, for the relief, rehabilitation, and reconstruction measures that will accelerate a rapid return to normal conditions. Many different government departments and agencies may be involved in this process, as well as those voluntary agencies, such as the Red Cross, which traditionally provide succour in time of need. It will be evident that the closest co-ordination between those responsible for the forecasting and warning service and those with important roles in disaster prevention and preparedness constitute a prerequisite for the successful operation of the total system.

As already stated, national procedures and measures should normally be enshrined in a national disaster or emergency plan. The importance of firm control at the government level is an essential ingredient if the plan is to operate successfully under the stresses inseparable from the chaos and destruction all too often brought about by severe tropical cyclones.

Although more and more countries are enacting legislation to combat the disastrous impact of tropical cyclones, full integration of all aspects of the system has not everywhere progressed as rapidly as might be hoped. The essentially national nature of these arrangements has been stressed but, here again, the broader activities of the Tropical Cyclone Programme have been designed to assist at a variety of levels, including the national and local.

The Human Response to Threat of Danger

In many respects the human response to the threat of danger is the very core of disaster prevention and preparedness. Ultimately, the success or failure of the warning system depends upon its weakest link—man himself. An accurate forecast, a well-designed disaster prevention system, and all the aids that technology provides count for little if the human response is not geared to the realities of the occasion.

Every cyclone brings forth a crop of stories demonstrating the endless diversity of human reaction to the disaster threat. Age, health, education, family situation, previous disaster experience and many other factors play a role, but a role so complex that no clear-cut pattern of behaviour emerges for general application to future disaster situations. The aerospace engineer in Texas can be as obstinate as the Bengali farmer in refusing to leave his home when advised to do so.

It is not surprising therefore that a public education and information component bringing together the efforts of the technical agencies and those in the social welfare field is progressively being embodied in relevant plans and programmes.

WMO's Tropical Cyclone Programme

The primary objective of the WMO's Tropical Cyclone Programme is to establish national and regionally co-ordinated systems to minimize the loss of life and damage caused by tropical cyclones. It has three main elements—meteorological, hydrological, and prevention and preparedness—whilst for convenience, its activities are divided into two categories, general and regional. The general component deals with those activities applicable to all WMO member states in tropical cyclone areas. It consists mainly of work directed towards providing up-to-date technical guidance material for the benefit of those concerned with the forecasting and warning systems in developing countries. This work is mostly carried out with the help of groups of experts having special knowledge of the subject matter. Publications emanating from these activities, or the transfer of technology as it is sometimes called, cover many aspects of the tropical cyclone problem, such as forecasting techniques, radar, automatic weather stations, the application of satellite data, storm surges, etc.

Under the regional component, the principal advances have been made by grouping together countries in specific tropical cyclone areas to carry out co-operative programmes designed to improve the warning system as a whole. These programmes cover meteorology, hydrology, disaster prevention and preparedness, training and research.

The regional cyclone bodies, as they have become known, cover nearly all the world's tropical-cyclone areas—the typhoons of the Pacific, the hurricanes of the Caribbean and Central America, the tropical cyclones of the Bay of Bengal and the Arabian Sea and of the southwest Indian Ocean (see Figure 2). Though much remains to be done, the years of operation of these bodies have seen immense improvements in observation and telecommunication systems, most notably in the radar and satellite facilities, which are of such vital importance for forecasting and warning. The installation of modern flood forecasting systems has been another major innovation in some areas.

The need for disaster prevention and preparedness measures to parallel technical advances in the meteorological and hydrological capabilities of members has received particular attention. The view that, in the end, the effectiveness of the system in saving life and reducing damage depends upon these measures has secured wider recognition. The participation of all national agencies responsible at the socio-economic level has been a major objective of this work, with limited but measurable progress. In these activities WMO works closely with three other international organizations such as the Office of the United Nations Disaster Relief Co-ordinator (UNDRO) and the League of Red Cross Societies, thus bringing their particular expertise and experience into the Tropical Cyclone Programme (TCP).

It can readily be visualized that the introduction of modern technology and techniques brings with it a continuing need for training, if those concerned are to remain abreast of developments. The TCP, through symposia, seminars, workshops, training courses, expert visits and fellowships, aims to meet this need. Similarly, the TCP has fostered a number of activities of a research nature, despite the limited resources available in many of the developing countries.

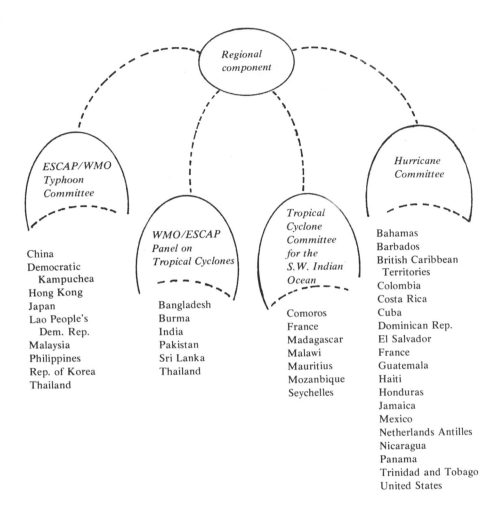

Figure 2. Regional cyclone bodies of the WMO Tropical Cyclone
     Programme (ESCAP = United Nations Economic and Social
     Council for Asia and the Pacific)

Appraisal of Progress Made to Date

What progress is being made in the effort to reduce the impact of
tropical cyclones on human society? It must be said immediately that it
is far from easy to find a satisfactory yardstick to measure this
progress. Experience over the years confirms that prevention and
preparedness measures can substantially reduce the death toll of
tropical cyclones, but we cannot easily show that x lives have been

saved or that the cost of damage has decreased by y millions of dollars. Indeed the cost of damage continues to rise inexorably, as has been demonstrated earlier. Even allowing for rising prices and the penalties of development—and the higher the level of development of a country the greater will be the cost of destruction—the figures must be a disappointment. However, model studies of the probable destruction caused by a tropical cyclone today and in the year 2000 in the United States indicate that while the destruction and loss of life may be expected to grow considerably as a result of population growth, coastal development, and rising prices, the projected estimates of damage, death, and injuries could be reduced by about a quarter if the most effective measures to minimize losses were to be applied without delay.

What is certain is that the capabilities of many countries to produce timely early warnings of tropical cyclones have been appreciably improved. There has been a noteworthy growth in the awareness of the adverse impact of natural disasters on the national economies of developing countries that has served to unlock extra funds from a variety of different sources. These are encouraging signs that mankind, which has suffered the ravages of tropical cyclones through the centuries, has decided that it is time to counteract the increasing vulnerability that accompanies the growth of population and the development of national economies. This change of heart is, perhaps, an indication that a foundation has been laid from which more positive benefits will accrue.

Future progress will inevitably depend largely upon the resources nations and the international community are prepared to devote to the major outstanding problems. So far, authorities and the public have been reluctant to accord these problems sufficiently high priority, perhaps understandably, taking into account the multitude of other problems faced by most developing countries. More efforts should therefore be directed to demonstrating the humanitarian and economic benefits deriving from a long-term planned programme. However, it is not only a question of resources; the will to perceive the advantages of protective action must also be present.

NOTES

1. Pressure reduction plays a relatively minor role in the storm surge. The main rise in level is through high winds piling water up, and because of the sloping sea-bed's topography as the surge nears the coast.
2. I. Sinnamon, *Cyclone-resistant Rural Primary-school Construction—A Design Guide*, Bangkok, Unesco Regional Office for Education in Asia, 1977.

With an average of 50 million cloud-to-ground flashes striking the U.S. each year, lightning is among the nation's most severe weather hazards. Basic research findings discussed here concern the interactions of an individual lightning flash: the damage caused by the large current that flows in the return stroke of a flash; the heat this generates, or the resulting shock wave; the protection of a building through diverting the current of a direct strike or through shielding a structure from transients. However, the overall phenomenology of lightning in thunderstorms—the total number of flashes, what fraction strike the ground, flashing rates, etc.—needs further research.

Chapter 14
Lightning Damage and Lightning Protection

E. Philip Krider

E. Philip Krider is Professor in the Department of Atmospheric Sciences and Institute of Atmospheric Physics of the University of Arizona. He is also Executive Vice President and Chairman of Lightning Location and Protection, Inc. His research on the physics of lightning and thunderstorm electricity has been supported by grants from the Office of Naval Research and from the National Aeronautics and Space Administration (NASA). He serves as scientific adviser to the NASA Kennedy Space Center on lightning hazards to launches and lightning protection methods and is a member of committees of both the American Geophysical Union and the International Commission on Atmospheric Electricity. He holds seven patents relating to devices for study of lightning.

Introduction

Lightning is a transient, high-current electric discharge whose path length is measured in kilometers. The most common cause of lightning is the electric charge that is generated by thunderstorm clouds, and well over half of all discharges occur within the clouds. Cloud-to-ground lightning is less frequent than intracloud, but flashes to ground are the primary hazard to people or objects on the ground. A recent estimate of the annual frequency of cloud-to-ground flashes, based on thunderstorm-hour statistics, is given in Figure 1 (Maier, 1983). Note that most of the continental United States has at least two cloud-to-ground flashes per square kilometer per year on average and that half of the United States has at least 4 km^{-2} yr^{-1}. In more familiar units, a flash density of 4 km^{-2} yr^{-1} is equivalent to about 10 discharges per square mile per year. Altogether, an average of about 50 million cloud-to-ground flashes strike the United States each year. Lightning is among the nation's most severe weather hazards.

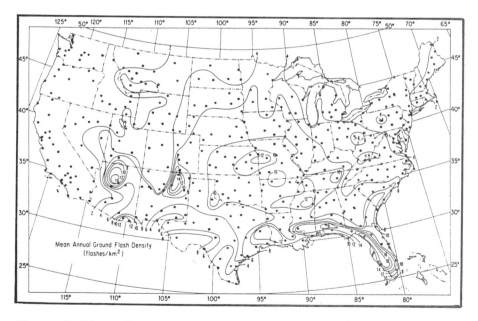

Figure 1. Map of the annual frequency of cloud-to-ground lightning over the continental United States, based on thunderstorm-hour statistics (courtesy of M.W. Maier).

The luminous development of a cloud-to-ground lightning flash, the mechanisms of lightning damage, and the fundamentals of lightning protection are reviewed briefly. Although the interactions of an individual lightning flash are discussed, it is worth noting that the overall phenomenology of lightning in thunderstorms—e.g., the total number of flashes, the fraction of all discharges that strike the ground, the time evolution of the flashing rates, etc.—needs further research (see, for example, Livingston and Krider, 1978). The questions of whether the characteristics of individual flashes depend on the geographical location, the ground characteristics, the season, the meteorological environment, etc., are also still to be answered. Although the average flash is probably similar throughout the world, there are important differences within a given region. For example, frontal storms are thought to produce higher flashing rates and more strokes per flash than air-mass storms (Schonland, 1956); topography affects the channel lengths and perhaps other properties of the discharges (McEachron, 1939; Winn et al., 1973); and there are important seasonal effects, such as in the frequency of positive discharges to ground (Brook et al., 1982).

Cloud-to-Ground Lightning

Here it may be helpful to review the terminology used to describe the luminous processes that occur in a typical cloud-to-ground lightning flash (for more detailed discussions of these phenomena, see Viemeister, 1961; Schonland, 1964; Uman, 1969, 1971; Salanave, 1980; and Uman and Krider, 1982). A typical discharge begins within the cloud with a process called the *preliminary breakdown*. The preliminary breakdown usually lasts several tens of milliseconds and eventually initiates an intermittent, highly branched discharge, called a *stepped leader*, that propagates downward. The stepped leader usually lowers negative charge, and the direction of the branches in a photograph indicates the direction of stepped-leader propagation. Successive stages in the geometrical development of a stepped leader are shown in Figure 2.

When the tip of any branch of the stepped leader comes close to the ground, the electric field at the surface under the leader becomes very large, and one or more upward propagating discharges form at the ground and start the *attachment process* (see Figure 2c). These

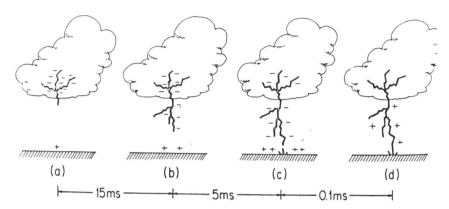

Figure 2. Sketch of the time development of a lightning stepped leader and the ensuing return strokes.

upward-propagating discharges rise until one or more attach to the leader a few tens of meters above the surface. When contact occurs, the first *return stroke begins.* The return stroke is a very large current pulse that starts at the ground and propagates back up the previously ionized leader channel to the cloud. The peak currents in return strokes are typically tens of kiloamperes, and the speed of upward propagation is usually about one-third the speed of light.

The last few steps of the stepped leader, the onset of a connecting discharge, and the beginning of the return stroke are illustrated in Figure 3. The distance between the object that is about to be struck and the tip of the leader when the connecting discharge is initiated is called the *striking distance* and is an important consideration in lightning protection. The distance to the actual junction between the leader and the connecting discharge is often assumed to be about one-half the striking distance. In Figure 3c the striking distance is labeled SD, and in Figure 3d the junction point is labeled J.

A photograph showing upward streamers near the ground during two strikes to mountainous terrain is reproduced in Figure 4. There point *d* shows what is probably the striking distance (about 39 m above the ground); point *e* is the junction between the connecting discharge and the leader (16 m); and points *a, b,* and *c* are upward discharges that did not contact the leader (8, 10, and 10 m long, respectively). Further details about this photograph are given in Krider and Ladd, 1975.

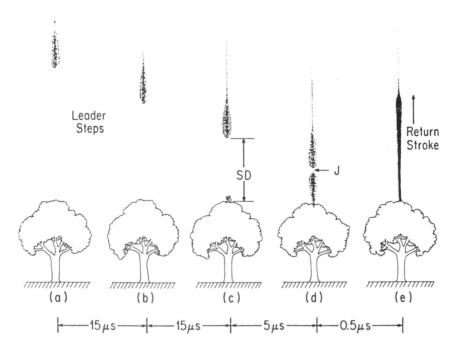

Figure 3. Sketch of the luminous processes that occur during a lightning strike. An upward-connecting discharge forms in (c) when the stepped leader is at the striking distance (SD).

After a pause of typically 40 to 80 ms, most cloud-to-ground flashes produce a *dart leader* that without stepping propagates down the previous return-stroke channel and initiates a subsequent return stroke. Most flashes contain two to four return strokes, and lightning often appears to "flicker" because the human eye can just resolve the time intervals between these bright components. In roughly 20 to 40 percent of all cloud-to-ground flashes, the dart leader propagates down only a portion of the previous return-stroke channel and then forges a different path to ground. In these instances, the lightning actually strikes the ground in two places, and the channel has a characteristic forked appearance that can be seen in many photographs.

The currents in return strokes have been measured in direct strikes to instrumented towers. Peak currents of typically 20 to 40 kA usually occur within 1 to 3 μs, and the maximum rate of rise of current during the initial onset may be 150 kA/μs or higher (Weidman and Krider, 1980). The current falls to about half the peak value in about 50 μsec,

Figure 4. Photograph of upward streamers near the strike points of two flashes in mountainous terrain. Point *d*, striking distance; *e*, junction between the connecting discharge and the leader; *a, b,* and *c,* upward discharges that did not contact the leader (Krider and Ladd, 1975).

and following this, many strokes have a *continuing current* on the order of hundreds of amperes that persists for tens of milliseconds after the stroke peak. Table 1 shows a summary of the current characteristics of return strokes that lower negative charge toward ground. Flashes that lower positive charge are much less frequent than those that lower negative charge; positive flashes do sometimes transfer very large amounts of charge to ground (Berger et al., 1975; Brook et al., 1982).

Recent analyses of the broadband electromagnetic power radiated by lightning indicate that the peak power during a first return stroke is at least 2×10^{10}w and that subsequent strokes produce at least 3×10^{9}w (Krider and Guo, 1983). These are large power values, but since

Table 1. Parameters of Return Strokes that Lower Negative Charge to Ground*

Parameters	Unit	Percentage of cases exceeding tabulated value		
		95%	50%	5%
Peak current (minimum 2 kA):				
First stroke	kA	14.0	30.0	80.0
Subsequent stroke	kA	4.6	12.0	30.0
Total charge:				
First stroke	C	1.1	5.2	24.0
Subsequent stroke	C	0.2	1.4	11.0
Entire flash	C	1.3	7.5	40.0
Impulse charge:				
First stroke	C	1.1	4.5	20.0
Subsequent stroke	C	0.22	0.95	4.0
Stroke duration				
First stroke	μs	30.0	75.0	200.0
Subsequent stroke	μs	6.5	32.0	140.0
Action integral:				
First strokes	A^2s	6.0×10^3	5.5×10^4	5.5×10^5
Subsequent strokes	A^2s	5.5×10^2	6.0×10^3	5.2×10^4
Interval between strokes	ms	7.0	33.0	150.0
Flash duration:				
Including single stroke flashes	ms	0.15	13.0	1,100.0
Excluding single stroke flashes	ms	31.0	180.0	900.0

* Adapted from Berger et al., 1975.

the duration of a stroke is limited to just a few tens of microseconds, the total energy is thought to be on the order of 10^8 to 10^9 J, or roughly 10^4 to 10^5 J per meter of channel (Hill, 1979; Few, 1981).

During a return stroke the large current heats the channel to a peak temperature on the order of 30,000 K in a microsecond or less. As a result of this heating, the channel pressure reaches 20 atm or more, and the channel expands behind a strong shock wave. The shock decays rapidly with distance to a weak shock, which then decays to an acoustic wave that we eventually hear as thunder (see Few, 1981). Ultimately, most of the input energy to a return stroke probably goes into heating the air and the mechanical work of the channel expansion (Few, 1981).

Lightning Damage

By the term *lightning damage* we mean any undesirable physical effect caused by any lightning process. Here the discussion is limited to the electrical effects caused by direct and nearby strikes, and we do not discuss the subsequent damage that can occur as a result of lightning-caused fires, lightning-caused power outages, etc., even though this subsequent damage can be very great.

Before we consider damage and methods of protection, it is useful to estimate how often a normal-sized structure, such as a house, might be struck, on average. We assume that the house is situated in a geographic region that has about four cloud-to-ground flashes per square kilometer per year (see Figure 1). We also assume that the physical area of the house is about 10 X 20 m² and that there will be a direct strike any time a leader comes within about 10 m of this area. In this instance the effective area of attraction is about 30 X 40 m², and the house will be struck, on average, (1200) (4) (10⁻⁶) = 4.8 X 10⁻³ times a year, or roughly once every two hundred years. Another way to think of this hazard is that under these conditions, on average, one house in two hundred will be struck directly at least once a year.

The electrical effects induced by a nearby flash can often be severe. If we assume that any strike within about 100 m of the house can be deleterious, then, in our example, we would expect such a strike about once every five years, on average. Of course, if the geographic region has a higher flash density than 4 km⁻² yr⁻¹, the strike frequency will be higher, and vice versa.

Direct Strikes

Most direct lightning strikes cause damage as a result of the large current that flows in the return stroke or the heat that is generated by this and the continuing current. If lightning strikes a person, for example, the current can cause serious burns and damage the central nervous system, heart, lungs, and other vital organs (Lee, 1977; Golde, 1975, Chap. 12). Many types of electronic circuits are damaged or destroyed when exposed to an excess current or to a current of the wrong polarity.

If nearby lightning strikes overhead electric power or telephone lines, large currents flow in one or more of the lines, and these currents can do considerable damage both to power and telecommunications equipment and to anything else that is connected to the system. If a lightning surge enters an unprotected residence by way of a power circuit, the voltages can be large enough to cause sparks in the house wiring or appliances. When these flashovers occur, they short-circuit the power system and the resulting AC power arc can start a fire. In such cases the lightning does not start the fire directly but causes a power fault; the power system itself does the damage.

The detailed mechanisms whereby lightning currents cause damage are often poorly understood and depend on the specific materials involved. In the human body the current heats the tissue and causes various electrochemical reactions. In metals large currents heat the conductor by electron collisions with the metal lattice, and if this heat is great enough, the metal melts or evaporates. We now examine the thermal effects of lightning on metals and semiconductors in more detail; then we consider mechanical effects. Much of the discussion follows that given by Golde (1975).

Damage Caused by Heating: When a current of amplitude, i, is passed through a resistance, R., the electrical heat deposited in the resistance is proportional to the time integral of the power dissipation, $\int i^2 Rdt$. If we assume that R is independent of current and temperature, and if the duration of the current is short enough that the effects of thermal conduction and convection can be neglected, then the temperature rise in R is proportional to the "action integral" $\int i^2 dt$. In Table 1 we see that a typical action integral for a return stroke is about $5 \times 10^4 A^2 s$.

Calculations of the temperature rise of copper wires of varying cross sections for various action integrals are shown in Figure 5. For aluminum conductors the temperature rise is about 1.5 times the values for copper, and for steel it is about 10 times the values for copper. From these curves we can conclude that an action integral of as much as $10^7 A^2 s$ will raise the temperature of a $50 mm^2$ (8mm diameter) steel conductor only about 150°C, a value that is readily acceptable in most situations. If a metal conductor is connected to another conductor, it is important that there is good electrical contact or a low resistance at the junction. A high-resistance bond can produce substantial heating and sparking and must be avoided when overlapping metal sheets, corrugated roofing, or similar construction materials.

The penetration, or burn-through, characteristics of metal sheets are important when there is a direct strike to a metal roof or to the skin of an aircraft. If a lightning current, i, strikes a metal surface, the heat deposited at the point of contact is approximately $\int Vidt = vQ$, where v is the surface potential of the metal, usually only 10 to 15V, and Q is the charge transferred by the lightning current. Therefore, we might expect that the amount of melting damage will be proportional to the charge transfer, Q, at least to first order.

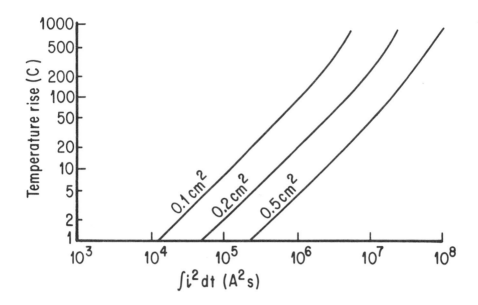

Figure 5. The temperature rise of copper conductors of various areas versus the action integral of the current (adapted from Golde, 1975, Figure 23).

Figure 6 shows the relation between the size of holes burned in metal sheets and the total charge transfer, Q. In Table 1 we see that lightning can transfer several tens of coulombs; therefore, we can expect millimeter-sized holes burned in thin sheets. If the duration of the charge transfer is long, the effects of thermal conduction reduces the damage, and the time required for a burn-through increases (see Golde, 1975, Figure 26).

If lightning strikes a relatively poor conductor or an insulator, the point of contact can be raised to a very high temperature and result in a burn-through. There are, for example, many reports of centimeter-sized holes burned in glass windows (McIntosh, 1973). If the insulator contains a trace of water or some other conducting material, the current tends to follow the path of least resistance. When moisture is evaporated and converted to steam, the resulting pressure can cause explosive fractures that are sometimes said to be the equivalent of 250 kg of TNT (Golde, 1975, 55).

An example of the explosive effects of a lightning strike to a stone wall and the associated currents in the ground is shown in Figure 7 (see

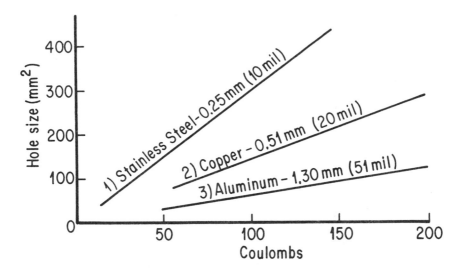

Figure 6. The hole area burned in metal sheets versus the total charge
transfer (adapted from Golde, 1975, Figure 25).

also Idone and Henderson, 1982). Note that the current flowed close to
the surface and that the explosive effects of soil heating blew clumps of
dirt and sod several meters from the channel. The largest trench was
3.0 m long, 0.8 m wide, and 0.4 m deep (Idone and Henderson, 1982).
If the soil density averaged about 2 gm/cm^3, then an energy of at least
2×10^3 J-m was required to excavate this amount of material, a value
that is consistent with the channel-energy estimates given in "Cloud-to-
Ground Lightning" above.

Damage Caused by Mechanical Effects: The shock wave produced
by the expansion of a return-stroke channel and the magnetic forces
created by the lightning currents can cause mechanical damage. As
noted above, the shock wave is produced by the rapid heating of the
channel by the return stroke (to temperatures on the order of 30,000
K), and the peak overpressures are at least 20 atm. The shock wave
heats the air and can cause mechanical damage to distances of a meter
or more.

The magnetic forces produced by lightning currents can crush
metal tubes and pull wires from walls if they pass around sharp corners
(Humphreys, 1964, Chap. 18). If two parallel straight wires share the
lightning current, the force between them will be attractive,
proportional to the square of the current, and inversely proportional to

Figure 7. Lightning damage caused by a direct strike to a stone wall
(right, rear) and to the ground (Idone and Henderson, 1982).

the distance between the conductors. To minimize these forces in a
lightning-protection system, the lightning conductors should not be
placcd in close proximity to each other (see below, "Basic Principles of
Lightning Protection").

The Sideflash

When a large, rapidly varying current is injected into a lightning
conductor (see, for example, Figure 8 below), the inductance of the
conductor and the resistance of the ground connection are often large
enough to produce a *sideflash*, a discharge from the conductor to a
nearby grounded object. A sideflash occurs when the potential of the
conductor is raised to a value high enough to initiate a spark and is
present long enough for the spark to propagate to the object.

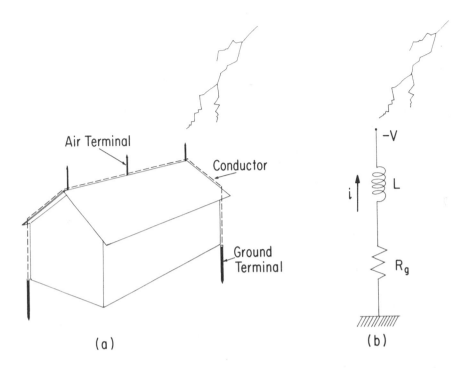

Figure 8. Sketch of a lightning-protection system that is appropriate
for small structures and its equivalent electric circuit.

A large variety of sideflash phenomena can occur during strikes to
other conducting materials or insulators. One of the greatest hazards in
standing near an isolated tree or any other tall object during a
thunderstorm is the exposure to a possible sideflash. The damage
caused by a sideflash is usually very similar to that of a direct strike.

Surface Breakdown

When lightning injects a large current into the ground, the resulting
voltage gradients usually exceed the breakdown strength of the soil
near the strike point, and the current propagates outward in a series of
well-defined channels (see Figure 7). These channels are often highly
branched and radiate outward for tens of meters or more. Figure 9
shows an example of the channels that were burned in the grass of a
golfcourse green after the flagpole was struck by lightning (see Krider,
1977, for a more detailed description of this photograph).

Figure 9.   Lightning damage to a golf-course green (Krider, 1977).

Since ground currents are often concentrated on the surface near the strike point and produce large voltage gradients on the surface, the hazards of standing close to an isolated tall object such as a tree or of lying stretched out on the ground when exposed to lightning are obvious. A person who is caught in open terrain should stay away from tall objects that are likely to be struck and should also crouch down or kneel so as to minimize both height and the area of the body that is in contact with the ground (Golde, 1975, Chap. 12).

Nearby Strikes

The electric and magnetic fields produced by nearby lightning can be very large and can induce damage in objects that are not struck directly. These induced effects can broadly be classified into two categories, electrostatic induction and electromagnetic induction.

Electrostatic Induction: When a conductor is exposed to an external electric field, a surface charge is induced on the conductor that is proportional to the strength of the field. If the field varies with time,

currents flow in the conductor to keep the surface charge in balance
with the field. Metal roofs and metal clotheslines should always be
grounded to prevent these conductors from reaching harmful potentials
in a thunderstorm and to prevent sparking to grounded objects during
lightning-field changes.

Electromagnetic Induction: During a direct or nearby strike, the
amplitudes of the fast-varying lightning fields are comparable to or
may even exceed those produced by a nuclear electromagnetic pulse
(Uman et al., 1982). If a closed loop of wire or any other closed
conducting path is exposed to a time-varying magnetic field, a current
is induced to flow in the circuit. The magnitude of the current is
proportional to the time derivative of the magnetic-flux density and
inversely proportional to the circuit impedance. This and more complex
types of coupling can cause large voltages and currents to flow in
conductors, such as power and telephone lines that are near lightning
but are not struck directly by it.

Basic Principles of Lightning Protection

The protection of a building and its contents against lightning can
be achieved by (1) diverting the current produced by a direct strike
away from the structure and letting it pass harmlessly to ground and
(2) shielding the structure and its contents against any lightning-caused
transients. Figure 8a shows the classical current-diversion system
employed since its invention by Benjamin Franklin, i.e., lightning rods,
lightning conductors, and a grounding system. The purpose of
a lightning rod, or "air terminal," is to initiate an upward-connecting
discharge whenever a stepped leader approaches within the striking
distance. During the ensuing return stroke the lightning conductors
keep the current outside the structure, and the grounding system keeps
the potentials of the entire system low enough to avoid sideflashes and
keeps the voltage gradients in the soil below the threshold for surface
breakdown. Thunderclouds usually produce high electric fields at the
ground, and under these conditions the rods (and any other tall objects
or points in the vicinity) may produce point discharges or coronas. The
point-discharge currents do *not* neutralize the thundercloud and
thereby make the cloud harmless. Again, the function of a rod is simply
to create a preferred strike point for any leaders that come within the

striking distance. Air terminals do not attract significantly more strikes to the structure than the structure would receive in their absence. A detailed description of the materials and procedures required to protect ordinary buildings from lightning is given in the Lightning Protection Code published by the National Fire Protection Association (NFPA, 1980), and further details are given by Golde (1975, 1977).

The space protected by a grounded air terminal or lightning mast is called the *zone of protection*. According to the U.S. Protection Code, this space can be visualized as a cone that has its apex at the highest point of the rod or mast and a radius at the ground that depends on the height of the mast as shown in Figure 10a. For small structures or masts not exceeding a height of 15 m, the radius of the base equals the height of the mast, and the angle of the cone is 45 degrees. If the building is particularly sensitive to lightning damage, it is best to protect it with an overhead ground wire, as illustrated in Figure 10b.

In general, the zone of protection depends on the striking distance, and the striking distance, in turn, depends on the distribution of charge being lowered by the stepped leader and the geometry of the leader channel. If the leader has a large charge near the ground, the striking distance is large, and vice versa. In most instances the striking distance is thought to exceed 30 m, and if this is true, the U.S. code indicates that a large structure, such as a tall mast, will protect a curved zone as illustrated in Figure 10c.

When thinking about the zone of protection, the reader should bear in mind that lightning is an unpredictable phenomenon and that this concept is valid only in a statistical sense. That is, the zone will be protected only *on average*, and individual flashes or upward streamers may occasionally strike within the zone. To illustrate the unpredictable nature of individual flashes, Figure 11 shows lightning striking close to the side of a tall television tower. In this instance the flash struck an insulated guy wire, and the final 70 m of the discharge was nearly horizontal even though the altitude of the channel was only about 80 m above ground. Further details of this photograph have been discussed by Krider and Alejandro (1983).

When lightning strikes a protection system, the effects are often modeled by assuming that the leader channel is a pure current source; that is, the current that flows is assumed to be independent of the impedance of the circuit to ground. The equivalent circuit of the system shown in Figure 8a is given in Figure 8b. Normally the DC resistance of

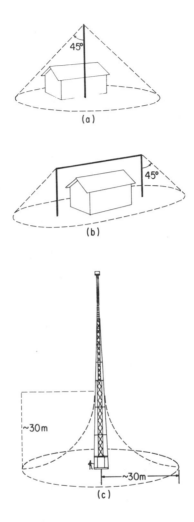

Figure 10. The zones of protection provided by (a) a vertical mast not
          exceeding a height of 15 m, (b) an overhead ground wire
          above a small structure, and (c) a tall tower.

the wires in a protection system is much less than the inductive
impedance of the wires or the ground resistance. In this case the
magnitude of the voltage, V, at the air terminal is

$$V = iR_g + L\frac{di}{dt},$$

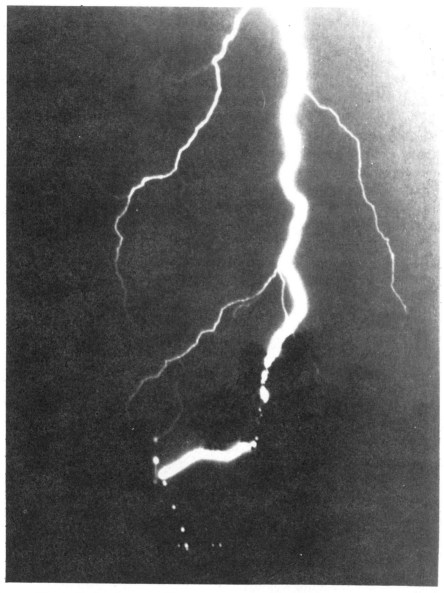

Figure 11. A lightning strike to a tall television tower in Tucson, Arizona. The trees in the foreground obscure the channel on the right. Note that the tower was struck below the top and that the channel was nearly horizontal before the strike. Colinear bright points are insulator flashovers on a guy wire (Krider and Alejandro, 1983).

where i is the lightning current (a function of time), Rg is the ground resistance, and L is the total inductance of the lightning conductors. If we assume that the ground resistance is about 30 ohms, that the wire inductance is 15 microhenrys (10 m of wire at 1.5 microhenry per meter), that the lightning current has a peak of 40 kA, and that the average di/dt is about 30 kA/μs, then V is on the order of 1.6 million volts for about 1 μs. If there is a grounded object nearby, this voltage and duration can be large enough to cause a sideflash.

All protection systems should be designed so that, as far as is possible, any lightning-caused potentials are the *same* everywhere within the structure and no potential *differences* can develop that will cause sideflashes. This practice, called *bonding*, is implemented by connecting any large metal objects that are close to the conductors in a protection system to that system. Ideally, if we eliminate all harmful potential differences within the building, there can be no arcing or equipment damage. This could be accomplished by completely enclosing the structure and all of its service wiring, plumbing, etc., within a perfectly conducting shield (a Faraday cage). With this, all lightning currents should flow on the low-impedance *outside* surface of the shield rather than inside. In practice such a shield is rarely possible because even an all-metal building has windows, doors, and other apertures and because power lines, telephone lines, pipes, etc., enter the structure and often are poorly shielded or not shielded at all. General topological concepts that can be applied to most lightning-shielding problems are discussed by Tesche (1978).

In practice, protection can usually be obtained by combining what building shielding does exist with proper grounding and bonding. A good grounding system, for example, usually has sufficiently low resistance and inductance that lightning currents cannot produce potential differences large enough to cause a sideflash. Where power lines, communications lines, pipes, or any other conductors enter the structure, they should be equipped with protectors, suppressors, or filters to hold or clamp any lightning-induced transients to a harmless level. Among these devices are such products as lightning arresters, surge arresters, surge suppressors, and transient suppressors. Most of these are *varistors*, which embody a variable resistance that decreases sharply when the applied voltage exceeds some threshold. This electrical behavior can be approximated by the following algebraic expression:

$$i = kV^n,$$

where k is a constant and n provides a measure of the nonlinear relationship between the current, i, and the voltage, V. Silicon carbide has an n in the range from 2 to 7. The zinc-oxide varistor has an n ranging from 20 to 70, and the silicon zener diode has an n that ranges from 100 to 500.

Variable resistors absorb the energy of the transient by transforming it into heat. Zener diodes can absorb up to about 1 J (1 watt-second) of energy, and silicon-carbide and zinc-oxide varistors can absorb 1 to 100 J or more, depending on their size. Since direct lightning strikes produce more energy than can be dissipated by most varistors, other devices, known as *switching protectors*, are often used to short-circuit the lightning current and reflect some of the surge energy away from the system before it can reach the varistors.

Switching protectors and varistors are frequently used together to provide optimum protection against induced surges. Figure 12 shows a typical protection circuit that might be used on an AC power line. Here a spark gap is used as the switching protector and reflects much of the incoming surge back down the line. The varistor in series with the spark gap prevents a line fault after the spark gap turns on, and the varistor on the right is used to absorb any fast transients that pass the first network during the time it takes the spark to develop in the gap. Surge capacitors and other high-voltage filters can also be used to reflect lightning energy, but these devices must be carefully designed to avoid flashovers.

The last matter considered here is the grounding system. Basically, a lightning ground or earth-termination network provides a sink where the lightning current can be discharged harmlessly into the earth. To minimize sideflashes, the ground impedance should be kept as small as possible, and the geometry should be arranged so as to minimize surface breakdown. Many technical articles and books have been written about grounding electric-power systems and associated equipment (see, for example, Sunde [1968] or *Military Handbook*, 1982). Much of this information also applies to a lightning-protection system, though the rapid lightning impulse sometimes poses special problems. For example, if a large current is injected into a short ground rod, the soil surrounding the rod usually breaks down as though it were an insulator. If the current is injected into a long, buried

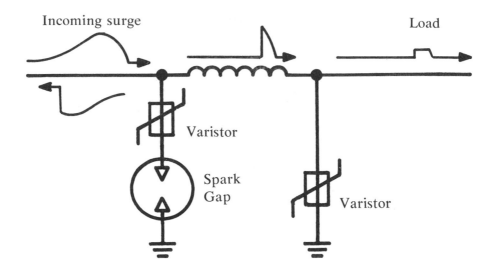

Figure 12. An example of a circuit that might be used to protect an AC
power circuit from a lightning surge. Most of the incoming
surge is reflected by the low impedance of the spark gap, and
the rest is removed by a second varistor. The delay between
the spark gap and the second varistor is necessary because
the latter is a faster-acting but lower-powered device.

conductor, however, the conductor reacts with its surge impedance,
usually about 150 ohms, rather than its steady-state ohmic resistance,
and goes into corona. As the initial impulse propagates along the
conductor, an increasing fraction of the conductor discharges current
into the surrounding soil, and the effective surge impedance decreases
with time. The steady-state impedance of the ground is not usually
reached until there has been time for several reflections of the current
pulse along the buried conductor.

REFERENCES

Berger, K., R.B. Anderson, and H. Kroninger, 1975. Parameters of lightning flashes.
  Electra 80:23-37.
Brook, M., M. Nakano, P. Krehbiel, and T. Takeuti, 1982. The electrical structure of
  the Hokuriku winter thunderstorms. *J. Geophys. Res.* 87:1207-15.

Few, A.A., 1982. Acoustic radiations from lightning. In *CRC Handbook of Atmospherics*, Vol. 2, H. Voland (ed.). CRC Press Boca Raton, Fla., 257-90.

Golde, R.H. (ed.), 1977. *Lightning*, Vol. 2, *Lightning Protection*. Academic Press, New York.

Hill, R.D., 1979. A survey of lightning energy estimates. *Rev. Geophys. Space Phys.* 17:155-64.

Humphreys, W.J., 1964. *Physics of the Air*. Dover, New York.

Idone, V.P., and R.W. Henderson, 1982. An unusual lightning ground strike. *Weatherwise* 35:223-24.

Krider, E.P., 1977. On lightning damage to a golf course green. *Weatherwise* 30:111.

———, and S.B. Alejandro, 1983. Lightning: an unusual case study. *Weatherwise* 36:71-75.

———, and C. Guo, 1983. The peak electromagnetic power radiated by lightning return strokes. *J. Geophys. Res.* 88:8471-8474.

———, and C.G. Ladd, 1975. Upward streamers in lightning discharges to mountainous terrain. *Weather* 30:77-81.

Lee, W.R., 1977. Lightning injuries and death. Chap. 16 in *Lightning*, Vol. 2, *Lightning Protection*, R.H. Golde (ed.). Academic Press, New York.

Livingston, J.M., and E.P. Krider, 1978. Electric fields produced by Florida thunderstorms. *J. Geophys. Res.* 83:385-401.

McEachron, K.B., 1939. Lightning to the Empire State Building, *J. Franklin Inst.* 227:149-217.

McIntosh, D.H., 1973, Lightning damage. *Weather* 28:160-61.

Maier, M.W., 1983, Private communication.

Military Handbook, 1982. *Grounding, Bonding, and Shielding for Electronic Equipments and Facilities*. Vols. 1, 2. MIL¶HDBK-419, U.S. Government Printing Office, Washington, D.C.

NFPA, 1980. Lightning Protection Code, NFPA-78. National Fire Protection Association, Inc.

Salanave, L.E., 1980. *Lightning and Its Spectrum*. University of Arizona Press, Tucson.

Schonland, B.F.J., 1956. The lightning discharge. *Handbuch der Physik*, 22:576-628. Springer-Verlag, Berlin.

———, 1964. *The Flight of Thunderbolts*. Clarendon Press, Oxford.

Sunde, E.D., 1908. *Earth Conduction Effects in Transmission Systems*. Dover, New York.

Tesche, F.M., 1978. Topological concepts for internal EMP interaction. *IEEE Trans. on EMC.* EMC-20, 60-64.

Uman, M.A., 1969, *Lightning*. McGraw Hill, New York.

———, 1971, *Understanding Lightning*. Bek Technical Publications, Inc., Carnegie, Pa.

———, and E.P. Krider, 1982. A review of natural lightning: experimental data and modeling. *IEEE Trans. on EMC.* EMC-24, 79-112.

———, M.J. Master, and E.P. Krider, 1982. A comparison of lightning electromagnetic fields with the nuclear electromagnetic pulse in the frequency range 10 4-10 7 Hz. *IEEE Trans. on EMC.* EMC-24, 410-16.

Viemeister, P.E., 1961. *The Lightning Book*. Doubleday, New York.

Wiedman, C.D., and E.P. Krider, 1980. Submicro-second risetimes in lightning return-stroke fields. *Geophys. Res. Letters 7* (2):955-58. See also C.D. Weidman and E.P. Krider, 1982. Correction. *J. Geophys. Res.* 87:7351.
Winn, W.P., T.V. Aldridge, and C.B. Moore, 1973. Video-tape recordings of lightning flashes. *J. Geophys. res.* 78S:4515-19.

The following News Release dated December 30, 1983, from the National Science Foundation shows the applicability of Dr. Krider's basic research on the physics of lightning to such an urgent matter as air travel safety.

LIGHTNING RESEARCH NETWORK HELPING
CONTROLLERS MAKE AIR TRAVEL SAFER

A federally-funded network for basic studies of lightning, used by an air traffic control center in Virginia to make air travel safer in the mid-Atlantic states, is being expanded with private funds to broaden its research function, the National Science Foundation (NSF) said.

The first lightning observing network of its kind on the East coast, the system features devices that locate lightning which strikes the ground by identifying the unique magnetic "fingerprint" produced by each flash. Like a giant radio antenna, each lightning bolt radiates electromagnetic signals which are, in effect, identifying signatures.

Dr. Richard E. Orville, an atmospheric scientist at the State University of New York at Albany, who started the network with NSF funding in 1982, explained that for locating lightning the system produces better data than radar or satellites because it deals directly with lightning. Radar and satellite data are based on information gleaned from convective clouds—the birthplace of lightning—and not on lightning itself.

Research using lightning location systems has shown that radar can locate rain and vertical motions, but cannot show where the lightning is located.

"Thus," Dr. Orville said, "radar alone can't be considered an unambiguous measure of lightning hazard in a thunderstorm."

Moreover, he added, if a storm is far away, radar might not be able to observe the cloud at all, whereas the lightning location system can.

The network already has given scientists new insights into some puzzling occurrences in thunderstorms. For example, researchers were astounded on August 22, 1983, to learn of the tremendous number of lightning bolts that zigzag across the sky in just a few hours of a single storm. More than 25,000 lightning flashes struck the ground during that storm, many more than had been expected, according to Dr. Orville.

He reported that many other flashes remained in the clouds and therefore were not recorded.

Air traffic controllers at Leesburg, Virginia, can be alerted by meteorologists that an area is filled with thunderstorms as much as 30 minutes earlier than they are with radar or satellite data. They can use this information to route air traffic around a potentially dangerous region. The Leesburg station—some 25 miles from Washington—controls air traffic in a 144,000 square mile area, including Maryland, Virginia, parts of Pennsylvania, West Virginia, and North Carolina.

"Until basic research on the physics of lightning—funded by the NSF and other Federal agencies—made possible the development of the system, there was no reliable technology available to detect severe lightning in remote areas," Dr. Orville said. The research was done by Dr. Martin A. Uman of the University of Florida and Dr. E. Philip Krider of the University of Arizona.

An increasing awareness of the physical, chemical, and biological consequences of fire in the ecosystem places this violent force of nature in man's hands as a creative tool in moulding his habitat.

Chapter 15
Fire: Catastrophic or Creative Force

Peter C. Moore

Peter Moore is Senior Lecturer in the School of Biological Sciences of King's College, University of London. He obtained his Ph.D. from the University of Wales in 1966 for work on the history of vegetation in central Wales. His research interests centre largely on the influence of man upon his environment, especially in prehistoric times.

Fire has been an important factor in the earth's ecology since communities of plants first colonized the land surface. By late Devonian times (about 350 million years ago), vegetation of a forest type had evolved, and it is at this stage in the earth's history that the rocks contain the first evidence of forest fires (Cope and Challoner, 1980). Contemporaneous sediments include small fragments of charcoal derived from the combustion of land plants, thus indicating that fire, as a natural occurrence, is of very considerable antiquity.

Since those early times in the earth's geological history, fire must have had a very considerable influence upon the balance of plant populations, hence upon the composition and structure of land vegetation. It may, in this way, have affected the environment in which man evolved, and then, as a tool in the hands of man, it became an increasingly profound factor in determining vegetation patterns and in moulding the habitats that man constructed around himself.

In a great variety of ecosystems in many different parts of the world fire is an important factor, either in the form of natural catastrophe or as a consequence of regular and deliberate human manipulation. In either case, it is important for ecologists and land managers to be aware of the physical, chemical and biological consequences of fire within the ecosystem in order to predict and, where possible, control the outcome of both natural and deliberate fire.

Fire in the Ecosystem

The ecosystem is a unit of plant and animal life within a non-living environment, the components of which are linked together by a variety of processes, including the flow of energy through the system and the cycling of nutrients within it. Obviously, the effect of fire upon an ecosystem is to disrupt many of these processes, to accelerate others and to destroy or modify some of the components as a consequence of the high temperatures generated.

Temperatures in Fires

Many attempts have been made made to measure the temperatures attained in fires. In heath fires in the British Isles, temperatures up to 940°C have been recorded (Kenworthy, 1963), with mean maximum temperatures of 670°C. Temperature varies with such factors as height above ground; a canopy temperature of 500-800°C may be accompanied by a ground temperature of only 300-500°C, and just one centimetre below the soil surface the temperature may be raised only thirty degrees (Whittaker, 1961). Such a stratification of temperature is naturally of great importance to the living organisms within the system. Canopy dwellers are most at risk, whilst subterranean animals, plant roots, and buried seeds may survive the conflagration. Also of importance is the period of time for which the high temperature is maintained, since this may determine the extent of damage, particularly to living plant tissues. In heathland, a fast burn (with the wind) may produce high temperatures for only two minutes or less.

Studies by Ahlgren (1970) in the jack pine forest of Minnesota in the United States have recorded canopy temperatures of 800°C lasting for one minute, followed by 500°C for nine minutes and 300°C for seventeen minutes. Any above-ground tissues which survive such a fire must therefore be resistant to these prolonged durations of high temperature.

Biomass, the total living matter of the ecosystem, is obviously reduced by fire, but may not be totally destroyed. In the case of heathlands, 90 percent of the biomass may be removed by an intense fire, whereas only 30 percent may be destroyed in a brief, low-temperature fire.

The bulk of living tissues consist of the elements carbon, hydrogen, and oxygen and these are largely converted into carbon dioxide and water vapour during fire and are lost to the atmosphere. But the biomass contains smaller quantities of other elements which are also liberated on combustion, some being lost in smoke and others being left as ash. Allen (1954) has made a detailed study of such mineral release processes in British heathlands and he has found that about 70 percent of the original nitrogen in the biomass (largely in the form of proteins) is lost as smoke, the remainder being left as ash. For sulphur, over 50 percent is lost in smoke. In the case of both of these elements, a high-temperature fire (over 800°C) results in greater losses than occur in a cooler fire.

Apart from nitrogen and sulphur, other elements are largely deposited as ash following a fire, including calcium, potassium, magnesium and phosphorus. Less than 2 percent of the original quantity of these is released in smoke from a cool burn (600°C), though this may rise to 2-5 percent in a hot fire (800°C).

Mineralization of Elements

One of the major ecological effects of fire, therefore, is the mineralization of many elements previously stored in the biological reservoir; this can be regarded as an acceleration of the normally slow release processes. The subsequent fate of these elements varies with local geographic and climatic conditions; sulphur and nitrogen are inevitably lost in large quantities through air movements, and the ash minerals may also leave the ecosystem by wind-borne or water-borne erosion of ash or soil, or by leaching through the soil.

Some estimates have been made of total losses to the ecosystem as a consequence of fire. For example, it has been calculated that the burning of moorland in upland Britain may release 1 kg/ha^{-1} of potassium (Allen, 1954), whereas 15 kg/ha^{-1} may be lost from the burning of North American forests (Wright, 1976) and 25 kg/ha^{-1} from the burning of boreal forest in Scandinavia (Viro, 1974). Rapid Mineralization of elements, therefore, inevitably leads to considerable loss from the ecosystem, which is increased by higher fire temperatures.

Nutrient retention within the ecosystem is enhanced if the soil is able to absorb the free ions on to the surface of its colloidal clay and humic components. In soils with a low clay content (such as sandy soils) and in those with a low organic content (which may, of course, itself have been incinerated during the fire), there are higher losses of the liberated nutrients.

Rapid regrowth of vegetation can create a nutrient demand which will absorb nutrients from the soil and will reduce leaching losses, but again a severe fire which has reduced biomass to a low level will lower the rate of recovery.

Although the overall effect of fire is the reduction of the nutrient capital of the ecosystem, its initial outcome is the mobilization of elements previously bound in the organic biomass and their release into the soil. Thus, for a short period, perhaps a few years, the soil may actually be enriched in nutrients. Viro (1974), in his studies of fire in Scandinavia, found that the soil becomes more alkaline for a few years after fire, the pH in his study area being raised from 4 to 5.5; calcium and phosphorus are also raised in these early stages before leaching reduces their abundance in the soil.

Much of the supply of nutrients released into the soil is washed out and departs from the ecosystem in drainage water and run-off.

Obviously, these nutrients must reappear in the sites to which the enriched waters percolate, often the streams, rivers, marshes, and lakes lying further down the catchment. In this way fire may have considerable influence upon ecosystems beyond those immediately affected; recurrent fires can result in the eutrophication of aquatic systems downstream. Wright's (1976) studies of a lake in North America which was affected by a fire in its catchment found that inputs of nutrients were increased as follows: calcium, 26 percent; magnesium, 29 percent; potassium, 265 percent; sodium, 65 percent; and phosphorus, 93 percent. Such an increase in the nutrient load of a lake's waters inevitably results in enhanced algal and aquatic macrophyte productivity.

Organic Molecules

Fire results not only in changes in the mineral ions of the ecosystem, but also in some important organic molecules. For example, fire in the Californian chaparral destroys the aromatic terpenoids which build up in the leaf litter on the surface of the ground (Harborne, 1977). These terpenoids act as inhibitors to the germination and growth of many other plant species, so that when they are removed by burning, the suppression of these other plants ceases, and they consequently flourish for a few years. It is only when the shrub species which are responsible for building up these terpenoids (such as the sagebrush, *Salvia leucophylla*) re-establish themselves that the toxic effect begins to develop once more and many species are extinguished. The entire cycle takes about twenty-five years to complete.

A similar, but even more complex, system of biochemical control has been described in *Pinus ponderosa* forest (Lodhi and Killingbeck, 1980), where organic molecules in the decomposition products of the litter (particularly polyphenols and tannins) are thought to suppress the activity of certain microbial populations in the soil. Of particular importance are the bacteria concerned with nitrification (*Nitrosomonas* and *Nitrobacter*), that is, the conversion of ammonium ions to nitrate ions. If this process is inhibited, then the rate of nitrate production diminishes and thereby the nitrogen resources of the environment become less available to plants. This can act as a competitive mechanism on the part of the pines, which reduces the risk of invasion by other species. Burning destroys the litter, together with its contained toxins, and releases the ecosystem from this plant-induced constraint, which initiates the development of a new vegetation.

Recovery from Fire

The recovery of vegetation following fire involves the accumulation of biomass and the concurrent buildup of the ecosystem's nutrient reserves. The rapidity with which recovery can take place depends upon the productivity of the remaining vegetation (which in turn is influenced by the proportion of biomass removed as a consequence of the fire's intensity), and also upon the supply of nutrients to the system.

Following fire, there may be changes in the vegetation of an area involving the invasion of new species, which are encouraged in their growth by the temporary enrichment of the soil. In many temperate parts of the world, the fire weed (*Epilobium augustifolium*) is an important colonizer; this species is demanding in its soil-nutrient requirements, enjoys full sunlight, thereby benefiting from the clearance of woodland canopy, and has light airborne seeds that permit rapid and extensive dispersal. It is therefore a species well fitted to avail itself of the new opportunities offered by fires. Such species do not normally survive for more than a few years because soil leaching renders conditions progressively less suitable for their continued growth.

If the original vegetation is not totally destroyed, its recovery may be relatively rapid. In a grassland ecosystem, for example, a number of benefits can result from a light burn. In the first place, much tissue may be removed which actually represents an energy drain upon the ecosystem. This can be illustrated by reference to the simple, hypothetical model in Figure 1. If we consider a grassland canopy as a series of leaf layers (a gross simplification), then each layer can be considered in terms of its productive potential, P, and its respiratory requirement, R (Watson, 1956). The former will vary with incident light intensity and the latter will be relatively constant until senility results in reduction. In a mature grassland canopy (Figure 1a) with high biomass and several (five in this case) leaf layers, lower layers may conduct very little or no photosynthesis, but may still respire. Thus, although these layers are expensive for the plant to maintain, they are required to develop a tall, competitive canopy.

The removal of the biomass by fire, if it permits survival of the basal shoots, leads to recovery stages in which the net productive

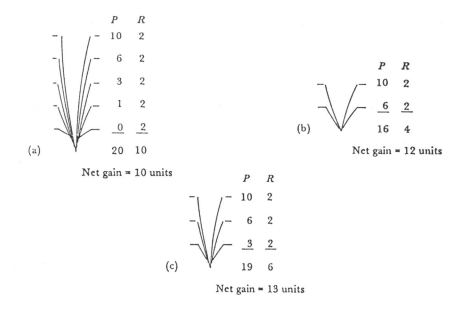

Figure 1. Simplified model demonstrating a possible influence upon net productivity of a grass canopy of biomass removal by fire: (a) before fire; (b) and (c) recovery stages. P = arbitrary units of gross photosynthetic production; R = units of respiration.

potential of the vegetation is greater than that of the original vegetation. Obviously, this is of considerable interest to the consumers of this primary production and especially to man, who can thus increase the stocking levels of domestic herbivores on lands thus treated.

Importance of Basal Shoots

An important consideration is the assurance of survival of the basal shoots of the plants and their subsequent rapid recovery. This depends not only upon the intensity of the fire, but also upon the condition and age of the original plants. As a perennial plant ages, it often passes through a series of predictable phases in its life-cycle: pioneer, building, mature, and degenerate phases (Watt, 1947). Its growth is most rapid during the building and mature phases and declines in the degenerate phase. The degree of recovery after burning depends upon the growth phase of the original vegetation. For example, in experimental burning of British moorland at 400°C for two minutes' duration, Kayll and Gimmingham (1965) found that building-phase heather (twelve to thirteen years old) showed a 58 percent survival, mature phase 14 percent, and degenerate phase only 10 percent. Thus burning is best performed during the immature, building phase as this permits a high level of recovery and a rapid development of young shoots duly enriched with the flush of mineralized nutrients from the soil.

The time taken for a total recovery of a mature ecosystem may be limited by nutrient supply, particularly if this is slow. New nutrients may become available in the ecosystem by the weathering of soil particles and a release from rock minerals or by input from rainfall. Nitrogen can be fixed directly from the atmosphere by such organisms as certain free-living microbes and cyanobacteria. Deforested hardwoods in the United States may take sixty to eighty years for recovery (Likens et al., 1978), and Scandinavian spruce forest thirty-three to fifty years (viro, 1974). In the case of heathland, much depends upon the stage of development at which burning took place. Chapman (1967) has examined the question of whether the rate of input of nutrients in rainfall may limit the process of heathland recovery, for this type of ecosystem is usually developed on sandy soils which yield little in the way of weathering products. He found that the nutrients contained in twelve years of precipitation were adequate to compensate for the losses resulting from a fire in the case of sodium, potassium, calcium, and magnesium. Nitrogen gains from this source were not sufficient to make up the deficit, but gains from biological fixation would probably compensate for this. Only in the case of phosphorus did there appear to be a serious shortfall, only about 5 percent of the loss during burning being renewed by the rainfall over the following twelve years. In nutrient-poor ecosystems of this type, phosphorus may thus limit biomass recovery following fire.

The Traces of History

It has already been pointed out that fire has a history on this planet which extends back as far as that of land vegetation itself. Cope and Challoner (1980) consider lightning strikes to have been a frequent source of forest fire throughout geological history and there are many descriptions of detailed palaeontological evidence for fire (Harris,

1958). It is difficult to determine, however, how frequent such fires have been in the past, particularly in times prior to the use of fire by man (which dates back at least 400,000 years). One approach to this problem has been provided by the examination of charcoal bands and soil inwash into lake sediments in the past (Cwynar, 1978; Swain, 1980).

Cwynar (1978) has worked on the sediments of a lake in Ontario, Canada, which is surrounded by a mixed forest of conifers and hardwoods. In a detailed study of the sediments laid down between A.D. 770 and 1270, he found evidence of fire approximately every eighty years. Yet, despite this, the general vegetation of the area showed no overall trends (as determined by pollen analysis) apart from the oscillations associated with the fire-recovery cycle. This suggests that the vegetation has achieved an equilibrium which is itself maintained by the fire cycle. Other sources of information concerning the more recent frequency of fire in this same area are the scars left in the wood of trees. Cwynar (1977) has shown that over the last 225 years the mean frequency of fires has been one every fourteen years, underlining the effect which intensive human activity has had upon the incidence of fire.

Evolution of Ecosystems

It is now generally accepted among ecologists that certain ecosystems have evolved under the constant and regular influence of fire, which results in the selection of fire-tolerant species. Such ecosystems require regular firing in order to maintain their long-term equilibrium. Fire resistance may involve coarse, thick bark which protects the living tissues of tree trunks and permits the sprouting of buds following fire, or underground survival organs such as rhizomes, or seeds that survive burning and may even be stimulated into germination by it. Many North American pine species regenerate effectively only after fire; burning removes the thick accumulation of needles and litter which prevent germinating seedlings from extending their roots into the underlying mineral soil. In the case of the jack pine (*Pinus banksiana*), the cones remain closed upon the trees until the resinous coating of the cone is destroyed by fire, which requires temperatures of at least 120°C. The seeds, which are then shed from the open cone, can remain viable even if the fire temperature reaches 1,000°C.

The regular use and misuse of fire by man has often led to the spread of fire-resistant species of this sort. For example, if one examines the rate of spread of spruce in Scandinavia and Switzerland over the past 10,000 years, it can be seen that its major advances are closely correlated with the arrival of agricultural developments in human culture, which in turn led to increased rates of forest modification (Moore, 1981). In some Finnish sites, the phases of expansion of spruce in the boreal forest (starting around 5,000 years ago) were accompanied by bands of charcoal at corresponding levels in lake sediments (Tolonen, 1980), thus confirming the association between man, fire, and spruce. In modern silvicultural practice in Scandinavia, burning is used prior to the establishment of young spruce trees to destroy the litter layer and liberate its nutrient load into the soil (Viro, 1974). Biochemical changes may also take place involving the level of toxins in the litter, similar to those described above for Californian chaparral.

In some ecosystems, the effects of recurrent fire have totally changed the original vegetation. In the British Isles, the effects of fire on vegetation can be traced back to the Hoxnian interglacial, about 400,000 years ago (Turner, 1970), but at that time it is questionable whether the human occupants of Britain (Swanscombe Man) were responsible for its occurrence, although man and fire coincided both spatially and temporally. But in the present inter-glacial, the use of fire by man as a means of modifying vegetation to his own ends is now firmly established.

Even before the advent of agriculture with Neolithic cultures (arriving about 5,500 years ago in Britain), landscape changes may have been brought about by man's use of fire. The massive expansion of hazel (*Corylus avellana*) in the early post-glacial, about 9,000 years ago (Rawitscher, 1945), and that of alder (*Alnus glutinosa*) about 7,000 years ago (Smith, 1970), have both been linked with burning by man. The development of heathland on the lowland, sandy areas of Britain has clearly been linked with burning by Mesolithic peoples, between 10,000 and 5,000 years ago (Dimbleby, 1962).

New Vegetation Types

Recently it has been proposed that burning of upland vegetation in Britain has destroyed the forest cover and has produced hydrological changes which have resulted in the now extensive blanket bogs of these areas (Moore, 1975), and again these changes may have begun in some areas as early as Mesolithic times, but certainly became more extensive in the Neolithic and Bronze Age (7,000 to 2,500 years ago). The effects of forest burning and destruction in these upland areas with their poor soils, high rainfall, and low overall temperatures would be (a) further loss of nutrients, and (b) increased water movement through the soil, resulting from reduced transpiration and rainfall interception. These two effects would lead to the waterlogging of soils and a reduction in the microbial decomposition rate as a consequence of which peat would begin to develop. The ultimate outcome of these changes is the development of a new vegetation type, relatively insensitive to further fire, within which the original tree species such as oak (*Quercus petraea*) would be unable to regenerate because of the wetness, acidity, and nutrient poverty. A total and permanent change in the ecosystem structure and composition has thus resulted from the effects of recurrent fire. Evidence for this process has been accumulated from detailed pollen analyses, coupled with the persistence of charcoal in the basal layers of blanket peats (Simmons, 1969).

In drier parts of the world, fire has also been an important factor in modifying vegetation types. This is particularly true of temperate and tropical grasslands in many of which total biomass has been reduced and the composition of species considerably modified as a consequence of frequent fire. There is evidence that the prairies of central North America were clothed with forest during the last glaciation of the higher latitudes and that this forest persisted locally into more recent times. Its destruction and replacement by grassland was in part due to climatic changes involving more prolonged summer drought, but fire could well have played an important role in its final demise, in the absence of which it may well have persisted (Wells, 1970).

The degree to which the tropical grasslands have depended upon fire for their development and maintenance is questionable, but it seems that interactions between increasing climatic aridity over the past 10,000 years, coupled with regular burning (which could be the product of natural lightning strikes) has resulted in a savanna environment. Man has undoubtedly increased the frequency of fires in these areas and has led to burns taking place before the biomass of the system is adequate to support a natural fire (Harris, 1980). In this way, human activity has modified the savanna plant communities and has led to their spread.

Conclusion: Fire an Environment Tool

From the above discussion of fire and its consequences, certain general features emerge concerning the consequences of fire which are of importance to man when he faces fire as a catastrophe or when he manipulates fire as an environmental tool:

- Biomass is immediately reduced. Crop species may be among those suffering loss and if this biomass has taken some while to develop, as in the case of forests, this may represent serious loss to man.

- In some systems productivity of the regenerating vegetation may be higher than that of the original system. This can be of value in pastoral systems where primary productivity determines carrying capacity.

- Organically bound nutrients are mineralized. Some losses result, both in smoke and leaching, but some ecosystems benefit from bringing more nutrients from the biomass reservoir back into circulation.

- Biochemical suppressants may be destroyed, releasing the system from toxic constraints and permitting the diversification of vegetation.

- The temporary change in flora resulting from fire may bring benefits if the species are preferred by grazing animals or by man.

The catastrophic and deleterious effects of fire, therefore, are limited to the immediate losses sustained by an ecosystem. Often the interests of agricultural man are served by the use of fire, for he is concerned chiefly with high productivity and carrying capacity for herbivores, or soil fertility for cultivated plants. It is for this reason that man has employed fire as an instrument for modifying his habitat on a grand scale since prehistoric and even pre-agricultural times, and why fire must generally be regarded as a creative tool rather than as a catastrophic agent.

GLOSSARY

Eutrophication—an enrichment of nutrients.

Macrophyte—a robust plant species, usually applied to aquatic species to differentiate from algae.

Chaparral—scrub vegetation developed in a Mediterranean type climate (hot, dry summers; mild, damp winters). The North American equivalent of *maquis*.

Terpenoids—volatile, oily, aromatic chemicals found in a variety of plant species.

Basal shoots—vegetative sprouts from the lower part of a plant.

Herbivores—animals feeding on plants.

Rhizomes—underground, root-like stems of a plant.

Boreal—northern.

REFERENCES

Ahlgren, C. 1970. Some Effects of Prescribed Burning on Jack Pine Reproduction in North-eastern Minnesota. *Minnesota Agr. Exp. Sta. Misc. Rep.*, No. 94, pp. 1-14.

Allen, S. 1954. Chemical Aspects of Heather Burning. *J. Appl. Ecol.*, No. 1, pp. 347-67.

Chapman, S. 1967. Nutrient Budgets for a Dry Heath Ecosystem in the South of England. *J. Ecol.*, No. 55, pp. 677-89.

Cope, M.; Challoner, W. 1980. Fossil Charcoal as Evidence of Past Atmospheric composition. *Nature*, No. 283, pp. 647-9.

Cwynar, L. 1977. The Recent Fire History of Barron Township, Algonquin Park. *Can. J. Bot.*, No. 55, pp. 1524-38.

———. 1978. Recent History of Fire and Vegetation from Laminated Sediment of Greenleaf Lake, Algonquin Park, Ontario. *Can. J. Bot.*, No. 56, pp. 10-21.

Dimbleby, G. 1962. The Development of British Heathlands and their Soils. *Oxford Forestry Mem.*, No. 23, pp. 1-121.

Harborne, J. 1977. *Introduction to Ecological Biochemistry*. London, Academic Press.

Harris, T. 1958. Forest Fires in the Mesozoic. *J. Ecol.*, No. 46, pp. 447-53.

Harris, D. 1980. Tropical Savanna Environments: Definition, Distribution, Diversity and Development. In: D. Harris (ed.), *Human Ecology in Savanna Environments*, pp. 3-27. London, Academic Press.

Kayll, A.; Gimmingham, C. 1965. Vegetative Regeneration of *Calluna vulgaris* after Fire. *J. Ecol.*, No. 53, pp. 729-34.

Kenworthy, J. 1963. Temperatures in Heather Burning. *Nature*, No. 200, p. 1226.

Likens, G.; Bormann, F.; Pierce, R.; Reiners, W. 1978. Recovery of a Deforested Ecosystem. *Science*, No. 199, pp. 492-6.

Lodhi, M.; Killingbeck, K. 1980. Allelopathic Inhibition of Nitrification and Nitrifying Bacteria in a Ponderosa Pine (*Pinus ponderosa Dougl.*) Community. *Amer. J. Bot.*, pp. 1423-49.

Moore, P. 1975. Origin of Blanket Mires. *Nature*, No. 256, pp. 267-9.

———. 1981. The Spruce Invasion. *Nature*, No. 289, pp. 223-4.

Rawitscher, F. 1945. The Hazel Period in the Post-glacial Development of Forests. *Nature*, No. 156, pp. 302-3.

Simmons, I. 1969. Evidence for Vegetation Changes Associated with Mesolithic Man in Britain. In: P. Ucko and G. Dimbleby (eds.), *The Domestication and Exploitation of Plants and Animals*. London, Duckworth, pp. 113-19.

Smith, A. 1970. The Influence of Mesolithic and Neolithic Man on British Vegetation. In: D. Walker and R. West (eds.), *Studies in the Vegetational History of the British Isles*, pp. 81-96. Cambridge, Cambridge University Press.

Swain, A. 1980. Landscape Patterns and Forest History in the Boundary Waters Canoe Area, Minnesota: A Pollen Study from Hug Lake. *Ecology*, No. 61, pp. 747-54.

Tolonen, M. 1980. Pollen Stratigraphy of Lake Lamminjärvi, South Finland. *Ann. Bot. Fennici.*, No. 17, pp. 15-25.

Turner, C. 1970. The Middle Pleistocene Deposits at Marks Tey, Essex. *Phil. Trans. R. Soc. Lond.*, No. B.275, pp. 373-440.

Viro, P. 1974. Effects of Forest Fire on Soils. In: T. Kozlowski and C. Ahlgren (eds.), *Fire and Ecosystems*, pp. 7-45. London, Academic Press.

Watson, D. 1956. Leaf Growth in Relation to Crop Yield. In: F. Milthorpe (ed.), *The Growth of Leaves*, pp. 178-91. London, Butterworth.

Watt, A. 1947. Patterns and Process in the Plant Community. *J. Ecol.*, No. 35, pp. 1-22.

Wells, P. 1970. Postglacial Vegetational History of the Great Plains. *Science*, No. 167, pp. 1574-82.

Whittaker, E. 1961. Temperatures in Heath Fires, *J. Ecol.*, No. 49, pp. 709-15.

Wright, R. 1976. The Impact of Forest Fire on the Nutrient Influxes to Small Lakes in Northeastern Minnesota. *Ecology*, No. 57, pp. 649-63.

A Committee of the National Research Council reports on the state of knowledge of low-altitude wind shear, the hazards of low-altitude wind variability, and recommends actions to reduce the hazards. Needed research is identified in a number of areas. The Committee found that wind shear and associated downbursts and microbursts are an "infrequent" but highly significant hazard to aircraft while landing or taking off.

Chapter 16
Wind Shear and its Hazard to Aviation*

The author is the Committee on Low-Altitude Wind Shear and Its Hazard to Aviation, aided by staff of the National Research Council. The Council is the research and operating agency of the National Academy of Sciences, the National Academy of Engineering and the Institute of Medicine.

* Excerpted from *Low Altitude Wind Shear and Its Hazard to Aviation*, 1983. Reprinted with permission of the National Academy Press, Washington, D.C.

Introduction

Low-altitude wind variability, or *wind shear*, has long been recognized as a potential hazard to aircraft landing and taking off. Although wind shear can result from a number of basically different meteorological conditions, pilots have been trained to avoid thunderstorms in particular because of often associated severe wind variability and turbulence near the ground and aloft.

It has recently been recognized that small, short-lived *downdrafts*, called *microbursts*, are serious hazards to aircraft during landings and takeoffs. In some microbursts the air carried downward strikes the ground and spreads out in a shallow layer—sometimes only a few hundred feet in thickness. The parent cloud from which the microburst descends is a convective one but one that has not necessarily grown to thunderstorm size and strength.

Thunderstorm outflow and accompanying downdrafts, some of the scale and intensity that have recently been named microbursts and *downbursts*, were identified by the Thunderstorm Project nearly 40 years ago (Byers and Braham, 1949). Such outflows and downdrafts were newly emphasized as the cause of some serious accidents after a quantitative analysis of the winds encountered by Eastern Airlines Flight 66 while landing at John F. Kennedy International Airport on June 24, 1975. Analysis of the flight recorder data from another aircraft operating in the immediate vicinity provided a wind model considered to be very similar to that encountered by EAL Flight 66.

A detailed map of the wind-shear patterns at the time of the crash was constructed from an analysis of available data, including meteorological satellite photographs and surface weather observations and measurements (Fujita, 1976; Lewellen et al., 1976). The analysis provided valuable insight into the characteristics of violent downburst cells within thunderstorms, the need to detect their presence as early as possible, and the need for immediate communication of warnings to air traffic controllers and flight crews in the vicinity.

The Nature of Low-Altitude Wind Shear

Wind variability is a perennial and inescapable problem for aviation. Meteorological circulations or terrain-induced airflows can on occasion induce large and rapidly changing variations in air velocity over small distances. These variations produce correspondingly sudden changes in the relative flow of air over an aircraft's wings and other lifting surfaces, with attendant changes in an aircraft's flight path. Thus, small-scale wind variations and turbulence can pose hazards to aviation, particularly when they occur in the lowest few hundred feet of the atmosphere, the zone that aircraft must penetrate while landing or taking off. To eliminate—or at least appreciably reduce—the hazards posed by low-altitude wind variability, it is necessary to understand the sources of wind changes and the risks they represent. It is also necessary to know how to detect, measure, and predict them and how to communicate useful information on wind variability to air traffic controllers and pilots in a timely fashion.

The wind changes not only with distance but also with time. As a result, the term *wind variability* is sometimes used when considering low-altitude flight hazards. Technically speaking, wind shear is the local variation, at a particular time, of wind velocity with distance. It is measured by dividing the velocity difference at two points by the distance between them. Strong wind variations over horizontal distances of 1 to 10 miles can cause particular difficulties for aircraft. Most often, in this report, we refer to wind variations as wind shears. In circumstances where time variations are important, they will be identified.

The three-dimensional airflow in the lower atmosphere, and the associated wind shears and turbulence, vary from place to place by season and by meteorological conditions. Based on experience, rough estimates can be made of the degree of hazard, frequency of occurrence, and difficulty of detection of various types of wind shear.

Atmospheric turbulence is generally defined statistically in terms of scale and intensity. Its effects are seen in an aircraft's ride and handling qualities and are taken into account in aerodynamic, flight control, and structural design criteria. However, patchy small-scale turbulence need not be present at low altitudes within layers of air with strong wind shear (Lee and Beckwith, 1981).

The most serious effects of wind shear are those that cause an aircraft to lose lift and altitude. This is particularly hazardous when an aircraft is close to the ground, either landing or taking off, when an aircraft unexpectedly flies from a region of headwinds into a region of strong tailwinds, and especially if the transition occurs in a strong downdraft. Turbulence and heavy rain, when occurring in association with wind shear, can contribute to flight hazards and increase the chances of an accident. The following paragraphs describe the types of wind-shear situations and the risks each poses to aviation.

Convective Outflows

Thunderstorms and other convective clouds are critically important sources of low-altitude wind variability. Many produce strong downdrafts that transport air downward, which then spreads out rapidly over the ground. The size and strength of the downdraft depend on the properties of the thunderstorm and on the humidity and temperature structure of the atmosphere. Thunderstorms occur most frequently in Florida, along the Gulf of Mexico coast, and over the central parts of the United States. Whenever there is a thunderstorm or precipitating convective clouds, hazardous low-altitude wind shear can be present. Some experts believe, however, that strong downdrafts and associated flight hazards are more likely when the thunderstorm cloud bases are high and the surface humidities are low.

Microbursts. Following the crash of Eastern Airlines Flight 66 at New York City's Kennedy Airport on June 24, 1975, the term *downburst* came into use to describe a strong downdraft that induces an outburst of damaging winds on or near the ground. Subsequently, studies of the EAL crash and of Continental Flight 426 at Denver on August 7, 1975, and Allegheny Flight 121 at Philadelphia on June 23, 1976, concluded that each of these accidents was related to downburst-induced wind shear (Fujita and Byers, 1977; Fujita and Caracena, 1977).

Results of the above studies indicated that the downbursts that contributed to these accidents were of small size and short life, and the term *microbursts* has been used to describe them. Microbursts are small downbursts, less than 2.5 miles in outflow size, with the peak winds lasting only 2 to 5 minutes. Some microbursts reach the ground, while others dissipate in mid-air and are not detected by ground-based anemometers. A critical point is that microbursts can come from convective clouds that are not accompanied by lightning.

The most recent wind-shear-related accident, the crash of Pan American Airlines Flight 759 in New Orleans, was reported by the NTSB (1983) to be a result of microburst-induced wind shear.

Climatology of Microbursts. Data on which to base averages of the frequency and intensity of microbursts are very limited. During a 43-day period in May and June 1978, ground-based anemometers associated with NCAR's portable automated mesonet (PAM) were deployed as part of the NIMROD Project near Chicago. PAM automatically measures wind speed and direction, dry- and wet-bulb temperatures, and pressure and rainfall at 27 surface stations (wind measurement is at 12 feet above the ground). Fifty microbursts were detected, 32 with rain (wet microbursts) and 18 without rain (dry microbursts) (see Table 1). Wind shear is apparently not related to rainfall intensity.

TABLE 1 Frequency of Microbursts Detected by PAM

	NIMROD	*JAWA*
Number of operational days	43	86
Number of microburst days	11	49
Number of wet microbursts *	32	31
Number of dry microbursts* *	18	155
Total number of microbursts	50	186
Number per operational day	1.2	2.2
Number per microburst day	4.6	3.8

* Equal to or greater than 0.01 inches of rain during the period of peak winds.

* * Less than 0.01 inches of rain between both the onset of high winds and the end of the microburst winds including the calm period if any.

The PAM deployed in the Joint Airport Weather Studies (JAWS) Project near Denver detected 186 microbursts on 49 days of an 86-day observation period from May to August 1982 (Fujita and Wakimoto, 1983). This amounts to 2.2 per day, nearly twice the rate found in the NIMROD Project. Of the total 186 microbursts, 155 were dry and only 31 were wet. Most were not associated with active cumulonimbus clouds but rather occurred under streaks of evaporating precipitation (virga) from dissipating cumulonimbus or dissipating cumulus congestus clouds. Because of their association with convective clouds, microbursts tend to occur most often between noon and midnight, but, the diurnal pattern differed at the NIMROD and JAWS locations.

Aircraft passing through the center of a microburst will experience a change in wind velocity that can be specified as the vector difference of the headwind and the tailwind along the flight path. The maximum wind difference of the JAWS microbursts, measured by ground-based anemometers, exceeded 95 knots on one occasion.

The JAWS Project used Doppler radar primarily to observe microbursts. With three wind-measuring Doppler radar systems, three-dimensional pictures of microbursts were obtained. Figure 4 shows the horizontal and vertical velocity profiles of a particularly strong microburst. The classical profile of headwind, downdraft, and tailwind are clearly seen in this figure.

Because the Doppler radars were used to concentrate on specific cases of interest and because they were not operated continuously, their data cannot be used to establish a microburst climatology. Nevertheless, the Doppler radars detected and observed 75 microbursts on 33 of the 86 operational days (McCarthy et al., 1983).

The Doppler radar data allowed for an examination of the time history of JAWS microbursts observed near Denver. It shows the percentage of microbursts that reached maximum velocity differential as a function of time from the detection of the initial velocity divergence near the ground. Approximately half of those observed reached maximum intensity within 5 minutes, and nearly all reached maximum velocity within 10 minutes. This figure dramatically illustrates the extremely short duration of these events.

Gust Fronts

A gust front is the leading edge of a mass of cool air that has recently descended from a thunderstorm or convective cloud. There is a large amount of literature on this subject, which was examined for the

Thunderstorm Project (Byers and Braham, 1949) and has since been much studied at the NSSL and by many researchers (Brandes, 1977; Charba, 1974; Goff, 1976, 1977; Sasaki and Baxter, 1982). The cool air near the gust front, which may be up to 1 mile in depth, is characterized by strong turbulent winds. The cool air sinks, while the warm air rises. The depth of the gust front, the associated wind shear and turbulence, and its speed of advance over the ground depend on the nature of the parent cloud and the wind distribution through the layer in which the cloud is imbedded.

. . . .

When there is strong vertical wind shear through the atmosphere and a severe long-lasting convective storm, the associated gust front tends to be maintained at the leading edge of the parent storm. The pattern of its advance can be very asymmetric with strong outward-blowing winds in those sectors coinciding in direction with the strongest winds aloft in the cloud layer.

Gust fronts, as they sweep over the ground, can usually be detected by radar, by a sufficiently dense network of ground-based anemometers (such as LLWSAS), and by microbarographs. Once detected, it is possible—largely through extrapolation—to predict their position anywhere from a few minutes to perhaps one-half hour in advance. Also, radar echoes often indicate the presence of deep convective clouds and the possibility of a gust front.

Gravity and/or Solitary Waves

As a gust front moves away from its parent storm, the temperature contrast across it is gradually reduced. The resulting circulation, when it exists in a shallow surface layer capped by a temperature inversion, can persist as a strong clear-air circulation that usually moves at speeds of 15 to 40 knots over long distances. Known variously as gravity waves or solitary waves, these motions are caused not only by gust fronts but also by downslope winds and by sea-breeze fronts. Solitary waves occur most often during the night and early morning. Over northern Australia, where they have been studied extensively, they occur throughout the year but are most frequent during the late winter and early spring (August to November). Corresponding climatic information for the United States is almost totally lacking. In vertical cross section, a typical solitary wave can have a horizontal dimension of several hundred feet to 6 miles with a 15-knot updraft at the leading section and a downdraft of similar strength on the trailing part. Because of the relatively long-lasting nature of solitary waves, their distinctive wind shifts, and associated pressure patterns at the ground, it should be possible to detect, track, and predict their arrival over an airport, given a surface-observing network of sufficient density.

Sea-Breeze Fronts

A sea breeze is a local wind that blows from sea to land. It is caused by the temperature differences that occur daily between the sea surface and the adjacent land. It usually occurs on relatively calm, sunny summer days. Often, the onset of a sea breeze occurs suddenly as a sea-breeze front, separating the cool air from the warm air, moves inland. Sea-breeze fronts cause a sudden change in wind velocity, from near calm to a brisk cool breeze. At the onset, the sea breeze flows across the coastline, but as time goes on it turns to its right (in the northern hemisphere) and has a component along the coastline.

Wind shear associated with sea breezes can prove to be a hazard at airports that are located along coastlines, such as Logan International Airport in Boston and the John F. Kennedy International Airport in New York City. For example, the occurrence of thunderstorm downdrafts and outflows when a sea breeze could have been expected caused some confusion about the wind velocity over the approach to runway 22 at Kennedy Airport when EAL Flight 66 crashed on June 24, 1975.

In some areas, sea breezes occur regularly during the summer and can be predicted with a fair degree of accuracy. Ground-based anemometers and airborne detectors should be able to detect wind shears, so that pilots can take appropriate action.

Air-Mass Fronts

Separate air masses do not mix readily when they come into contact if they have different temperatures and humidities. Instead, the colder, more dense air mass passes under the warmer, less-dense air mass. The zone of transition between the two air masses is called a front. When

the cold air advances, forcing the warm air to retreat and pass over the
wedge of cold air, it is called a cold front. When the warm air advances,
the frontal boundary moves toward the cold air and a warm front is
said to exist.

All fronts have some degree of wind shear across the zone of
transition between the air masses, but the narrower the zone the
stronger the wind shear is likely to be. When the transition zone is
perhaps 300 or more feet deep, the wind-velocity change with height is
gradual and turbulence is weak or nonexistent. Nevertheless, an
aircraft taking off or landing through such a zone experiences changes
in wind velocity.

. . . .

The following pilot report is typical of a flight through a frontal
zone with high wind variability. It was recorded at the Madison,
Wisconsin, airport.

Have report on wind shear forecast for Madison. Took off on
Runway 18 on 0233Z. Hit base of front at 1500 ft. Rate of climb
pegged with excessive pitch-up, and moderate turbulence lasted
through 5000 ft. (Sowa, 1974)

One U.S. air carrier has been forecasting low-altitude wind
variability associated with frontal conditions since 1962 (Sowa, 1974).
The forecasts give wind direction and speed on either side of the front,
tell whether the front has an abrupt or gradual transition zone, and
give the intensity of turbulence, if any. This technique is now used by
many airlines. The NWS provides forecasts for low-altitude wind
variability for warm and cold fronts, low-altitude jet and nocturnal
inversions, cold surface inversions, friction-surface slowing, inversions,
and sea-breeze fronts.

Weather forecasters cannot now specify the altitude of the base of
the layer of strong wind shear beyond 4 hours. Techniques need further
refinement to improve such forecasts.

Frontal conditions and the accompanying wind shears occur in all
parts of the United States, but they are most frequent over the middle
latitudes during the colder months of the year. While Hawaii averages
about two shears per winter, the central and northeast portions of the

United States average four to five per month during the fall, winter, and spring. The southern states and those east of the Rocky Mountains average one significant frontal passage per month during the same seasons.

Terrain-Induced Wind Shear

Mountain terrain can cause significant low-altitude wind variability, depending on the nature of the large-scale wind field. Airports located close to mountains, near breaks in mountain ranges (known as gorges), or on hills with sharp dropoffs near the ends of runways are subject to steady-state winds that break down into chaotic gusts that are constantly changing. The presence of turbulence, often severe, can compound the problem of operating aircraft in or out of these airports.

The following is a typical pilot report of this condition. It came from a Boeing 707 airplane that had just taken off from the Anchorage, Alaska, airport:

> Take-off on Runway 06R. Light turbulence right after lift-off. At 500 ft., turbulence changed to what I can only describe as massive bursts. The aircraft pitched, yawed, and slipped. The cockpit became a capsule of ricocheting manuals, log books, and debris. Aileron control was stop-to-stop, air-speed changes of plus or minus 50 knots. I made a slow left turn, established a slow climb attitude and, at 4000 ft., the shearing action subsided and turbulence became moderate.*

Because of the pulsing nature of terrain-induced winds, another aircraft on the same approach several minutes later might encounter winds much different from those described above.

This type of low-altitude wind variability may or may not have clouds or precipitation associated with it. The synoptic weather patterns that cause terrain-induced wind shear and turbulence are known and their occurrence can be predicted, but it still is not possible to adequately predict precise wind values at specific altitudes and locations (Sowa, 1977). Wind shear induced by terrain occurs most often in late fall, winter, and early spring. It may happen only three to

---

* Sowa, 1977, Copyright American Institute of Aeronautics and Astronautics

four times per season in some places but as often as 20 days per month in places where the terrain and the prevailing weather patterns are favorable.

Mountain Waves

Mountains induce high-amplitude undulations or waves in air currents flowing over them (Lilly, 1978; Lilly and Zipser, 1972). They are associated with strong shears and turbulence, and their influence can extend from near the ground to very high altitudes. Mountain waves are typified by descending air over the lee side of the mountain range. The descending air has acquired distinctive names in various parts of the world—"Santa Ana" in the Los Angeles Basin; "chinook" along the Rocky Mountains of western Canada and the United States; and "foehn" in Switzerland, Norway, and Sweden.

These strong, gusty winds at the earth's surface produce low-altitude wind shear and turbulence at airports located in the lee of mountains. It is not unusual to have gust velocities double that of the steady-wind values. In extreme cases these gust velocities can exceed 100 knots. Under certain meteorological conditions, a strong temperature inversion existing near the ground restricts the downslope winds from reaching the surface. Instead, the air glides along the top of the inversion, producing wind shear and turbulence about 300 to 1,500 feet above the ground.

Mountain waves can be predicted. It is not possible, however, to precisely forecast the steady-state wind velocity, the gust factor, or the turbulence intensity of such winds. These have been observed during every month of the year in Alaska and in the western mountainous regions of the United States and Canada. Mountain waves are most frequent in the fall, winter, and spring. In an average year, to the lee of the Rocky Mountains, in Montana and southern Canada, there are 15 wave days a month. In Colorado and the more southern states there is an annual average of 7 wave days a month. The mountains in the eastern United States usually do not produce strong downslope winds because their lee slopes are not particularly steep.

Low-Level Jet Streams

The strength of the wind near the ground is tightly linked to diurnal processes in the lower atmosphere. During daytime the earth's surface is heated by the sun, and the planetary boundary layer is marked by vertical air motions. This process causes the frictional influence of the ground on the wind to be transmitted through a deep layer of air. Thus, wind velocities near the ground tend to be relatively high in the form of a concentrated current called a low-level jet stream. The formation of such a jet stream depends also on the distributions of heating and cooling and their daily variations over sloping terrains (see, for example, McNider and Pielke, 1981).

In a typical low-altitude jet stream situated over an airport, the wind at the surface tends to be light and to come from the same direction as the stronger flow immediately above the airport. Consequently, an aircraft that is landing will typically approach the runway into the jet stream wind. As the aircraft descends below the jet stream, headwinds decrease, often substantially, as the aircraft nears touchdown. The sudden loss of headwind can be a serious problem if the pilot is unaware of the situation. In a typical low-altitude jet stream situation, as described above, the event occurs often in clear air but at night when the visual perspective of the pilot may be inhibited.

Tornadoes

No discussion of low-altitude wind shear would be complete without at least a mention of tornadoes and other high-speed atmospheric vortices, such as waterspouts and dust devils. Most often dust devils, of the type commonly seen over desert areas during the hot, dry summer months, are too small to pose serious risks.

Because of the very strong wind shears that characterize them, tornadoes should always be avoided. Most of the time they can be seen by pilots flying below the bases of the parent thunderstorms. An appropriate radar should be capable of detecting existing and incipient tornadoes in sufficient time to allow pilots to fly around them.

Recommendations

The committee's recommendations are listed under four broad categories: general, detection and prediction, aircraft performance and operations, and research. The numbering of the recommendations does not signify any priority. The broad spectrum of specific recommendations reflects the complexities of the low-altitude wind-shear problem.

GENERAL

1. NEED FOR AN INTEGRATED WIND-SHEAR PROGRAM

2. WIND-SHEAR EDUCATION PROGRAM

The FAA and the industry should prepare and disseminate as widely as possible updated and authoritative information on wind shear. Informational materials should stress avoidance of wind shear and should describe flight control techniques for recovery from encounters. The information should encompass all of types of aircraft, with appropriate guidance for each class. It should include recommendations on the most effective means of training pilots.

3. PILOT/CONTROLLER COMMUNICATIONS

The FAA should promote the use of standardized terminology and improved communications between flight crews and control towers. A standardized system of pilot reports (PIREPs) should be developed for reporting low-altitude wind shear encounters.

4. WIND SHEAR DETECTION SYSTEM DEVELOPMENT

DETECTION AND PREDICTION

5. THE LOW-LEVEL WIND SHEAR ALERT SYSTEM (LLWSAS)

LLWSAS is the only system currently available in the near term for detecting low-altitude wind shear on an operational basis and every effort should be made to assess and improve its performance.

6. RECORD AND ANALYZE LLWSAS DATA

7. USE OF AVAILABLE RADAR DATA

The existing network of weather radars, operated by the NWS, should be used more effectively to judge the likelihood of wind shear conditions.

8. NEXT GENERATION WEATHER RADAR (NEXRAD)

The next generation Doppler weather radar system (NEXRAD) should be developed and installed with all possible speed. This long-range radar system will serve many national needs related to severe-weather detection, forecasting, and warning.

9. AIRPORT TERMINAL WEATHER RADAR

The FAA should take immediate action to develop a pulsed Doppler radar system that can be used to observe weather conditions at and around airport terminals.

10. USE OF AIRPORT TERMINAL WEATHER RADAR OBSERVATIONS

For terminal Doppler radar to be most useful to traffic controllers and pilots, a concerted effort should be devoted to developing procedures for analyzing, displaying, and using its observations.

11. AIRBORNE REMOTE SENSORS

Research should continue on the use of airborne Doppler lidars and microwave Doppler radars as a means for detecting low-altitude wind shear.

AIRCRAFT PERFORMANCE AND OPERATIONS

(Recommendations 12-17 are generally outside the interests of this chapter.)

RESEARCH

18. EFFECTS OF HEAVY RAIN

Investigations should continue on how heavy rain affects the low-speed aerodynamic characteristics of aircraft. Particular attention should be paid to the possible adverse effects of heavy rain on aircraft lift, performance, and controllability, including its effects on wind shear detection and flight sensor systems.

19. RESEARCH ON THE NATURE OF LOW-ALTITUDE WIND SHEAR

More must be learned about the various kinds of wind shear and the meteorological conditions that cause or are associated with them. This knowledge is needed to reduce the hazards represented by low-altitude wind shear. Research should include additional field observations and the construction of theoretical models over the relevant scales—from about 1,000 feet to 10-20 miles and from minutes to hours.

The existing body of data obtained by various research programs should be reexamined and augmented, at an appropriate time, by a field program in the humid southeastern United States.

The current drought in Africa has already caused great suffering for many people there and the threat of famine is real in many regions. The phenomenon of drought is linked to the difficult question of climatic variations. Its effects are associated in many ways with desertification. In recent years a substantial amount of research has been carried out on the interrelationships between climate, drought, and desertification.

Chapter 17
Climate, Drought and Desertification

Reprinted from *Nature and Resources*, 20, no. 2 (January - March 1984) by permission of Unesco, Paris.

Most climatic elements, especially precipitation, vary with time. The general word for such changes is *variation*. A climatic change is a variation that persists for at least several decades. A variation lasting several decades in which the elements then return to their original value is called a climatic *fluctuation*.

A *trend* is an upward or downward drift of a central tendency, such as the mean of successive values. If a trend is absent, the series of these values in time is said to be *stationary*. Climate is usually defined by means of thirty-year averages over standard periods. The *variability* of a climate is best defined as the typical pattern of variation within such standard periods. Most such variation is quite short-term (e.g. between successive years) and aperiodic. Some of it, however, is truly periodic. Such variation includes daily and seasonal changes forced by the regular behaviour of the sun. Some of the variation may appear quasi-periodic, but this is usually without value for prediction, especially as regards precipitation.

Drought has many definitions. *Meteorological drought* occurs when rainfall falls well below expectation in any large area for an extended period. In many cases such drought has economic impact because it impairs food production, streamflow, water supply, and other resource yields. *Agricultural drought* occurs when rainfall amounts and distribution, soil-water reserves, and evaporation losses combine in such a way to cause crop or livestock yields to diminish markedly.

Desertification is a term employed rather loosely but which refers specifically to the deterioration of arid and semi-arid lands that are used beyond their capacity for sustained production by cultivators, herdsmen, and others. Drought often accelerates such deterioration, but natural ecosystems usually recover from even prolonged drought. When human misuse of the land weakens the natural system, drought often leads to desertification.

Rainfall Trends in the Arid Zones

Annual rainfall curves (Figure 2) show that certain stations in the arid zone (e.g. Agadez, Abéché and Alice Springs) have recently experienced apparent downward trends in rainfall, whereas others (e.g. Jodhpur, Phoenix) show high variability from year to year, but no consistent trend. The question clearly arises: is there widespread evidence that rainfall in the arid zone is lessening? If so, is a fluctuation in progress, or is the decrease a lasting change?

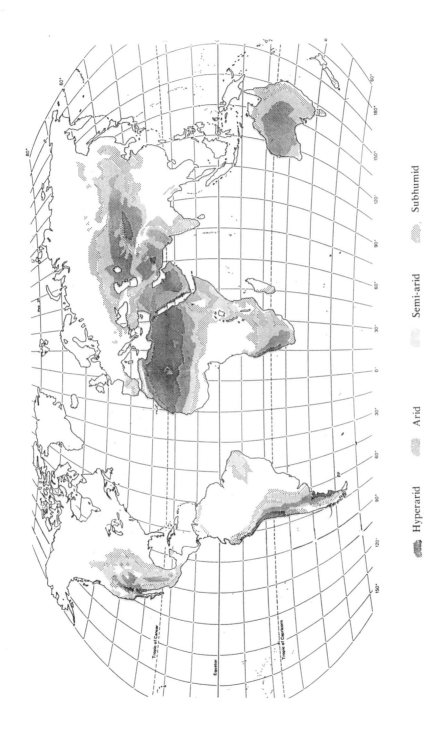

Figure 1. Map of world distribution of arid regions (Unesco).

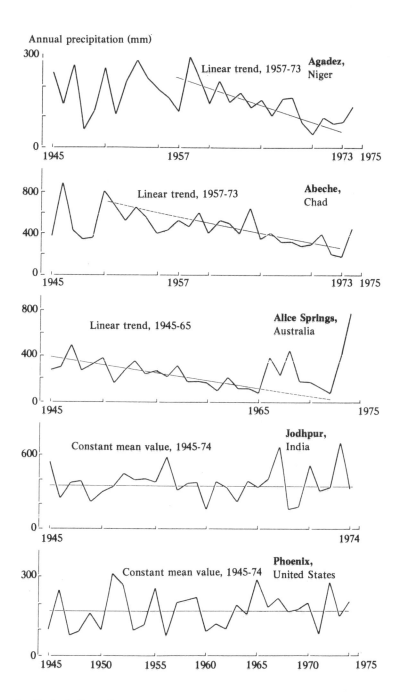

Figure 2. Rainfall variations at selected arid-zone stations since 1945.

On a very long time-scale there have certainly been great changes in many tropical and subtropical areas. In Africa, there was apparently a desiccation beginning about 8,000 years before present (B.P.) and culminating before 4,000 B.P. A similar sequence is visible in Australasia.

It is clear that there was a prolonged desiccation of these continents between 8,000 and 4,000 B.P. Prior to this desiccation, much of North Africa, for example, carried savanna or scrub vegetation capable of sustaining large numbers of game animals upon which human hunters preyed. Saharan cave-painters have made this tradition visible to modern observers.

The desiccation must, indeed, have influenced the origins of pastoralism and cultivation, which coincided with it in time, at least in Africa and the Middle East. Almost certainly, however, the resulting spread of desert surfaces was mainly of natural origin. It was part of the readjustment of world climates that followed the end of glacial climates about 10,000 B.P.

North America (and much of central and northern Eurasia) had a different history: desiccation came much earlier, chiefly in the epoch 12,000 to 8,000 B.P. North American lakes were falling as those of Africa and Australasia were at high levels or were still rising. This disparity emphasizes that middle-latitude deserts and semi-deserts have a different history from those of the intertropical and subtropical zones. Their rainfall (or snowfall) comes from travelling cyclones quite unlike the rain-generating systems of low altitudes.

There is thus plenty of evidence of *past* desiccations that led to the spread of desert surfaces and the extent of the arid zone. Is there evidence of a similar desiccation in progress today, as the charts in Figure 2 seem to indicate? Is the widespread desertification now in progress due to such a downward trend of rainfall?

No such worldwide trend has been observed, nor are there present grounds for expecting such a change. But severe and prolonged drought has affected many semi-arid areas. Northeastern Brazil, for example, has been a major victim. So has east-central Australia. Major drought episodes have affected inland China. The largest effects have been observed in Africa, initially along the southern edge of the Sahara (the Sahel and Sahelo-Sudanian belts), but more recently in many parts of eastern and southern Africa. From high levels in the 1950s rainfall declined progressively in west and central Africa south of the Sahara, to an extremely low level in 1972/73. Since then it has fluctuated, but has remained (into 1982) far below long-term mean values.

Climate-Desertification Linkages

This very prolonged drought has prompted the question: Is the climate being affected by human action? There are two mechanisms whereby this might happen.

First, overgrazing, unwise cultivation, and the stripping of trees and shrubs for firewood all tend to make the surface more reflective to solar radiation (i.e. to raise the albedo). Dynamical modelling indicates that such raised albedos tend to diminish rainfall further—a potentially disastrous positive feedback.

Second, in regions far from the oceans, much of the rainfall occurs from re-evaporated soil moisture. Faulty land-use practices may reduce storage capacity, and hence evapotranspiration.

Only in Africa does it appear possible that man-induced changes can have thus permanently altered the climate. The Sahelian drought has not ceased. People have absorbed the losses and adapted to it. The spread of diminished rainfall into other parts of semi-arid Africa has raised the spectre that the above feedbacks may be at work and that the desiccation may be lasting. Elsewhere, drought tends to be overridden by a return to normal or even excessive rainfall.

There is no doubt, however, that over-grazing and unwise cultivation alter the surface microclimates adversely. Reduction of perennial vegetation cover has the following consequences throughout the arid zone:

- Albedo is increased, leading to a lower level of absorbed solar radiation.

- Soil temperatures are nevertheless raised, and the stress on organisms increased.

- Fine materials, both mineral (clay and silt) and organic, are lost to erosion, and organic material is oxidized.

- Water-holding capacity is thereby reduced.

These four interacting processes represent a hostile change of surface micro-climate.

The Observed Facts in Africa

The semi-arid areas of Africa are regions with highly variable rainfall and histories of recurrent and intense drought. Nowhere is the situation as severe as in the Sahel and its neighbouring regions along the southern margins of the Sahara. The most notable characteristics of drought are a random distribution in time, spatial coherence over large areas and, in some regions, persistence for years on end. In some years there appears to be a spatial coherence which extends on a continental scale; simultaneous droughts in the Sahel and severe conditions in southern and eastern Africa occur more frequently than the continental drought.

It is well known that drought occurred throughout the sub-Saharan area in the years 1968-73. In the years 1974 and 1975 rainfall increased considerably in the region, leading to the belief that the drought had ended. In fact, although wetter than previous years, those two years were still below normal. In 1976 severe drought returned to the region and has continued in most areas up to the present time.

Not all African countries have been uniformly affected by this prolonged spell of deficient rainfall and run-off. Recent experience in Kenya and the United Republic of Tanzania, for example, has been more favourable. All of West Africa has also seen variable conditions. Extreme drought has affected the western Sahel for much of the past decade, but other countries have been more fortunate. In contrast to the very dry conditions of 1968 and 1973, the Sahelian zone of Nigeria has been enjoying satisfactory rainfall in recent years.

This general observation does not preclude delays in the onset of the rainy seasons, as was experienced in 1983. There also are localized drought conditions, but large-scale drought has been absent. This is in contrast with the widely reported severe drought conditions in some other parts of the Sahel zone of West Africa, for example Mauritania.

The full significance of the recent rainfall anomalies is most evident when compared with variability throughout the last three decades. Since the 1950s changes in Sahelian rainfall have been particularly dramatic (Figure 2). Wet conditions prevailed during that decade, with decadal averages ranging from 15 percent above normal in the southern areas to 35 to 40 percent above normal along the Saharan fringe. Favourable conditions ended in 1960 and by 1968 the situation was very bad. Average deficits for the six years 1968 to 1973 matched the excesses of the 1950s: 15 to 40 percent below the mean. The extremes were reached in 1972 and 1973, with deficits of 50 to 60 percent in the northern Sahel and 30 to 35 percent in the more humid southern areas, where mean rainfall ranges from 400 to 1,200 mm. In 1974 and 1975, when drought reportedly had ended, rainfall was still about 25 percent below the mean in the north and about 10 percent below in the south. Larger rainfall deficits occurred in subsequent years and continued until 1983, deficits of 1976 and 1977 matching or exceeding those of 1972 and 1973 in many areas. Thus, the drought which began in 1968 in the sub-Saharan regions never really ended, though some areas were luckier than others, notably because of a favourable distribution of rainfall throughout the season so that the consequences for agricultural production were not as detrimental.

Sahel droughts sometimes coincided with abnormally dry conditions over much of the continent. Although the wet episode in the Sahel during the 1950s was paralleled by above-normal rainfall through much of southern Africa, it was a decade of generally dry conditions in east Africa. The 1960s were abnormally wet throughout east Africa and in many other equatorial regions, but drier conditions commenced then in the semi-arid subtropical regions of the continent. Drought conditions occurred early in that decade in southern Africa, a few years before they began in the Sahel. The early 1970s were a special case, however, in that they were years of nearly continent-wide drought affecting northern Africa, east Africa, and especially northern margins of the Kalahari (but not those on the southern Kalahari). The last eight years have variously seen drought not only in the Sahel, but also in east Africa and in southern Africa, although the most severe periods have not been synchronous in all three regions.

The spatial coherence of rainfall anomaly patterns is particularly marked in the semi-arid regions of northern Africa, generally extending across the east-west expanse of the continent and including areas with winter rains north and those with summer rains south of the Sahara. Thus, the rainfall fluctuations tend to manifest themselves as contractions and expansions of the dry zone. To a lesser extent, such coherence can be observed across the entire continent, especially on multi-year time-scales. In the 1950s, for example, rainfall was above average in 65 of 84 regions; sub-normal rainfall was limited to equatorial regions, such as east Africa. In a later period, 1968-1973, drought prevailed and rainfall averages for the six years were below average in 68 of 84 regions; positive anomalies were generally small and confined to equatorial regions.

Streamflow Decreases

The meteorological droughts are of course also reflected in streamflow regimes. In large parts of West Africa runoff is not perennial and presents great interannual variability. There is a close link between floods and rainfall rates: a rainy year may give manageable runoff if rains are properly distributed in time and a dry year may induce high floods from rain concentrated in a few days. Nevertheless, the persistence of deficient rainfall for fifteen years in the whole Sahel has led to an overall stream-flow deficit that is very severe; also, runoff has varied widely in time and space. The year 1968 presented the greatest deficit (except in Chad), with amounts of less than 20 percent of normal. In Chad the years 1972 and 1977 were the weakest. Some years had local excess runoff, for example the case of the Niger in 1974, 1976, and 1980. The deficits of 1982 and 1983 are very strong, especially in basins with shallow water tables.

Much of the streamflow in the Sahel comes from outside the Sahel zone—the Senegal, Niger, and Chari rivers coming from wetter regions to the south. These rivers have undergone a severe decrease of runoff during the last fifteen years. For instance, the mean annual discharge of the Senegal river at Bakel has been below normal since 1968 (excepting 1969 and 1974). The situation is almost the same for the Niger river at Koukiloro, and the discharge of the Chari river at Ndjamena has been systematically below normal since 1965.

The average annual total water yield for all the rivers reaching the Sahel is 125 billion m^3 approximately. For the period 1968 to 1982, this average falls to 95 billion m^3. Such a deficit of 25 percent represents each year the equivalent of three times the assumed stored water of the Manatali Dam in Upper Senegal basin.

The systematic weakness of annual floods is particularly catastrophic for the crops normally watered by overflow. In the lower valley of Senegal where the yield of sorghum is directly linked to the area of overflow, the annual maximum height of floods since 1968 has been below the mean for thirteen years out of fifteen. The situation is the same for the inner lakes in the Niger's interior delta (15°-17° N).

For all these rivers the present drought appears more severe in duration than the two others of the century (in the 1910s and 1940s).

Lake Chad has shown a systematic decrease of its level since 1963. At that time the lake surface covered 23,500 km^2 and the volume of stored water was 105 billion m^3. In 1973, ten years later, the surface area had been divided by three and the volume by four. Since this date, the lake has been cut into two parts. The northern part dries up every year, with only a small inflow through the Grande Barrière.

Time series of precipitation in the subtropics are quasi-periodic in nature. Analysis of such series may contain periodicities which are statistically significant. However, as these time series exhibit apparently random changes in phase, they have no predictive value, and are unlikely to be useful unless we can gain some insight into the underlying physical mechanisms. Similarly, apparent trends in such time series have no predictive value. What is clear is that drought is a normal component of climate in parts of the tropics and subtropics. Economies, in particular the agricultural production systems, have to be versatile enough to endure them.

In summary, the observed fact about rainfall over Africa since 1968 is that drought has been widespread, especially in the western part of sub-Saharan areas (west of 5° W), and that this has been reflected in diminished streamflow. In the northern Sahel there has been an apparent downward trend of rainfall since the high values of the 1950s, and there is no sign that this downward trend is about to be reversed. The analysis of available statistical data—admittedly not complete—does not support the idea that such a trend can be relied on to continue, nor is there evidence of any kind of cyclical behaviour.

Causes of Drought—Can it be Predicted?

The basic requirements for rainfall are the presence of water vapour in the air, condensation nuclei around which water droplets form, and rising air motion which promotes condensation (through cooling by transport of moisture to cooler air aloft).

The factors promoting drought are thus absence of available water vapour or condensation nuclei, or the presence of sinking air motions (called subsidence, which arises from large-scale atmospheric flows as part of the circulation of the entire atmosphere). Also, rainfall tends to form in organized atmospheric disturbances (squall lines), so that an additional promoting factor of drought is the absence of such systems.

While meteorologists are aware of these general conditions necessary for formation of drought, the quantitative details of the conditions necessary for the onset and duration of drought are not yet known.

Studies with numerical models of the atmosphere have supported the hypothesis that changes in surface properties (such as reflectivity or soil moisture) may contribute to the persistence of drought in the Sahel. An increase in surface reflectivity over a limited area (caused for example by a decrease in vegetation from overgrazing) produces a relative cooling of the surface and atmosphere and a reduction in precipitation. Other modelling work has demonstrated that a reduction in soil moisture could also lead to a reduction in rainfall. When the surface becomes dried, there is less evapotranspiration and less moisture available for precipitation. In one such modelling study, the formation of rain-bearing disturbances was inhibited when part of the land surface was assumed to be initially dry rather than wet. However, upper-air observations just before, during and just after the passage of rain systems in the Sahel indicate that some portion of the water vapour that produces rainfall has its origin in upper air masses that move from the Atlantic Ocean towards the Sahel. More complete information on the origin of water vapour that falls as rain must be obtained as a prerequisite for further study of the incidence of drought.

Two cautionary remarks on the use of models should be made. First, in order that the model's response may be distinguished from the fluctuations which are part of the model's natural variability, the imposed changes are made much larger and more extensive than, for example, those observed recently in the Sahel. Second, many of the relevant physical processes are represented in the models in a simplified manner. Although numerical models can thus be used to identify qualitatively the processes contributing to drought, they cannot yet be used quantitatively.

A possible further mechanism for the occurrence of a drought situation may be the presence of a deep layer of dust. Such a layer, i.e. the Saharan Dust Layer, can reduce the downward radiative flux into the desert, while at the same time increasing the heating of the atmosphere. This indicates a stabilizing effect of dust on the rate of lower-level temperature decrease with height, leading to a possible positive feedback mechanism, i.e. the stable layer inhibits convection, thus preventing removal of the dust layer, and perpetuating the thermally stable situation. This hypothesis, however, should be tested by a numerical model, and a start has been made in this direction.

Sea Temperatures, CO_2 and Drought

One area of active research is the effect of changes in tropical sea-surface temperatures on atmospheric circulation. It has been calculated that the amount of energy transported over large distances by ocean currents is of the same order of magnitude as that transported in the atmosphere by latent and sensible heat transfer. Since sea-temperature anomalies may persist for several months, they may have some predictive value for atmospheric processes. It is known that warming of the equatorial East Pacific (El Niño) is associated with changes in the longitudinal circulation in the tropics, and many of these changes have been reproduced in numerical models. Although several major El Niños have coincided with dry summers in the Sahel (1972, 1982), other events (for example, 1957) have occurred when rainfall in the Sahel was above normal (but below normal in the two subequatorial belts).

Further observational and numerical work has considered the effects of anomalous sea temperatures in the tropical Atlantic and Indian Oceans. As yet, no clear relationship has emerged between tropical sea-surface temperatures and drought in Africa, although some of the results have been encouraging, for instance in Senegal. Natural climate variability in the tropics is less marked than in high latitudes, so there is some potential for predicting the mean behaviour of the tropical atmosphere for the periods of a month to a season ahead. However, changes in sea-surface temperature do not account for all the variability in the tropics.

In the long term, i.e. many decades from now, it is possible that carbon dioxide increase may alter climates in Africa. Studies of the effect of such increase give no consistent picture of regional changes in precipitation, though there is qualitative agreement on latitudinally averaged changes. It is highly improbable, however, that the increase of carbon dioxide to date has contributed significantly to the recent dry conditions.

The Need for Drought Planning

At present, it is not yet possible to predict either the onset of drought or the end of the present phase of dry conditions in Africa. Hence it is good strategy for all African nations to take measures to protect themselves as far as possible against the continuation of drought or the recurrence of drought in those areas that are currently better off.

Drought is an inevitable part of climate in many parts of Africa and in other continents too, and all available scientific evidence indicates that its temporal and spatial occurrence is still unpredictable. At the same time, no practical method for appreciably enhancing precipitation is yet on hand.

There is a need, therefore, for all countries concerned to establish drought-control plans that are capable of mitigating the consequences of drought.

Such drought-control plans are necessarily the work of an interdisciplinary team, comprising economists, agriculturalists, hydrologists, experts in human sciences and health services, and many others, as well as meteorologists. Emphasis should be placed on the establishment of climate research groups to monitor continuously the occurrence and progress of drought, at least on a seasonal basis. Such monitoring of drought could be used to forewarn farmers and the governments of possible severe drought.

The drought-control plans should contain provisions for the implementation of specific actions to detect drought and to help alleviate its effects on agricultural production.

Conclusions

A summary of the major findings contained in the two documents on which this article is based, is given below.

- The climates of the desert fringe are everywhere subject to high variability to which natural ecosystems and traditional livelihood systems are both well adapted. But there is little evidence of persistent trend towards a different climate. Nor is there convincing evidence of any useful periodicities.

- The drought in Africa which began in 1968 has not yet ended everywhere in 1984, especially in the Sahel; in recent years drought has spread to southern Africa and some parts of eastern Africa. However, some countries in East Africa and in West Africa have had much less severe drought conditions during this period.

- Drought is a common occurrence in many parts of the tropics and subtropics in Africa. The general meteorological causes of drought are well known but the specific quantitative conditions necessary for the onset and cessation of the African drought are not yet fully understood. Further developments to explain the causal mechanisms can be expected in the next few years if active research continues.

- No known periodicities or trends exist in the climate of Africa which cause or ameliorate drought. Although rainfall amounts in the sub-Sahara have indeed markedly decreased over the past fifteen years, there is no certainty that these deficiencies will continue or cease.

- No known method exists to predict reliably the continuation, cessation or recurrence of drought in Africa.

- Reliable and continuous weather data do not exist in many parts of Africa; these data are necessary to permit the analysis and warning of droughts.

- Rain-making has not been convincingly demonstrated to be able to alleviate the current drought in Africa.

- Several positive actions can be taken by African countries and others to improve the detection of drought and to help alleviate its effects on agricultural production.

- Poor land-use practices have led to deterioration of local and surface microclimates in the arid and semi-arid zones. Even though the general climate may be little affected, the removal of a good vegetation cover fundamentally alters the microclimate, and hence changes the effective environment of human beings, plants, and animals.

The overriding priority, therefore, from the standpoint of climate-desertification relationships, is to avoid further destruction of surface cover by poor pastoral and agricultural practices. Whether or not such practices are really leading to a lasting deterioration of large-scale arid-zone climates is still open to question. What is certain is that these bad forms of land-use worsen their own local climates, and therefore exaggerate the bad effects of any prolonged drought that may occur. It may not be true that "desert feeds on desert," as is often said. But it is profoundly true that drought feeds on poor land-use, and is thereby worsened. Thus the key to the future in the arid zone lies in land-use control.

TO DELVE MORE DEEPLY

Conant, F., et al., (eds.). *Resource Inventory and Baseline Study Methods for Developing Countries*. Washington, D.C. American Association for the Advancement of Science. 1983.

Reining, P. *Challenging Desertification in West Africa*. Athens, Ohio, Ohio University Center for International Studies, Africa Program, 1980.

Reining, P. (ed.). *Desertification Papers*. Delivered at the Science Association Seminar on Desertification, Nairobi, Kenya, 1977. Washington, D.C., American Association for the Advancement of Science, 1978.

Reining, P. *Handbook on Desertification Indicators*. Washington, D.C., American Association for the Advancement of Science, 1978.

This article is based on two sources: the report of an expert group meeting on the climatic situation and drought in Africa, convened by the World Meteorological Organization in Geneva on 6 and 7 October 1983 in the framework of the World Climate Programme, which was chaired by Professor F. Kenneth Hare of Trinity College, University of Toronto; and a more general paper prepared by Professor Hare for the Agricultural Meteorology Commission of WMO, on climatic trends and desertification.

PART V

Preparedness and Rescue

A comparison of societal response to disaster in a developed country (Romania) with that in a developing country (Nicaragua) reveals significant differences. suggesting the latter to be disaster-prone. The sheer poverty of people in developing countries induces a risk-taking propensity and a fatalism that explains their continued occupancy of hazard areas.

Chapter 18
Consequences of Disasters for Developing Nations

Charles H.V. Ebert

Charles H.V. Ebert. who is professor of physical geography at the State University of New York at Buffalo. was born of American parents in Europe but. after the Second World War. completed his university studies in the United States. obtaining his Ph.D. in geography and geology from the University of North Carolina. He joined the newly created Department of Geography in Buffalo in 1963. becoming its first chairman. Dr. Ebert's professional interest in soils. environmental impact studies. and land development has taken him to Afghanistan. Australia. Guatemala. Israel. Nicaragua. Peru, and Saudi Arabia.

General Considerations

Change is an integral part of all natural systems and is an ongoing component of our global evolution. Natural systems include the lithosphere, the hydrosphere, the atmosphere, and all living things. A change in any one of these results in adjustments in some or in all of the others as energy is transformed, expended, or shared. Life on earth is marked by such processes.

When these occurrences take place in sudden, violent events, they may have a cataclysmic impact on the environment and on people, as witness volcanic eruptions, earthquakes, avalanches, seismic sea waves, and major floods. Other processes may result in slow adjustments, almost unnoticeable changes, and with an environmental response time too long to be of immediate significance to the untrained observer.

Disasters Plague the Entire World

It is not surprising that the violence of some of these events terrified our ancestors who were entirely at the mercy of nature's fury. Their token weapons against nature in revolt were flight, passive suffering, and the offering of sacrifices to pacify the unknown forces. The destruction of crops, sudden deaths, and widespread suffering soon exceeded the level of stress mankind could tolerate. Earthquakes, volcanic eruptions, and other criteria of nature in revolt were not perceived as natural processes but as calamitous events written in the stars: disasters.

It is true that modern science and technology have liberated mankind from the absolute powerlessness that our forefathers experienced. This is, of course, particularly true for developed nations. Yet, disasters plague the entire world. They do not stop at political boundaries, so that the peoples of the continents are not truly separated by distance and time. The effects of major planetary upheavals may reach all of us. Yet, as we shall see, the impact of disasters is much more devastating on developing nations than on technologically advanced societies. Nevertheless, disasters plague the entire world, though many do not receive the international publicity associated with commercial sensationalism of most news media. Many events pass unnoticed because they occur in more remote areas. It is believed that during forty years alone, from 1938 to 1977, more than 1,000 catastrophic happenings have been recorded in which ten or more people were killed.[1]

On the surface it appears that worldwide catastrophes are on the increase; yet, this is difficult to judge. Major upheavals must have shaken our planet since primeval times. Scientists agree that eras of unusual earth activities have taken place, such as periods of violent volcanism, tectonic disturbances, as well as severe climate changes. These processes have not always been identified with the concept of disaster. The plausible reason for this is that the presence of human beings, in large numbers, and eventually in structured societies, is requisite to call a natural process a disaster. Thus it can be said that, as the world's population increases, the likelihood of natural catastrophes will continue to increase as people move closer to volcanoes, build near or across geologic faults, and so on. It seems that no earthquake ever discouraged people from rebuilding their city, nor have recurring floods ever convinced man to move out of dangerous floodplains along the world's rivers and deltas. For example, Managua, Nicaragua, has had fourteen destructive earthquakes since 1772, four of which took place between 1926 and 1972; yet, the city is being rebuilt once more on the same site.[2]

Varied Response to Disasters

Does this insistence simply reflect ignorance, social inertia, or even reckless abandon? Or is it that mankind has reached the dangerously false conclusion that science and human experience have made it possible to stand up successfully to the fury of natural forces? The answers to these and related questions are difficult to find. There simply are no universally valid parameters that clearly define the critical stress levels which exceed the normal capacities of different people.

Human response to disasters varies from culture to culture, from society to society, as well as from individual to individual. Such reactions depend, at least in part, on sociological, psychological, economic, and even political differences. In view of the innumerable varieties of disasters, sites, circumstances, and cultural settings it is just about impossible to establish a meaningful hierarchy or classification. It is quite clear, however, that the impact of a major disaster on developing countries quickly narrows the parameters within which survival and recovery are possible.

In many cases it may be difficult, though, to distinguish sharply developing from developed countries. The reasons are (a) that development is a transitional phenomenon and (b) it is an ongoing process. When it comes to the attitudes toward disasters, the situation is further obscured by the massive growth of relatively inexpensive and worldwide communication systems that break down barriers between peoples. In the past, the lack of such communications isolated people from the rest of the world. This isolation prevented a society from questioning the conditions which prevailed in its midst and which it accepted as being normal to its setting. In modern times, people's views of what ought to be is strongly shaped by political, economic and technological conditions observed elsewhere in the world.[3] Therefore, perception is frequently out of step with existing realities. This could mean that in adjusting to disasters, folk societies and less developed countries, which usually are more flexible and more variable over short distances, become less dependent on their ability to deal with disasters because they expect the outside world to provide assistance in various forms.[4]

Responses in Developed and Developing Countries: A Comparison

It was stated previously that some natural disasters occur in sudden, cataclysmic ways while others may at first go unnoticed though they eventually reach the level of a catastrophe. Thus each disaster has its unique implications but they all turn into true disasters when the stress placed on a given system becomes too great for such a system to sustain such an impact.

Various disasters could be selected to illustrate how societal responses differ from place to place. Considering the extreme complexity of such an inquiry, it appears to be more practical to look at a few examples of recent disasters to find some common denominators of disaster response in developing nations compared to those of technologically more advanced countries. Two events, the 1977 Bucharest and the 1972 Managua earthquakes, serve to give us some valuable insights.

Bucharest

The Bucharest earthquake occurred on a Friday evening (4 March 1977), when a great number of people were in their homes. The severe quake, measuring 7.2 on the Richter scale, lasted slightly over one minute and did great damage to the city of 2 million people. Over 1,400 people were killed, more than 10,000 were injured, and up to 80,000 lost their homes. The total damage was estimated at a minimum of $1,000 million.[5]

The response of the highly structured society, and the strong, central control on the part of the Romanian Government, may explain the swiftness and effectiveness of the reactions to the disaster. Within forty-eight hours food was delivered to the stricken city from the surrounding regions. Local clean-up teams were organized to begin immediate rescue and repair work. Clothes were distributed to needy people and small cash grants were made available to encourage quick reconstruction of homes. Within a year a great deal of the damage had been repaired and the reconstruction of Bucharest had taken place at an impressive pace.

The way a national government is capable of responding to a disaster obviously depends on a variety of factors. Such determinants include the type of government, the resources available, the effectiveness of communications, the magnitude of the catastrophe, and the human reaction in a given society. It seems that in the case of the Bucharest event the response time was short, the measures were effective, and the society reacted in a disciplined and purposeful way.

*Managua**

Few earthquakes of recent occurrence have been studied more thoroughly than the Managua earthquake of 23 December 1972, which struck the Nicaraguan capital about twenty minutes after midnight. The *Proceedings* of the Earthquake Engineering Research Institute Conference, held in San Francisco in 1973, contains a wealth of information dealing with the technical and sociological aspects of the earthquake.[6]

On the surface, and referring back to the Bucharest earthquake, it seems that a strongly centralized government is able to deal more effectively with disaster conditions. As a matter of fact there have been instances where governments revert to totalitarianism and declare martial law to prevent a breakdown of law and order.[7] There is little

* The writer visited Managua just before the earthquake, immediately afterwards, again in 1974, and has completed a study for publication.

question that the former government of General Samoza must be viewed as a strong, centralized government. Yet, the fact that Nicaragua still was in a developing phase reduced the effectiveness of this government's intervention.

The earthquake struck with a devastating force. The shallow depth of the quake's focus allowed the various types of seismic waves, usually separated by considerable time intervals, to reach the epicentre in the city almost simultaneously. The result was massive and sudden destruction. The central fire station was immediately destroyed; most channels of communications and almost all public utilities broke down instantaneously. Neither the government nor the people were prepared to deal with this sudden catastrophe. The government, although strong and centralized, could not rely on an effective civil service system of adequate size to continue administrative and operational functions. When communications broke down, and when directives from the sole source of power were not received, the formerly effective system of government began to fail.[8]

The Managuan population, generally poor and to a large extent inadequately educated, to a considerable degree fended for itself. Intensive looting broke out in many parts of the devastated city, fires raged through large sections of Managua, and there seemed to be very little effective governmental action. Indicative of this self-help situation was the fact that an estimated 75 percent of the homeless found shelter in and around the homes of relatives on the fringes of Managua or in distant towns.[9] The latter pattern seems to be typical of disaster situations in developing countries. There, most of the elements of an industrial society tend to be centralized in a capital which is still surrounded by a predominantly rural countryside. Thus, a great number of the Managuan people, mostly on their own, and poorly prepared to deal with the disaster within a well-organized plan, had to adjust by modifying human behaviour more than by controlling nature. This they did individually or in small groups.[10]

Developing Nations are Less Prepared

Developing nations, generally speaking, are less prepared to deal with natural disasters and also do less to prepare for them. The Managuan earthquake certainly illustrated this. Many aspects of an early destructive earthquake in 1931 repeated themselves after an intervening period of forty years: no significant planning for disaster emergencies and no emphasis on seismic-resistant construction, with the exception of a few government or bank buildings of modern design (Figure 1). The dangerous *taquezal* construction so typical of thousands of small homes proved disastrous to many people because of its inability to resist earth tremors. The fragile wood-frame buildings, supported by earth-filled walls and weighted down by heavy-tiled roofs, turned to death traps for many victims.

Without wishing to over-simplify a very complex set of interrelated factors, one can state that the poorer people of the developing countries are more disaster-prone. The more developed technology of industrially advanced countries, with inherently greater total resources, offers a cushion against some of the worst disasters. It is a recurring fact that, on a worldwide basis, the greatest death tolls occur in the overcrowded shanty towns and cramped quarters of socially marginalized people. [11] In many instances the areas of great suffering are struck repeatedly by the same type of disaster, and the casual observer may ask himself why the population of such endangered places will not abandon such high-risk locations.

The Problem of Recurring Disasters

A good example to illustrate recurring disasters is the Bay of Bengal where tropical cyclones have repeatedly spread havoc and death in the coastal regions of Bangladesh. On 12 November 1980, this low-lying deltaic region, including many densely populated offshore islands, was exposed to a major storm surge in connection with the passage of a violent tropical cyclone.* Ironically, this was the second storm system to threaten the area within a month. Despite warnings by radio, a great part of the population remained in dangerously exposed locations. The first storm had not been too severe and there was no immediate indication that the second cyclone would be more dangerous than the preceding one. In consequence, the loss of life and property became staggering. Between 200,000 and 400,000 people drowned, more than 500,000 cattle were killed, 9,000 fishing-boats were destroyed, thousands of small dwellings were swept away, and 80 percent of the rice crop was lost. [12]

---

* See article by Peter Rogers in this book.—Ed.

Figure 1. This modern building of reinforced concrete successfully
withstood the severe shocks of the 1972 Managua
earthquake. (C.H.V. Ebert)

Here is an area of about 18,000 square kilometres occupied by over 6 million people within a chronically endangered region. Are these people foolhardy, exceptionally brave, or simply not aware of the potential recurrence of danger? The answers to these questions are certainly complex; yet, it is clear that a considerable risk-taking propensity and some fatalism enter the picture. [13] Poor people, even if they are aware of the dangers to their lives, are reluctant to leave their homesteads because they realize that they can do very little to change the situation. This may explain, at least in part, the general fatalistic attitude. [14] Unfortunately it is a recurring pattern in developing nations that the badly housed, poorly educated, often isolated and immobile rural populations are mercilessly exposed to natural hazards.

Behavioural Responses to Stress

There is no question that many known and unknown factors enter the picture when a key to the behavioural response of people to stress and disasters is being sought. Some of these, without distinction, may affect both developed and underdeveloped countries. However, human occupancy of areas subject to recurrent hazards seems to be justified in the minds of the local people concerned for a number of reasons, which include: (a) superior local economic opportunities such as good soil, water resources, and favourable access to transportation and established trade patterns; (b) lack of other alternative opportunities; and (c) variations in hazard perception. [15]

It is especially the last factor that still requires a great deal of research and interpretation. In his study of the Galachipa community in Bangladesh, M. Islam concluded that people forget easily, that a carefree attitude prevails between disasters, and that there is a naive faith in government promises for improvements in the future. [16] Thus it is evident that personal attitudes and perceptions help to explain human behaviour in the face of the ever-present threat of disaster. Furthermore, such response is shaped by the recency of the personal experience, the frequency and magnitude of the events, the personal propensity of risk-taking, and weighing the existing hazard against the local advantages.

Concluding Thoughts

It was stated that with an ever-increasing population and more industrialization and urbanization, the likelihood of disasters occurring appears to be on the increase. Yet, the relationship with nature, with emphasis on the impact of nature's violence on man, also follows a law of reciprocity. The depletion of natural resources, coupled with a general environmental deterioration, reflects mankind's relentless encroachment on nature, which leads to what some observers call a widespread environmental crisis.[17] Therefore, man's interaction with the environment may set up additional stresses and imbalances which may also lead to disasters. Human activities causing such stresses include massive deforestation, uncontrolled soil erosion, open-strip mining, and the various forms of pollution that lower the effectiveness of the atmosphere, the hydrosphere, and the biosphere. To what extent man-induced disasters occur depends partially on the same factors discussed before: personal attitudes and perceptions, economic advantages, individual as well as collective willingness to face risks, levels of education, and values, as well as political and governmental systems.

The law of reciprocity, however, does not apply equally to all people. There is no question that the most basic difference between the impact of disasters on technologically advanced and developing countries is that the latter are predominantly in marginal social, political, and especially precarious economic situations. This makes them more vulnerable, as was demonstrated by the repeated mass death meted out to the people of coastal Bangladesh.

Another example of regional mass suffering was presented to the world in the sub-Saharan Sahel which clearly showed the concept of marginalization of developing nations. Drought, starvation, and diseases, through 1973, killed hundreds of thousands of people and more than a third of their livestock in this band of poor nations that extends across Africa, from Ethiopia on the east through Sudan and the Sahelian countries of Niger, Senegal, Mauritania, Mali, Upper Volta, and Chad.[18]

It is clear that the scope of most natural disasters, often reaching far beyond the political boundaries of countries, extends far beyond the capabilities of developing nations to deal effectively with them. Without massive outside aid such disasters would grow into completely uncontrollable situations. International organizations such as the Red Cross, the United Nations Relief and Works Agency (UNRWA) for Palestine Refugees in the Near East, and the United Nations Food and Agriculture Organization (FAO), to mention a few, as well as many private, religious, and national organizations have tried to stem the tide of death and suffering in many parts of the world. Unfortunately, there are also stories of incompetence, mismanagement, and even of corruption of the local infrastructure.[19] Furthermore, even a casual glance at the amount of financial resources entering the international arms race, compared to the means available to international disaster aid, illuminates the questionable priorities set in today's world.

The world must recognize the pressing need for studying the causes and effects of disasters, their non-parochial nature, and the staggering impact they have, especially on developing nations. Given the political and economic realities, it is sadly evident that no magic wand can quickly erase the existing crass differences in wealth, education, and technology. Yet, these facts should not discourage the continued struggle for knowledge and means needed to offer all people a life without unnecessary suffering.

NOTES

1. Encyclopaedia Britannica (eds.), *Disaster! When Nature Strikes Back*, p. 258, New York, Bantam/Britannica Books, 1978.
2. C. Santos, *Proceedings of the Earthquake Engineering Research Institute Conference* (San Francisco), Vol. I, 1973, pp. 58-9.
3. *Man's Impact on the Global Environment. Report of the Study of Critical Environmental Problems*, p. 250, Cambridge, Mass., Massachusetts Institute of Technology Press, 1970.
4. G. White, *Natural Hazards*, New York, Oxford University Press, 1974; R. Cates et al., *Proceedings*, op. cit., p. 949.
5. Encyclopaedia Britannica, op. cit., pp. 41-2.
6. *Proceedings*, op. cit., Vols. I and II.
7. J. Whittow, *Disasters*, Athens, University of Georgia Press, 1979, p. 27.
8. *Proceedings*, op. cit., Vol. II, p. 947.
9. Ibid., p. 946.
10. Ibid., p. 931.
11. Whittow, op. cit., p. 371.
12. J. Butler, *Natural Disasters*, Richmond, Heinemann Educational Australia, 1978.
13. M. Islam, Report in *Natural Hazards*, op. cit.; White, op. cit., p. 19.
14. Whittow, op. cit., p. 371.
15. White, op. cit., p. 5.
16. Islam, op. cit., p. 27.
17. D. Coates, *Environmental Geology*, New York, John Wiley & Sons, 1981.
18. R. Bryson and T. Murray, *Climates of Hunger*, Madison, Wis., University of Wisconsin Press, 1977.
19. Whittow, op. cit., p. 27.

In the long run, it is only through appropriate physical planning, urban design, and building measures that it will be possible to offset the effects of severe natural hazards in a world of rapid urbanization and population.

Chapter 19
Settlement in Disaster Prone Regions

L. van Essche

The author, L. van Essche, is an architect planner with UNDRO specializing in disaster prevention and mitigation for housing and human affairs.

Reprinted from *UNDRO News*, May-June 1984.

The earthquake in the Erzurum region of Turkey in 1983 has, once again, raised the question of how we can prevent such events from resulting in major disasters. Beyond a certain threshold, the forces of nature are such that nothing can be done, short of moving out of the way of the threat altogether. Volcanic eruptions illustrate this most vividly. For the majority of natural hazards, however, much can be done in theory to control risk, not only by preparing to face emergencies, but also in planning and building settlements in a sounder manner or in safer locations than in the past.

Risk Management

Unfortunately, planning is a long-range activity highly vulnerable to conflicting priorities and demands, especially if these are economic. Buildings have relatively long economic lives ranging from 50 to 100 years; historical monuments and settlements and other cultural property are immutable. To move existing settlements of any significant size is, without exception, prohibitively expensive and unrealistic both in social and economic terms. In the end, one is left with fairly limited possibilities of modifying what exists, while calling the attention of decision makers to the potential consequences of prevailing hazards when the development is planned.

And yet so much more would probably be done if the risks of disaster were more clearly evaluated by architects, engineers, economists and planners, and more keenly appreciated by both the public and the authorities. In the long run, it is only through appropriate physical planning, urban design, and building measures that it will be possible to offset the effects of severe, natural hazards in a world of rapid urbanization and population growth.

Physical planning is less a problem of designing the layout and distribution of human activities than a problem of resolving the sectoral conflicts of development planning at the national and local levels. The purpose of disaster prevention, therefore, is not merely to identify the physical parameters of risk reduction. Perhaps, a more meaningful substitute for the term "Disaster Prevention" might indeed be "Risk Management." Preventing disasters from occurring altogether is, in many instances, neither technically nor economically feasible. Ultimately, society accepts a compromise between exposure to hazard and economic or social necessity. Such compromise may be expressed as that society's "acceptable level of risk." While setting an acceptable level of risk is essentially a political decision, it is nonetheless essential to understand its parameters, both in physical and socio-economic terms.

Definition of Risk

To avoid conflicts of nomenclature and to establish a set of terms for practical use which will be widely understood and accepted, definitions of the concept of risk and its constituent parts have been proposed by UNDRO for international use* :

- *Natural Hazard* meaning the probability of occurrence, within a specific period of time in a given area, of a potentially damaging natural phenomenon.

- *Vulnerability* meaning the degree of loss to a given element at risk or set of such elements resulting from the occurrence of a natural phenomenon of a given magnitude and expressed on a scale from 0 (no damage) to 1 (total loss).

- *Elements at risk* meaning the population, buildings and civil engineering works, economic activities, public services, utilities and infrastructure, etc., at risk in a given area.

- *Specific risk* meaning the expected degree of loss due to a particular natural phenomenon and as a function of both natural hazard and vulnerability.

- *Risk* meaning the probability of loss, i.e. the expected number of lives lost, persons injured, damage to property, and disruption of economic activity due to a particular natural phenomenon, and consequently the product of specific risk and elements at risk.

UNESCO, Habitat, other agencies of the U.N. system as well as a number of Member States, have used these definitions regularly in their scientific planning and decision making activities. All the artifacts of

---

* "Natural Disasters and Vulnerability Analysis," UNDRO, Geneva, July 1979.

man can be classified as elements at risk. They can be divided into different functional categories, and can further be categorized into structural systems which for the purpose of vulnerability assessment is essential.

In assessing the interaction between disasters and development, however, direct loss of function or investment is not the only disaster-related criterion to worry about. There are chains of secondary effects which in the long-run can lead to irreparable national economic damage: loss of production and income, loss of serviced land, deterioration of certain natural resources, pollution etc.

The rapid growth and spread of population in hazardous areas is rapidly contributing to the mounting costs of disasters in terms of lives lost and damage to property and investment. Most developing countries double their populations every 20 to 25 years (assuming national population growth rates of 2 percent to 3 percent), while the urban populations in these countries double every 12 to 15 years (assuming urban growth rates of 4 to 7 percent).

The rate of expansion of slums and squatter settlements around major urban agglomerations is even larger, growing at about twice the average urban rate. In settlements such as these there is a doubling of population every 5 to 7 years. Densities are usually very high: up to 100,000 persons per km^2 and more. Even the average densities for urban areas as a whole are high enough to cause concern.

Little Evidence of Firm Action to Reduce Disaster Risks

The problem of exposure to disaster risk among rural populations, however, should not be underestimated as experience notably in Turkey has shown. Although the population growth rate in rural areas is usually lower than the national average, due to rural urban migration, the scarcity of arable or developed land in many developing countries, combined with the fact that on the average more than 70 percent of total national populations are still rural, can create significant risks. Rural population densities can exceed 1,000 persons per km^2 in areas where rainfall and soil conditions limit the amount of arable land. Wherever rural populations are sedentary and engaged in agriculture or animal husbandry on hazardous land, the risk of substantial disaster cannot be ignored.

Thus, the list of potentially negative interactions between the built and the natural environments appears to grow longer with the passage of time. However, there is little evidence to suggest that a sufficiently large number of countries are taking firm action to reduce disaster risks substantially at all levels of development planning and programme implementation. The mere existence of technology, building codes, land-use regulations, and other provisions for risk reduction do not in themselves suffice. Risk management is of very much wider concern and implies a systematic approach both to the analysis and the control of all the factors liable to cause disasters. In short, there is a need to create hazard analysis and risk management techniques which will operate at all levels of planning, for which implementation can be assured through adequate legislative and administrative means.

Much work has been done in the earth sciences to define the physical characteristics of earthquakes, storms, floods, etc. Less has been done to carry the analysis one step further, i.e., to increase the basic understanding of how these natural phenomena, by their severity, can affect lives and property. It is necessary to estimate the casualty and damage potential of geophysical events on existing or future populations and properties at risk using whatever pertinent information is currently available since operational decisions must be made on a day-to-day basis.

Magnitude of Hazard Impact

The basic requirement is to understand and collect data on the interaction of four factors determining the magnitude of natural hazard impact:

- The first factor is the geographical pattern of the severity of the phenomenon;

- The second factor is the number, spatial distribution, and density of population and property exposed to the effects of the various natural hazards;

- The third factor is the vulnerability of the elements at risk when they are subjected to different frequency, intensity and distribution relationships of hazards;

- The final factor is the effect of local conditions in modifying the severity of the event at a given location. For example, as regards earthquakes, local ground conditions can markedly affect the severity of ground motion.

The spatial interactions of these factors determine the loss-producing potential of the natural hazard.

Estimating Future Losses

The interest of the third factor, *vulnerability* lies in the fact that it is the determinant of risk. It is therefore an important tool for economic planning, investment programming, physical planning, design and building. Vulnerability, it must be understood, refers to classes or categories of structures and not to individual structures. The degree of loss can be expressed as loss of function or loss of value. It measures the degree of damage due to past events. It estimates degrees of future loss to the existing building stock in probabilistic terms. It can even be used to estimate the loss potential of future development, given sound information on building methods. It is a commentary on the prevailing quality of design, materials, and workmanship. It measures, or at least evaluates, the extent to which building, land use and other codes are applied or require modification. It permits economists and engineers to carry out cost-benefit analyses of repair, reconstruction, and new development. In sum, it is essentially a tool for the economic analysis of risk reduction policies and programmes. The concept of vulnerability has been studied in detail since the Montenegro earthquake of 1979. Today it forms the planning basis for earthquake risk reduction in that region.

It should be emphasized that vulnerability assessments can prove to be unreliable and even severely misleading if they are based on observations following a single event. It is most important that data on damage be collected for as many past disasters as possible for a given type of hazard.

In the absence of clear information on vulnerability, existing building codes should be applied to design and the supervision of construction. It has been observed that even in the absence of hazard-specific codes, the mere observance of good building practice can reduce vulnerability by as much as 50 percent. In the absence of severe environmental or ecological consequences, siting need not systematically be a determining factor provided that the additional costs of structural resistance can be met. Siting only becomes an imperative criterion for risk reduction in the face of extreme hazards (such as landslides, rockfalls, direct faulting, frequent flooding, ground instability, etc.).

Where traditional building practices prevail, especially in rural areas, it is not always possible, nor even relevant, to impose official codes and regulations. Poverty, climate, and scarcity of suitable materials for earthquake-resistant construction may also combine to perpetuate or aggravate risks. For example, in parts of the Balkans, the Middle East, Central America and North Africa, traditional buildings consist of dry-stone or adobe walls and heavy tiled or flat mud-filled roofs. These buildings have the thermal capacity required to protect both man and beast from extreme diurnal and seasonal fluctuations of temperature. They often have great architectural merit, expressing the culture and traditions of a people. Unfortunately, their low resistance to shaking makes them extremely vulnerable to earthquakes. In cases such as these, the communities concerned can nevertheless benefit from technical assistance and training in "hazard resistant" methods of construction allied to traditional patterns of building. Professional groups of architects and engineers have emerged in a number of industrialized and developing countries, out of concern for the conservation of cultural heritage and the protection of deeply rooted traditions and ways of life. Instruction booklets have been compiled describing simple measures for strengthening traditional buildings.

Acceptable Risk

We may now ask "where does risk management fit in?" Risk is the convolution of hazard, vulnerability, and elements at risk. It is an expression of total expected loss due to a particular natural phenomenon. Risk thus is the output value of the estimation and interaction of several variables. It is, therefore, a tool for modelling disaster scenarios, from which risk management policies can be formulated. By creating varying scenarios of total expected losses, it becomes possible to evaluate different levels of risk *vis à vis* social, economic, and other criteria—and from this, to estimate locally acceptable levels of risk.

Acceptable risk is, of course, never explicitly stated. It exists implicitly in building codes and regulations. The richer the society, the lower the acceptable risk, the lower the threshold probability of exceedance admitted in the code. Knowing the life expectancy of buildings and the relative economic prosperity of a nation or community is therefore important in formulating a risk policy.

This consideration in turn affects the manner in which settlements are likely to evolve: there are intricate relationships between hazard, vulnerability, replacement costs, society and risk policies. These relationships must be examined regionally as much as locally. In so doing one enters the domain of pure planning—probably one of the more intuitive professions. It is extremely difficult to manipulate quantitative and qualitative parameters simultaneously, or to express one in terms of the other. For this reason, clear, explicit and quantifiable risk management policies will continue to elude us to some extent and for some time to come. It is probably important to remember that science, technology, and objective knowledge can only carry us to a certain point in the decision making process. Ultimately policy and planning decisions depend as much on human factors as they do on objective scientific criteria and technology. This is perhaps an important observation to make to scientists and engineers. Indeed, experience shows us that it is most important and urgent that "hard" scientific data on earthquake risk be adapted to the needs and language of planners, architects, and those responsible for the protection of the population in times of earthquake emergencies. In effect, the problem is that of the transfer of technology. UNDRO is working on this very question with a number of governments in the Balkan Region, notably in Yugoslavia. Following the 1979 earthquake, the revision of the physical development plans for the Socialist Republic of Montenegro has incorporated a re-evaluation of seismic risk and the development of a methodology to apply such evaluation to current physical planning activities.

Against a backdrop of many destructive natural disasters, the Caribbean island states established the Pan Caribbean Disaster Preparedness and Prevention Project (PCDPPP) in 1981 to develop the individual and collective capacity of the participating countries to mitigate the disastrous effects of natural hazards. To date, the Project has invested about U.S. $2 million in disaster preparedness and prevention.

Chapter 20
The Pan Caribbean Disaster Preparedness and Preservations Project

Reprinted from *UNDRO News*, March-April 1984.

Initially, the work programme during Phase I focussed on establishing contacts, through country visits, with government officers responsible for the various aspects of disaster management. In some countries the responsibility for disaster management was vested in a committee which met only once a year, providing few opportunities to review existing plans or develop more extensive ones. In such cases, efforts were made to have at least one government official designated as national disaster co-ordinator on a permanent basis with responsibility for promoting disaster preparedness planning and prevention activities. In addition, surveys were made to establish what facilities and plans existed and what were the priority needs for help from the PCDPPP. Progress at first was rather slow, but after contacts were made with senior government officials, and workshops and training seminars were successively held in different countries, the Project gained momentum. In all, during the first phase of the Project, 23 seminars, workshops, or country-specific training programmes were organized (or co-sponsored) on topics which included air safety and crash simulation, air traffic control, disaster preparedness in school curricula, emergency management procedures, essential drugs for disasters, first aid, hospital emergency plans, mass casualty management, meteorological aspects of preparedness, public awareness, water supply after disaster, and vulnerability of structures. In addition, the Project reviewed the needs of each country in emergency telecommunications equipment, organized the installation and use of emergency radios to link national emergency offices, and provided audio-visual equipment to those offices which were ready to make use of it.

Project Activities: Phase II

A second phase of the Project based on new funding commitments began in April 1983 and will run to the end of 1984. Several important changes took place at the beginning of Phase II. Firstly, in line with the policy of fostering regional self-reliance, the responsibility for administration of the Project passed from UNDRO to the CARICOM (Caribbean Community) Secretariat. A separate post was created for a Disaster Preparedness Specialist, appointed by UNDRO. Under Phase I, disaster preparedness had been one of the many duties of the Project Manager, and it was felt that, as a result, this important component had received insufficient attention. In addition, a Sanitary Engineer was appointed under WHO/PAHO supervision. All others posts and executing agency responsibilities remained unchanged. However, after the first Project Manager retired at the end of Phase I, the Health Adviser assumed the post in addition to health duties.

Activities under Phase II are intended essentially to broaden and deepen those initiated under Phase I. With an expert working full-time in preparedness, this component developed strongly. It includes three main types of activity, namely:

a) Country visits by the expert to identify priorities for and assist in the development of national emergency plans. During 1983, the expert visited seven island states of the region (Anguilla, British Virgin Islands, Dominica, Grenada, Montserrat, St. Kitts-Nevis, St. Lucia) and published reports on the level of their preparedness.

b) Regional or sub-regional workshops and seminars were held on topics including the role of the mass media, evacuation and emergency shelter, and the role of the security forces in disaster management. These workshops, each with 20 - 40 participants, provided opportunities for persons responsible for disaster preparedness in the different countries to receive instruction from experts and to exchange ideas and experiences, and hence to develop a stronger commitment and capacity to furnish mutual assistance during future disasters. Reports including presentations by consultants were prepared for several of the larger workshops.

c) The sending of Caribbean disaster preparedness officers to specialized training courses outside the region.

Prevention activities have included a workshop for the construction industry to illustrate and discuss earthquake vulnerability, the preparation of public awareness and education material on ways of mitigating risks, a field survey of the suitability of designated hurricane shelters in four countries (Antigua, Dominica, St. Kitts-Nevis and St. Vincent), and a feasibility study for an earthquake monitoring network in Haiti.

The main objective of the emergency communications programme has been to complete the island-to-island emergency radio links and, in consultation with WMO, to provide for country-to-country links between the primary meteorological offices of the region and each of the national emergency offices. During 1984 links will be provided within each country between essential services and the national emergency headquarters. With the assistance of ITU, the necessary equipment will shortly be installed in the first six countries (Barbados, Dominican Republic, Grenada, Haiti, St. Lucia, St. Vincent). The outstanding needs of other countries will be met later in the year. A regional seminar has been held on communication and control in emergencies.

Under the PAHO/WHO-administered component of the PCDPPP, during Phase II country visits have been made to the Cayman Islands, Jamaica, the Netherlands Antilles and St. Vincent to develop disaster preparedness activities within health training programmes. The first aid component (administered by LRCS in close co-operation with the British Red Cross) has continued training activities in this area.

Benefits of a Comprehensive Approach

Among UNDRO's many involvements in disaster preparedness and prevention, the Pan Caribbean Project has been considerably larger in scale, longer in duration, and more complex than any previously undertaken. This complexity can be attributed only in part to the large number of missions, workshops, contracts, financial transactions, and executing agencies involved. The real problems stemmed from bringing together as many as 28 participating countries and territories, as varied in size as in their respective levels of disaster preparedness, some situated as far apart as 3,000 km and with three different languages. In fact, in the early days of the project, there were times when it seemed that it would have been more appropriate and effective to promote a number of independent small-scale activities in different parts of the region.

However, as the Project evolved and matured, the benefits of a long and integrated sequence of activities with Caribbean-wide participation have become increasingly evident. Most parts of the region are subject to the same spectrum of natural hazards. The buildings and infrastructure, being similar in style, have similar vulnerability. Thus the lessons learnt from a recent disaster in one country are directly and fully applicable to others which may become victims of similar future events.

Likewise, a demonstration in one Caribbean country of the effectiveness of careful pre-disaster planning acts as a source of motivation and encouragement to other countries that are less advanced in this respect. The repeated contacts which have taken place between the relatively few people working in disaster management in each of the smaller Caribbean states could only be provided through a regional project of long duration, and these contacts have served to create and maintain a feeling of commitment to a common cause.

By the end of 1984, nearly US $2 million will have been invested in disaster preparedness and prevention through the PCDPPP. This is a considerable sum, yet it remains very small in comparison with the losses suffered in a single major disaster or, more significantly, with the amount by which these losses can be reduced through good pre-disaster planning. The PCDPPP has become a significant landmark in the history of disaster management in the Caribbean and points the way towards a comprehensive approach to the subject which could be of benefit to other developing regions.

The Pan Caribbean Disaster Preparedness and Preservation Project

The proposal for a regional project in disaster preparedness and prevention for the Caribbean island States developed mainly from the recommendations made at a seminar on Caribbean Disaster Preparedness held in St. Lucia in June 1979 and attended by over 150 participants including representatives of 22 Caribbean governments. Two months earlier, a violent volcanic eruption in St. Vincent had forced the evacuation of over 20,000 people from the northern half of the island. Even as the seminar was in progress, widespread flooding of western Jamaica rendered 35,000 homeless. Ten weeks after the seminar, the worst hurricane for several years devastated most of the island State of Dominica and large parts of the Dominican Republic, killing over 1,400 people, injuring 6,000, leaving more than 260,000 homeless, and causing damage estimated at $830 million.

It was against this backdrop of destructive natural disasters that the Caribbean island States endorsed the idea of a regional project in disaster preparedness and prevention. While recognizing their national responsibility to improve disaster preparedness measures, the Caribbean governments fully appreciated the need for mutual co-operation within the region as well as the necessity to tap expertise and specialized assistance from abroad.

The 1979 disasters illustrated the typical problems of disaster management, including the need to issue warnings widely and rapidly, the difficulties of moving many thousands of people quickly away from the most vulnerable areas, the importance of establishing evacuation centres and feeding programmes, co-ordination centres, and emergency communication systems, and of setting up damage assessment and reporting procedures. In the case of hurricanes especially, they demonstrated the urgent need to apply simple preventive measures such as anchoring roofs securely to buildings and providing strong shutters to glass windows, in particular for buildings intended as public shelters. These disasters also made it clear, especially in the smaller states where devastation from a single event may extend over the entire territory, that the provision of immediate assistance from neighbouring countries is critically important and much more effective if planned in advance.

Development of the Pan Caribbean Project

The events of 1979 led to a resolution adopted by the U.N. Economic Commission for Latin America and endorsed by the General Assembly in November 1979 that "the United Nations, and more particularly the Office of the United Nations Disaster Relief Co-ordinator, should study ways and means of setting up specific machinery to cope with the natural disasters that periodically occur in the Caribbean Basin."

A final endorsement of the need to improve disaster preparedness and prevention was added by the first hurricane of the 1980 season: one of the biggest of the century, it ripped through St. Lucia, southwestern Haiti and northern Jamaica leaving 250 dead, 205,000 homeless, 525,000 deprived of their normal source of food, and 530 million dollars of damage to property, infrastructure, and agriculture. This further reminder of the destructive powers of Nature was neither welcome nor necessary: UNDRO was already busy, in close co-operation with CARICOM, CIDA, EEC, ITU, LRCS, OECS,

UNEP, UK/BDD, USAID/OFDA, WHO/ PAHO and WMO* , assembling the "specific machinery" which a year later became the Pan Caribbean Disaster Preparedness and Prevention Project (PCDPPP).

Objectives, Scope and Co-ordination

The long-term objective of the PCDPPP, as stated in the 63-page Project Document, is to contribute to socio-economic development and environmental protection by developing the individual and collective capacity of the participating countries to mitigate the disastrous effects of natural hazards, and to cope efficiently with disasters when they occur.

Its immediate objectives are to promote and facilitate the adoption of preparedness and prevention measures at the national and regional levels, and in particular:

a) to help governments plan preparedness and prevention programmes based on existing threats and the impact of disasters on the development of the countries concerned. These include in particular the formulation of emergency plans, the setting up of relief co-ordination machinery, and the application of prevention measures;

b) to help governments implement preparedness and prevention programmes on the basis of priorities agreed upon and the availability of resources from within and outside the countries concerned. The fields covered include, but are not limited to, the training of personnel in all aspects of disaster prevention, preparedness and relief, warning systems, vulnerability analysis, land-use legislation, zoning laws, building techniques and codes, public information and restoration of natural resources so as to achieve maximum protection of the vulnerable population at minimum cost;

---

* Caribbean Community Secretariat (CARICOM), Canadian International Development Agency (CIDA), European Economic Community (EEC), International Telecommunication Union (ITU), League of Red Cross Societies (LRCS), Organization of Eastern Caribbean States (OECS), United Nations Environment Programme (UNEP), British Development Division (UK/BDD), US Agency for International Development—Office of Foreign Disaster Assistance (USAID/OFDA), World Health Organization—Pan American Health Organization (WHO/PAHO) and World Meteorological Organization (WMO).

c) to provide a regional "pool of expertise" for relief, co-ordinated by UNDRO whenever a disaster occurs anywhere in the region;

d) to periodically re-evaluate risks in the Caribbean on the basis of a new inventory of resources and progress made in disaster prevention and preparedness.

The geographic scope of the project includes all the island states and territories of the Caribbean (*shown on the accompanying map*) together with four adjacent mainland states (Belize, French Guyana, Guyana, Suriname) which for reasons of language and through other associations have close ties with the Caribbean island countries.

Co-ordination of the Project has developed in close consultation with governments, regional and international organizations, and funding agencies. It is an evolutionary process and new organizations are being included as awareness of the importance of disaster planning to development activities increases. Responsibility for monitoring the progress of the Project rests with the Project Management Committee, which is composed of representatives of the member countries and executing and funding agencies. Observers are invited from other agencies from which technical advice is received or which have programmes or interests related to disaster preparedness in the Caribbean. The Committee meets once every six months to review past activities and approve future work programmes, budget, and staff appointments.

Financial support for the project or assistance in kind has come from numerous countries and agencies. The largest contributors to date have been CIDA, the EEC and USAID/OFDA.

Project Activities: Phase I

The Project formally initiated its activities in September 1981 with the appointment of the Project Manager and other team members and the establishment of an office in Antigua to serve as Project Headquarters. The first phase ran for 18 months, ending in March 1983, the overall supervision of the Project during this period being provided by UNDRO. The staffing of the Project during this period included six full-time professional posts as follows (the seconding or appointing agency is indicated in brackets):

— Project Manager/Preparedness Specialist (UNDRO)
— First Aid Advisor (LRCS)
— Health Adviser (WHO/PAHO)
— Meteorology and Communications Adviser (British Development Division)
— Prevention Specialist (UNDRO)
— Red Cross Specialist (LRCS)

In addition to these full-time posts (not all of which were occupied for the full duration of Phase I), consultants in air safety, civil engineering, public awareness, school education, seismology, and telecommunications were appointed for periods ranging from a few days to several months. Support staff for the project included an administrative assistant, three secretaries and a clerk.

Selections from a policy paper of the U.S. Agency for International Development on:

INTERNATIONAL DISASTER ASSISTANCE

Following the Skopje, Yugoslavia earthquake of July 1963, the U.S. Government determined that a central authority was needed to coordinate disaster assistance offered to foreign governments and peoples. The next year the Foreign Disaster Relief Coordinator's Office was established within the Agency for International Development.

Over the next few years it became evident that immediate disaster relief, while necessary and humane, wasn't the entire answer, and that costs, damage and human suffering could be better reduced by helping disaster-prone countries prepare for the inevitable. In 1976, with an amended charter from Congress incorporating the preparedness element, the renamed Office of Foreign Disaster Assistance began encouraging disaster-prone countries to prepare for and become more self-sufficient in dealing with disasters. Preparedness alone, involving prediction and early warning, has greatly diminished the relief burden on the U.S. Government in several disaster-prone countries.

Overview

The AID Office of U.S. Foreign Disaster Assistance (OFDA) coordinates U.S. Government assistance with that of international agencies, other donor governments, and private and voluntary organizations. Its Director reports directly to the Administrator of

A.I.D., the President's Special Coordinator for International Disaster Assistance.

From 1964 to 1984, the United States Government has, through OFDA, provided emergency relief for 772 foreign disasters which have killed over 2 million people and seriously affected more than 751 million others. Through fiscal 1983, $6.3 billion was provided in relief by the international community, of which about one-half was provided by the United States—$2.4 billion by the Federal Government and $281.5 million by the private sector.

OFDA responds to requests for emergency assistance an average of 37 times a year. This office monitors another 40 situations which could become disastrous, develops early warning systems, and provides technical assistance to strengthen relief agencies in disaster-prone countries. A 24-hour response capability is maintained to rush life support goods and services to disaster victims anywhere in the world.

The Congress authorized foreign disaster relief in Chapter 9 of the Foreign Assistance Act of 1961, as amended, which provides for assistance:

A. to preserve life and minimize suffering by providing sufficient warning of natural events which cause disasters;

B. to foster self-sufficiency among disaster-prone nations by helping them achieve some measure of preparedness;

C. to alleviate suffering by providing rapid, appropriate response to requests for aid; and

D. to enhance recovery through rehabilitation programs.

Disaster Operating Policies

AID Handbook 8, "Foreign Disaster Assistance," is the operational guide for anticipating and responding to disasters in the host country. The following is a brief overview.

The Ambassador or Chief of Mission (CM) has primary responsibility for providing U.S. assistance in the event of a disaster in a host country. The Office of U.S. Foreign Disaster Assistance, AID, is responsible for coordinating all United States Government international disaster relief. OFDA staff is available 24 hours a day to assist the Mission in determining whether assistance should be provided, in selecting the most effective forms of assistance, and in rapidly supplying the required relief specialists and commodities.

Disaster-Related Technology

New technologies are continually being assessed for adaptation and application to disaster avoidance or mitigation and enhanced early

warning. The OFDA Director can use International Disaster Assistance
Account resources to incorporate these technologies in development
programs and projects.

Disaster Assistance Staffing

Response to a disaster may require rapid temporary additions to
the U.S. Country Team in the stricken country or OFDA in
Washington. OFDA will, if practical, deploy qualified officers and
contracted specialists to disaster sites.

It is important that Assistant Administrators and AID principal
officers at field posts give highest priority to temporary duty assignment
to the Country Team of qualified individuals requested by the OFDA
Director. Bureaus and Offices will temporarily detail to OFDA
previously designated individuals whose skills and experience qualify
them for specific tasks during relief operations, as requested by the
Director.

In order to enhance U.S. response to foreign disasters and improve
disaster planning in country and regional development programs and
projects:

- disaster assistance (preparedness and relief) units will be
  incorporated in training programs for in-service AID employees
  and for International Development Interns;

- Washington training programs for selected International
  Development Interns will include rotational assignments in
  OFDA; and

- OFDA will conduct orientation sessions in disaster assistance for
  Washington employees. Employees should attend to help meet
  the needs of their bureaus in disaster management.

Lessons Learned Information System

The "Lessons Learned Information System" is a tool used to avoid
the mistakes of the past and forms the basis for much of OFDA's
operating policy. Hundreds of "lessons" from experience are routinely
referenced for policy and procedural guidance. These range from the
general (U.S. aid should often be self-contained, i.e., that it doesn't
place additional burdens on already strained host country resources), to
the specific (ship can openers with canned foods).

Source: *A.I.D. Policy Paper: International Disaster Assistance.* Issued
by Bureau for Program and Policy Coordination, U.S. Agency
for International Development, Washington, D.C. 20523, May
1985

The school is the largest building to be found in most rural settlements throughout the world. During the day, it houses most of the younger generation on which the future of every community depends. In a natural disaster therefore, the school has to survive since an entire generation in it may be at risk. Moreover, the school is usually the only building in a village whose design and construction may be controlled by the government. It is thus a building which can, if the government so decides, be made safe for children and which could, if government so wished, be designed as a short term, community refuge during and immediately after a disaster.

Chapter 21
School Buildings and Natural Disasters

D.J. Vickery

D.J. Vickery is an Educational Building Consultant, Langrick, United Kingdom.

This article is excerpted from a preparatory study for Unesco by D.J. Vickery, an educational building consultant, Langrick, United Kingdom, dated December 1980, contract #206 922.

Few governments in countries vulnerable to natural disasters have an adequate perception of the risks to schools. The problem is one of resources, of which the financial is not the most intractable. Lack of skilled designers and trained inspectors, little guidance from codes of practice and regulations, and a paucity of design material are but a few of the difficulties. Where these have been partly overcome, it is usually the urban schools that benefit while rural buildings continue to be constructed conventionally and are thus unlikely to resist a severe disaster. This is despite the fact that the vast majority of schools in vulnerable countries are in the rural areas, for that is where some 80 percent of the population lives.

It is simple enough to identify the countries of the world at risk; it is very much more difficult and, indeed, delicate, to identify the extent to which regulations governing earthquake-resistant school design are mandatory in the countries where they exist. The literature of disasters, which is now very extensive indeed, is mainly concerned with the physical and human aspects of the immediate events and it is rare to find material that deals thoroughly with the periods in between. Yet it is precisely these periods which, in the end, are of such importance. **School construction is part of the long-term planning of a country.** Programmes of construction are not usually linked to disasters but are part of the normal development of education. Disasters, in this context, are rarely seen as a matter of priority and, even when the risk is considered and reflected in new designs, only rarely is the action documented. Mexico and Peru are among the very few countries which are exceptions to this state of affairs.

The Importance of the School Building

A natural disaster comprises two components, *cause* and *effect* (on lives and property). There are, as far as is known, no natural phenomena or "causes" of disasters that uniquely affect school buildings. Strong cyclones, floods, and earth tremors affect all buildings in the area of occurrence. The "effects" of these phenomena on the nature of the disaster in relation to schools is also only infrequently unique. Buildings that have shape, construction, and internal space arrangements similar to schools, such as rural hospitals, are likely to suffer similar effects in respect of damage and destruction.

There are, however, some aspects of natural disasters which are uniquely related to school buildings. The first is that of their location.

Schools are generally distributed with the population and there is usually a school in every large village in the rural areas. The school is, moreover, usually the largest of the village buildings. Thus, in places subject to recurring disaster, a school which is designed to be disaster-resistant may provide the focus for relief activities and even temporary housing for those injured and uninjured and whose accommodation was unable to withstand the force of the phenomenon—whatever it may have been.

Secondly, school building, when they are occupied during the school day, have within them a concentration of human beings the density of which is matched only by buildings designed for public performances, such as cinemas. Thus, while a disaster to a dwelling may injure or kill an entire family, a disaster to an occupied school could kill or injure the entire younger generation from a village and the area around it.

The case for the design and construction of disaster-resistant schools is thus, on both counts, very strong indeed.

Case Studies

The effects on school buildings of a number of specific natural disasters are described below. Each case is dealt with very briefly indeed for the literature on the general subject of buildings is prolific and all that is required here is specific focus on the educational building aspect. The cases have been drawn at random from the thousands of reported and describe disasters to school buildings in Asia, Latin America, and Europe.

The Peruvian Earthquake of 31 May 1970

This was by far the most destructive earthquake recorded in the western hemisphere. Of intensity IX along the coast of Peru, it affected an area of some 83,500 square km, much of which was mountainous. The damage was extensive and included the destruction of 186,000 houses and a very large number of schools, with 54,000 people killed and 150,000 injured. The earthquake also triggered an avalanche of ice, rock, and mud in the mountains which buried two towns, killing 20,000 people. [1]

School buildings in Peru are constructed, depending on their location, in three different ways:

- *Quincha* construction, used in the more remote areas, consists of vertical poles interwoven with thin branches or canes. The roof is equally light and of similar materials. Flexible and light, quincha probably resisted the earthquake better than the more common and heavier forms of construction.

- *Adobe* construction is used in most rural areas and, were it not for earthquakes, would be durable and thermally comfortable. Adobe is sun-dried earth. In Peru it takes the form of either bricks or mud which is packed between boards until it is dry. Adobe walls are always plastered with mud on both sides. The roofs commonly found on schools with adobe walls are of eucalyptus poles overlaid by boards or reeds and covered with heavy clay tiles.

- Urban schools as well as those in the more accessible rural areas are constructed with reinforced concrete columns between which a filling of either brick or concrete block walling is built. The roofs are commonly of corrugated galvanized iron sheets on timber rafters, although reinforced concrete roofs are occasionally found in the more affluent communities.

The effects of the earthquake on these three forms of construction were, as might be expected, somewhat different. The quincha buildings were shaken but not seriously damaged unless they happened to be in the path of the avalanche or landslide. The adobe schools were more seriously damaged. Tiles slipped and fell from the roofs, walls bulged outwards, cracking appeared around doors and windows, and at the junctions of one wall with another or with the roof there was often total separation. New adobe buildings, it was noted, suffered a little less damage than old. The schools constructed with reinforced concrete columns were also often seriously damaged. The panel walls split off from the columns and collapsed while the tops of the columns cracked and the concrete spalled from the reinforcement. The total damage to the stock of schools in Peru was such as to make a review of school building design a matter of priority before reconstruction started.

An Afghan Earthquake Sequence

The Peruvian earthquake is an example of the sort of tremor that produces widespread disaster and loss of life. There are, however, many recorded tremors which attract less attention yet cause damage that increases the risk to school buildings. A typical earthquake sequence in Afghanistan is used to illustrate this particular problem.

In the year 1974 there occurred some 12 tremors of intensity ranging from II to VI in the eastern part of Afghanistan. No deaths, injury to persons, or damage to property were recorded. Yet in many of the small, four-classroom schools in the rural areas, there was good evidence of the tremors.

Typically, schools in the eastern part of Afghanistan are constructed either of brick or stone in mud mortar or, more commonly, sun-burned bricks or balls of dried mud set in a mud mortar. This material is used to make walls up to one metre thick on a foundation of stones set in mud mortar. The roofs are of poplar poles on which are laid boards or bundles or rushes. On top of the roof some 40 to 50 cm of mud made from specially selected earth is carefully trampled and then smoothed to a fine finish. Because of the scarcity of wood, windows and doors are usually small and often without frames. The characteristic of this construction is best described as "massive." However, this is not of great importance since the schools are closed in the long and bitterly cold winter months while the spring and autumn classes are often outside in the warm sun.

The earthquakes of 1974 gave these schools a thorough shaking. Although in almost all cases, the buildings remained structurally intact (the walls stood more or less upright and the roofs did not generally collapse), there was however, considerable minor damage. In many of the schools, cracking occurred at wall junctions and around most window and door openings. Substantial areas of mud plaster fell off, leaving the mud bricks or stones in mud exposed to the weather, and dust and mud was frequently brought down from the roofs.

Thus, while there was no collapse, most buildings were seriously weakened. In an area such as Afghanistan where there are many tremors throughout the year, this weakening process is almost continuous and school buildings become increasingly dangerous to use.

It will be recalled that in the Peruvian earthquake briefly described above, the older adobe buildings suffered more damage than the newer buildings. The Afghan earthquake sequence discussed here provides the reason for this—progressive weakening caused by low intensity tremors. The real difficulty in such a situation is the improbability of schools in the remoter, rural areas being inspected, repaired, and strengthened against subsequent earthquakes of strong intensity.

The Bangladesh Cyclone of 12-13 November 1970

At the time of this cyclone, much of the heavily indented coast of Bangladesh was protected by some 3,000 miles of earth wall about four or five metres high, two metres wide at the top, and sloped on both sides.[2] In addition, an elaborate warning system had been set up with Swedish assistance. Every local official in coastal areas was provided with a small radio to receive storm warnings, while flares and other visual signals were also available and an evacuation plan existed. Yet, familiarity with strong cyclones and, worse, with cyclones that had passed nearby but not over the district, meant that on 12 November most people went about their business as normal, including many fishermen who put to sea despite the warning signals that the sea itself offered.

The cyclone struck the coast towards the east of the country, slightly above the port of Chittagong and at the very head of the Bay of Bengal. High, spring tides and three great rivers in flood—the Padma, Ganges, and Brahmaputra—established the worst possible conditions.

The atmospheric pressure when the cyclone struck the coast was 986 mb, raising the sea 27 cm above mean sea level. The spring tide was estimated at 3 m above sea level and the cyclone brought 250 mm of rain in 24 hours. The land was already under the normal and beneficial flood waters of the three rivers, an annual event which deposits rich silt over the rice fields and encourages farmers to continue to live in the area despite the other risks. Thus, the rise in sea level was of the order of 5 to 6 metres and the existing earth wall was not high enough to keep back the waters brought by the cyclone. The surge of water, carried along at about 25 km per hour as the cyclone moved northeastwards, swept the wall away completely in many places. Many of the inhabited islands in the delta area were under 5 m of water and mainland districts were inundated for many kilometres inland. Where the wall remained intact after the surge, it prevented the waters running back into the sea and fierce winds whipped up large waves on what had become an inland sea. A 10,000 square km area was affected, 90 percent of the cattle were drowned, and property, houses, and crops were virtually totally lost. Over 4,000 educational institutions were damaged, many of them beyond repair.

School buildings in Bangladesh at that time were of five classrooms in a row, built of brickwork with piers at about 3 metres, centre to centre, and with a reinforced concrete or galvanized corrugated iron roof. Floors too were of brick, covered with a thin layer of cement. The effects of the cyclone on these buildings were dramatic. The force of the wind blew out windows, wooden shutters, and even window frames; the pressure of water washing on poor brickwork weakened it and the subsequent waves and strong winds caused partial collapse; the concrete roofs, many with reinforcement corroded over the years by warm salt air, collapsed progressively while the metal roofs were blown off; furniture, books, and other equipment were later found in a sea of mud.

The Dominican Republic and Hurricane David

On 31 August 1979, hurricane David swept over the Dominican Republic on its course westward.[3] At least 1,100 people were killed, 3,000 injured, and about one quarter of a million people were rendered homeless. Winds of 240 km per hour were recorded and rainfall averaging 300 mm fell over the country during the day.

Of the schools, 330 were totally destroyed, 250 seriously damaged, and a further 1,200 affected. The hurricane similarly affected other islands of the Caribbean that lay in its path—Dominica, Puerto Rico, Barbados, St. Vincent, St. Lucia, Martinique, and the Bahamas. After ravaging the coast of the United States, it finally, eleven days later, weakened over eastern Canada.

Of particular interest in the immediate post-cyclone period was the report by the Unesco mission to the Dominican Republic of the heavy damage caused to schools by the homeless that used them as places of refuge. Furniture was broken up to provide fuel for cooking and this, together with other damage, was estimated to cost some 20 percent of the final bill for repair.

The Earthquake of 6 May 1976 at Gemona di Friuli, Italy

The earthquake of magnitude 6.5 that occurred at Gemona di Friuli in northwest Italy in 1976 resulted in 965 deaths, 2,286 injured, and the total collapse of 41 schools. In addition, 45 schools were seriously damaged and 33 damaged slightly.[4] It was fortunate that the shock occurred at 9 p.m.; otherwise, the schools would have been the scene of mass death of children. The enrollment of children of school-going age was some 70,000. As it was, 70 children of school-going age were killed. Had they all been at school, considering the proportion of schools that collapsed, some 20,000 children might have been affected.

The schools in the area subject to the tremors were broadly of two types of construction. Those built early in the century consisted of two floors and had heavy masonry walls, wooden floors on wooden beams, and wooden roofs covered with clay tiles. Buildings of this type were almost totally destroyed, even at places well away from the epicentre of the earthquake. The more modern schools built during the past 40 years were similar in construction to the older buildings except that floors and sometimes roofs were of reinforced concrete. These newer schools suffered severe damage to the extent that either they could not be repaired or repaired only at a very high cost.

Strangely, the Gemona di Friuli area, despite its well documented seismic history of more than 800 years, was not officially classified as "seismic" and the regulations for earthquake resistant design were not applied to the schools. Even if there had been an attempt to design newer schools to resist earthquakes, there would still have remained a large number of older schools that would have been dangerous. The experience of the Gemona di Friuli earthquake is of particular interest for it highlights the need not only to design new schools to be earthquake resistant, but also, as was discussed in the Afghan case above, the need to examine the stock of existing schools for safety and, if necessary, to increase their resistance. It is also evident that, although Italy is a country well known for some of its modern buildings and the home of structural engineers some of whose names are world famous, their skills seem not to have spread beyond the large towns, leaving the more remote and rural areas with schools which are both traditional in character and dangerous in earthquakes.

Identifying Common Problems

These case studies are drawn from a very large number on which comprehensive reports are available. They are sufficiently typical in respect of school buildings to lend themselves to identification of some very common problems.

The first fact that is evident concerns the so-called marginalization syndrome. Peru, Afghanistan, Bangladesh, the Caribbean islands, and

Gemona di Friuli are places where, despite the very real risks of loss of life, the population is always likely to remain. The main reasons for this are that there is nowhere else to go and that in some of the cases cited, notably Bangladesh, the land is so rich that it would always attract farmers willing to risk the occurrence of a natural disaster.

The conclusion to be drawn from this is that it is absolutely essential that school buildings in all these places be designed and constructed to resist natural disasters.

This statement is by no means trite. In none of the cases cited were the schools designed against the natural disasters that could be expected in the countries concerned. Happily in Peru, this situation was swiftly amended and a programme of earthquake-resistant school construction commenced very quickly after the event of May 1970.

The second point that emerges from the case studies is the need to inspect and strengthen the older stock of school buildings in all countries where there is a risk of natural disasters. All too often attention is paid to improving the design of new buildings while the old stock is left to deteriorate. There is no cynicism in the suggestion that most architects and politicians would find it more exciting, respectively, to design and declare open a new school than to repair an older building. The stock of old buildings in most countries is far larger than that of the new, and the risks correspondingly greater in the event of an earthquake or cyclone.

The third point of importance in the case studies concerns the use of school buildings as places of refuge after disaster. The Dominican Republic experience is important in illustrating the need to design schools for this function. Indeed, in Bangladesh, in a cyclone prior to that of 1970, the people of villages near Chittagong fled to community centres which had actually been constructed with this dual function in mind. In the Andhra cyclone people fled to what were thought to be safe buildings but which subsequently collapsed. The need for refuges and the suitability of schools for this purpose needs thus to be considered.

Conclusions

This study suggests that at the technical level, the eventual production of disaster-resistant schools will depend: on the introduction in many countries of Codes of Practice and regulations for both urban and rural situations; on measures to ensure compliance with these regulations in all countries; on the training of architects, structural engineers, technicians, and builders in general; and on increased awareness in the offices of the construction agencies of the risk of natural disaster and its implications for school buildings.

There is such a large stock of existing buildings which are highly dangerous that the cost of any measures to strengthen them could not be met by most governments. In some countries, almost all the schools in the rural areas are at risk. One very practical measure that is adopted, for reasons of climate rather than safety, is to use the building as little as possible. Closed in the winter and with the children outside in the warm sun during chilly spring and late autumn, thousands of schools could collapse without hurting anyone. The educational planner, in assessing risks, will inevitably take note of the fact that when holidays, weekends, and periods in the spring and summer are added up, the use of the average rural school as a percentage of the 365 days in every year is very low indeed and the risk of collapse on the children correspondingly light. Such a view would be far from cynical for it is at *risk* that the planner would be looking. If the risk is thought to be high, then the problem of financing strengthening of existing schools has to be faced.

The second problem that will follow is that of making an estimate of the number of schools that need strengthening and the amount of work to be done on an average school. In this, the work of Testa and Habibzadeh[5] in Iran is of considerable assistance. They have developed a method of sample surveying educational facilities which includes, as a major feature, the development of standards and the measurement of the state of maintenance against the standards which enables a global view of the needs of the country as a whole to be assessed.

The principal agency concerned with any disaster is, however, always the government of the country in which it has taken place. It is thus primarily incumbent on governments to establish guidelines concerning all measures necessary to cope with natural disasters. Furthermore, governments must not only initiate satisfactory prevention policies, but also make public opinion aware of their importance. External agencies are able, at best, to offer consultative services to assist governments in improving preparedness for disaster prevention and in taking the essential operational measures.

NOTES

1. M. Cangiano, *Peru: Construcciones escolares*, Paris, Unesco, 1972.
2. Asian Regional Institute for School Building Research. *East Pakistan's primary schools.* Technical Notes no. 4, Colombo, the Institute, 1970.
3. Unesco. *Dominican Republic: Report of an interdisciplinary mission to evaluate the damage caused by hurricane "David" and the "tormenta," "Frederick" and to suggest possible immediate and longer-term action to the Directorate of Education, Science and Culture.* Paris, Unesco, 1979.
4. Unesco. *The Gemona di Fruili earthquake of 6 May 1976.* Paris, Unesco, 1976.
5. Institute for Research and Planning in Science and Education. *Sample survey of educational facilities in Iran* by Carlo Testa and Suzan Habibzadeh, Teheran, 1973.

TO DELVE MORE DEEPLY

Arya, A.S., et al. *Influence of natural disasters (earthquakes) on educational facilities.* Final report of a study. Roorkee, School of Research and Training in Earthquake Engineering, University of Roorkee, 1977.
Building Research Station, U.K. *Model regulations for small buildings in earthquake and hurricane areas.* Tropical Building Legislation, Garston, The Station, 1966.
Daldy, A.F. *Small building in earthquake areas.* H.M.S.O., 1972.
Fournier D'Albe, E.M. "Earthquakes: Avoidable disasters." Impact of Science on Society 16, No. 3 (1966), pp. 189-202.
International Association for Earthquake Engineering. *Earthquake resistant regulations: A world survey.* Tokyo, The Association for Science Documents Information, 1973.
Refauste, N.J. and Marshall, R.D. *FY 74 progress report on design criteria and methodology for construction of low-rise buildings to resist typhoons and hurricanes.* Prepared for the Office of Science and Technology, Washington, D.C., A.I.D., 1974.
Sinnamon, I.E. *Natural disasters and educational building design: An introductory review and annotated bibliography for the Asian region. Education Building Report 4.* Bangkok, Unesco, 1976.

Accounts of relief operations in many recent major disasters—Skopje in 1963, Pakistan in 1970, southern Italy in 1980—reveal the shocking waste, scandals, delays of uncoordinated efforts. A technologically efficient and timely response to disaster requires preplanning, stockpiling, a clear command structure and speedy communications, perhaps only possible when nations collaborate in an international rescue organization.

Chapter 22
Needed: An International Rescue Organization

Anthony R. Michaelis

Anthony R. Michaelis is the editor of Interdisciplinary Science Reviews *(London), a quarterly journal he founded six years ago. Committed to the communication of science, he has also been editor of* Discovery *and the science correspondent of the London* Daily Telegraph. *He has travelled very widely for his work and is proud to include the South Pole as one of the many unusual places amongst his date-lines. For many years he has been deeply concerned about the ineffectiveness of disaster prevention.*

It is certain that thousands, probably tens of thousands and possibly hundreds of thousands of men, women and children will die needlessly in 1982. Their deaths will not only be due to nature's violent forces, earthquakes, cyclones, floods and tsunami which will inevitably strike their home, but also because relief for their desperate plight will be too little, too late and of the wrong kind. This is a situation that our society must not accept. Furthermore—and this is the most ugly aspect of this complex problem—vast fortunes are frequently made out of disasters through inefficiency, greed, and the results of bureaucracy. This scandal is well summed up by a remark made recently by a well-qualified cynic. "Every earthquake makes a millionaire; big ones make two or three."

Natural disasters have always occurred on our planet, and will always continue, although during its last million years of history their number and severity must have somewhat decreased. To these natural catastrophes have in recent years been added man-made technological disasters, still small and often local, yet in the foreseeable future likely to rival those due to natural causes.

In the last 100 years, 9 million people have died from floods, 1 million from earthquakes, and 1 million from hurricanes, typhoons and cyclones. Untold additional millions died from diseases, the direct result of these disasters, and from catastrophic droughts. Yet during these last 100 years, the world population was only a small part of what it is today. Now an entirely new approach to disaster rescue, which is outlined here, is urgently needed.

Some Suggested Definitions

Accidents: 1-1,000 people dead, or in imminent danger of death.
Disasters: 1,000-1 million people dead, or in imminent danger of death.
Catastrophes: More than 1 million people dead, or in imminent danger of death.

Disaster Relief Calls for Wide Collaboration

Repeated pleas for an international rescue organization to stockpile, transport, and distribute relief fairly to disaster victims have so far failed, mainly for political reasons. Although voluntary organizations have each year collected and distributed millions in cash and gifts, their resources, even worldwide, are quite insufficient. Aerial photographic reconnaissance, emergency satellite communications, helicopter evacuation, mobile field hospitals, plastic igloos for housing survivors, pipelines for drinking-water, and large computer-controlled strategic stockpiles of food, blankets, and tents are only some of the modern rescue services which, in this age of advanced technology, should be available automatically for all disasters. Although most countries will accept disaster relief when it comes from reputable voluntary organizations, as such help presents no reflection on their own capacity for dealing with the emergency, relief from foreign governments may be accepted only grudgingly and sometimes diverted for political reasons, never reaching the victims at all.

Scientists, engineers, and doctors have a grave responsibility for efficient disaster relief. Their research has created the tools that should be used. All too often these lie idle, thousands of kilometres away from where they are desperately needed to alleviate suffering and so save lives. Unless and until this appalling situation is changed, they bear as much responsibility as the governments which send token relief for self-advertisement and those officials of the recipient countries who divert help, either for political reasons, or to line their own pockets.

Our planet is a restless one, not dead like the moon; there are 3,000 earthquakes a day and about 44,000 thunderstorms every 24 hours. Two factors have made disasters worse and brought them forcefully to our notice. The ever increasing speed of the population explosion means that present and future disasters will inevitably take a correspondingly greater toll of human life. Today knowledge of a disaster is flashed within minutes around the globe, and within hours detailed pictures appear on the television screens of hundreds of millions of viewers.

The need to consider major rescue operations from an international point of view has been greatly strengthened in recent decades. Scientific advances in both seismology and meteorology now allow us with a fair degree of accuracy to predict the location of future earthquakes and of the great circular winds. *Where*, but not yet *when*, is the present state of disaster prediction. A very large number of seismographs are distributed all over our planet and continuously monitored. Similarly satellite photographs of our atmosphere from above give us a constant picture of major turbulences, where they build up and in what direction they move. These pictures, and their rapid analysis have undoubtedly saved more lives than any other disaster-prevention technique. Although earthquakes have often small foreshocks, these may be followed by major disturbances of the earth's crust so shortly afterwards that no effective warning can yet be given. Only by close international collaboration can prediction be further strengthened, warnings issued in time, and when disaster strikes, rescue operations be organized on an efficient, modern, and technologically adequate scale.

The Heavy Toll of Past Mistakes

If any disaster is subjected to closer scrutiny—and a disaster is here defined as 1,000 to 1 million people dead or in imminent danger of death—the mistakes are uncountable; the circulars published by the Red Cross in Geneva record these only too abundantly. Undoubtedly, worst of all was the mismanagement which followed the cyclone and tidal wave disaster which devastated what was then East Pakistan on 12/13 November 1970. An estimated 1 million people lost their lives.

Some examples of mistakes and neglect follow:

The Earthquake in Iran 1 September 1962

There was extensive damage over a large area, 200 kilometres west of Tehran. Although massive help came from all over the world—a total of $2 million was collected by the Red Cross—a month later, on 9 October, the disaster victims were still 4,000 tents short. These were finally air-lifted by the United States Air Force.

The Earthquake at Skopje, Yugoslavia, 26 July 1963

Over 1,000 people lost their lives, 3,000 were injured, 170,000 were homeless. The *Final Report* of the Red Cross on this disaster states: "Due to the destruction of all communications with Skopje it was difficult to obtain precise information on the actual situation in the city after the earthquake and a listing of the most urgent needs." Within a week, the situation had completely changed: "Such a large quantity of relief supplies had reached Yugoslavia that a recommendation was circulated that for the time being no further shipments should be sent forward."

Waste, frustration, and the additional loss of life, or at a minimum hunger, thirst, and disease, are the obvious consequences of this type of situation, only too typical of many disaster reports. Communications are inevitably destroyed in all large disasters. After aerial photographic reconnaissance, communications with survivors or with its own experts parachuted onto the scene would have highest priority by an international rescue organization.

The Floods in Tunisia, September/October 1969

There were 540 dead, 261,000 homeless, 70,000 homes destroyed, caused by successive torrential rainstorms. The Red Cross observed:

"Two months after the disaster, part of the territory is still being provisioned by helicopters. Tents, blankets, clothing, footwear, and food have been distributed to the homeless, but in still insufficient quantities. Thousands of tents, tens of thousands of blankets, tons of clothing and footwear, especially for children, cooking utensils and heating appliances are still lacking. The approaching winter can only aggravate the conditions; sugar and baby foods are needed.[1]

This was the "forgotten flood," when it proved extremely difficult to rouse public interest. The Tunisian Air Force worked desperately with a few helicopters of its own, and some borrowed from the United States Air Force.

The Earthquakes in Iran, 31 August and 1 September 1968

Here there were 10,000 people killed, 4,000 injured and 15,000 homes destroyed. One report stated:

Bulldozers were ordered to level the ruins, leaving the bodies of the dead under them for ever. The extremely heavy casualties were blamed on the still unsuitable building practices. Indeed thousands of lives might have been saved had other types of construction been used, but mud and timber have been the basic building materials in Iran for centuries.[2]

This report also attributed the ineffectiveness of these operations to the following problems: initial failure of communications; inadequate maps and insufficient information on the location of villages affected; absence of roads and inability to maintain airstrips; lack of helicopters and airlift support; reluctance to take relief materials to villages and hamlets located in the farther reaches of the mountain areas and to relatively inaccessible areas.[3]

The Earthquake in Peru, 31 May 1970

In this earthquake there were 70,000 people killed, 50,000 injured and 200,000 dwellings destroyed. The earthquake provoked the fall of a gigantic cornice of ice from the upper glaciers of Huascaran, producing an avalanche of 80 million tonnes. It raced at a speed of 400 km/h down the valleys, burying whole towns and many villages. It was described by scientists as the single geological phenomenon of greatest magnitude in recorded history.

It was the usual story of far too little, far too late, although eventually aid reached the survivors:

"News of the scope of the disaster gradually started to come in by radio and other means. It was only 24 hours after the tragedy that reports came through of the total destruction of towns. . . .Still now (four and a half months after the earthquake) a large number of hamlets can only be reached by mules and in certain cases only on foot carrying relief supplies in sacks. Given to the Peruvian Air Force, 5,270 (only!) parcels were dropped by parachute. The total number of zinc sheets distributed was estimated to reach 65,000, used in the villages for roofing."[4]

Nevertheless, three important innovations in rescue work were tried. First, a special instrument aircraft belonging to NASA, the American space agency, overflew the area affected and handed the photographs to the Peruvian authorities, two months and six days after the disaster! Secondly, 500 plastic foam igloos, each providing shelter for a family with seven beds, were donated by the German Red Cross. They have excellent heat insulation and will last for several years, but they are still fairly expensive, costing $200 each. Thirdly, the Swedish Catastrophe Force of sixty-two engineers and technicians went into action for the first time, although only after lengthy delays. After their initial offer of assistance, it took two months for a tripartite agreement to be negotiated and signed between the Governments of Sweden and Peru and the United Nations. It took another month and a half before the first echelon reached Peru itself. Three mobile workshops accompanied the unit, which finally proved a great success.

There can be no doubt that thousands of lives could have been saved had rescue and relief reached the isolated villages by air, as it would have done had international rescue arrangements been in existence.

The Cyclone and Tidal Wave in East Pakistan, 12/13 November 1970

There were an estimated 1 million dead, the destruction of homes uncounted. If this was one of the worst natural disasters yet recorded, it was also the worst example of inefficient rescue operations. For several weeks afterwards, it was estimated that about 1,000 people were dying a day, simply because there was no official machinery to get to them the tons of supplies accumulating on and near Dacca airport. For example, a Boeing 707 of the German Air Force was the first to bring rice, blankets and drugs to Dacca, travelling 16,000 kilometres in mere hours, but these goods could not reach the needy a few miles away. They were moved to an open field next to the airport and then found their way onto the black market.

Neither the Pakistan Government, the international aid organizations, nor the foreign armed services were under a single directorate controlling all rescue operations. They were unable to control the movement of men, materials, and messages within the disaster area and could not secure the relevant expertise. These are the three most important elements in all rescue operations after a disaster, according to Lord Robens.

Six major cyclone disasters have hit East Pakistan in ten years; once in 1960, twice in 1961, again in May 1963, and in 1965 there were 36,000 people killed. In November 1970, the estimated deathroll was 1 million. There was thus plenty of warning that nature would strike again, and the Red Cross had purchased and erected a special radar system for storm detection. Yet a few days before the disaster on Friday, 13 November, it had been altered and was out of action. Another warning had however come from satellite cloud pictures of the tropical storm Opal. But because of lack of local communications, this could not be passed on to the people in greatest danger. Another report about the failure of the radar warning states that only three weeks earlier a smaller cyclone, killing a mere 300, had struck the same area and that then the warning system worked perfectly. Most of the villagers had however been left unaffected, and when the second warning came, it was to them another cry of "Wolf!" They did not bother to seek out their safety positions. Had they done so, 500,000 people might have been saved.

The sending of cash donations to countries afflicted by a natural disaster is a much debated question. It may help to start up a hard-hit local economy but, human nature being what it is, it might also easily lead to profiteering.

As so often happens with voluntary gifts for disaster relief, many were completely useless. Tins of apple sauce, jars of honey, woollen socks, greatcoats and tents too difficult to erect took up much valuable air-cargo space, when water-distillation units, collapsible rubber dinghies, even simple swim vests, should have reached the scene.

Only when modern technological tools were introduced, for example, the many inflatable life-boats donated by the Royal National Life-Boat Institution and the warships *Intrepid* and *Triumph*, did real relief begin. The lack of helicopters will always remain one of the greatest scandals during the East Pakistan floods. Apparently fifty helicopters of the Pakistan Air Force remained in their western territories, only one local and three from the Federal Republic of Germany being available during the early days.

Cyclone Tracy, Darwin, Australia, 25 December 1974

In Darwin, 50 persons were killed, with every building in the city destroyed. Darwin had known previous cyclones and had been ruined before, in 1878, 1897, 1917, 1937 and in 1942, when Japanese bombers killed 243 persons. To cope with the aftermath of Cyclone Tracy, General Alan B. Stretton was placed in absolute command and succeeded in re-establishing the foundations for a new city. He identified the lessons to be learned from this cyclone as follows: apathy of the potential victims and responsible authorities before the cyclone; breakdown of essential communications; failure of local broadcasting stations; the convergence of unwanted sightseers after the disaster; need for enabling legislation to cope with emergency situations; need for co-ordinating voluntary relief supplies; adequate facilities to trace disaster victims; need for national pool of essential disaster-relief supplies; need for centralized control during disaster-relief operations.[5]

As a result of his recommendations, the government set up the Australian Counter-Disaster College at Macedon, Victoria, which is briefly discussed below.

The Earthquake in Southern Italy, 23 November 1980

About 5,000 were killed, several villages being completely destroyed, with widespread damage and devastation, including Naples. About 250,000 people were without shelter; rain and snow fell soon afterwards and the plight was great. Only twenty-four hours after the disaster did the first helicopters arrive in the area. There was too much medical help in some villages, whereas in others there was none. In Conza, new clothes were lying by the roadside; in neighbouring villages there were none. The first warm meals were handed out by the army three days after the earthquake. Rather than using computers, elaborate handwritten lists of dead and missing were compiled locally and at ministries in Rome. As usual during earthquake relief operations, heavy lifting gear and bulldozers were missing, and soldiers appeared by thousands carrying useless rifles instead of spades and axes. Relief supplies were hijacked by criminals and looting started in the centre of Naples were damage had been severe. The Italian Parliament had passed laws in 1970 for disaster relief, but these had never been implemented. Nine months after the earthquake, in September 1981, those who had forcefully found shelter for themselves in schools and convents were still living there.[6]

Natural Catastrophes

Natural events producing a catastrophe with 1 million dead are extremely rare, and although their number will increase as the population explosion continues, there is no reason to believe that they will become a common event. Including the pandemic diseases, only the catastrophes shown in Table 1 have been recorded in recent history: It is doubtful if in prehistory anything but the Great Flood of biblical times can be called a catastrophe; the population of our planet was simply too small.

Table 1. Catastrophes recorded in recent history

Date	Catastrophe	Death (in millions)
1337-51	The Black Death (bubonic, pneumonic and septicaemic plague)	75
1918	Influenza epidemic	21
1770	Famine in India	10
1877	Famine in China	10
1919	Famine in USSR	5
1931	Flood, Hwang-ho River, China	4
1970	Flood in East Pakistan	1

One event that could easily cause a large catastrophe would be the fall of a giant meteorite onto a crowded city. About 2,000 meteorites of average mass of 100 kilograms fall upon our planet each year. The largest existing meteorite, nine cubic metres in volume, fifty tonnes in weight, lies where it fell in Southwest Africa. But this is by no means the largest that collided with the earth: the famous Tunguska meteorite, which fell in Siberia in 1908, was estimated to have weighed 1 million tons and to have exploded 400 times its own mass of rock, earth and water. Had it fallen onto any city, its impact would have been equivalent to a 1.2-megaton hydrogen bomb. This is equivalent to sixty Hiroshima-type atomic bombs or a pro-rata deathroll of 5.5 million. A somewhat smaller one hit the rocky slopes of the Alin Mountains in eastern Siberia in February 1947, scattering meteorite fragments over an area of several square kilometres. Large meteorite craters like the Barringer one at Winslow in Arizona with a diameter of 1.2 kilometres testify that such collisions have occurred in the distant past before there were any cities. They might occur again.

A quite different type of catastrophe, possibly the worst that could occur and one that has apparently already happened several times in the geological past, is the Antarctic ice surge. In a paper published in 1964, A.T. Wilson postulated that at the beginning of each ice age, there is a rapid but temporary rise in all sea levels of about 30 metres caused by the sudden slipping of the whole Antarctic ice shelf into the surrounding oceans. There is a gradual buildup of ice in the Antarctic during thousands of years until its own weight transforms the bottom layers into water under high pressure. This water, acting as a natural lubricant, allows the whole ice-cap to slide off the underlying rocky structure and "surge" rapidly outwards, forming huge floating ice shelves in the surrounding southern oceans. [7]

Such glacier surges have been measured elsewhere at a rate of 0.1 km/day. Apart from the cooling of the oceans and the gigantic tidal wave that causes ocean levels to rise by 20-30 metres all round the world, J.T. Hollin has suggested that such a surge would immediately double the brilliantly white reflecting surface in the Southern Hemisphere, now made up by the floating ice shelves, and the new snows on the Antarctic continent itself. The sun's heat received would thus be greatly reduced, leading perhaps to the beginning of a new ice age.[8]

The Concept of an International Rescue Organization

The essential concept of a technologically efficient and worldwide rescue operation, what we here shall call the International Rescue Organization (IRO), is preplanning and stockpiling, before the disaster, all the rescue supplies that will be needed. It will indeed be a long shopping-list including such obvious items as collapsible rubber dinghies, water stills and pills, and communication equipment by radio and satellite. Much can be learned from the stockpiling done by military and civil defense services who have by now long experience of what foods are most suitable, which radio transmitters are most efficient, and what type of tent most easily erected.

These great rescue warehouses would be strategically dispersed around the globe, near the equator to cut down north-south flying time to a minimum. Geneva, Singapore, and Panama may prove suitable, and the stockpiles should obviously be as near to an international airport as possible. Nine small warehouses exist, belonging to the League of Red Cross Societies, but unfortunately they may not always hold the correct supplies. This international body (IRO) itself would not own aircraft, but would, when disaster news is received, ask for free transport by either military or civilian cargo planes. There is by now a well-established precedent, sanctioned by IATA, a convention of the International Air Transport Association (IATA), that such cargo planes are lent free of charge for disaster-rescue work, and the prestige of the IRO would ensure that no misuse is made.

Regional Networks

The IRO would have a regional network with a central disaster office on each continent. It would be a small office whose main function would be information and communications. It would be among the first to receive news of a disaster, to alert its volunteer experts, and to channel requests for further help from the disaster to other regional offices. The office would naturally work on a twenty-four-hour basis and its location would be well known to all governmental and military authorities of the region.

The first news of a disaster in its region might well reach it by radio, or through the ordinary news-agencies, if disaster prediction had not already placed the centre on a stand-by alert. (Flood and typhoon warnings come today from satellite pictures, and earthquakes often have fore-shocks.) As soon as a disaster had been confirmed, a smooth and often rehearsed plan of operations would begin. Volunteer experts, doctors, and engineers, with previous experience in disaster work would be called up and if necessary flown on a priority basis half way round the world, to the site of the disaster.

Focus on Reserve Priorities

This international rescue organization would deal with only one of the three aspects of all disasters. Prevention would be just as much outside its scope as the inevitable rehabilitation which must follow. Only quick and efficient help immediately following a natural or man-made disaster is the business of the IRO.

All disasters have a basic similarity and the IRO would apply its carefully planned list of rescue priorities in each case. Ten priorities run as follows:

Chain of command. On receipt of the news of a major disaster, the appointment of a Disaster Commander, the DC, must have first priority. Normally he would be a high-ranking military officer of the country in which the disaster had occurred, someone familiar with the terrain, the customs of the people afflicted, and preferably trained in, or at least familiar with, rescue operations on the scale needed. The example of General Stretton in Darwin is here most relevant. If no such suitable DC is immediately available, the regional IRO office might offer one of its own experts. The DC would have absolute power over men, materials, communications, and supplies whether indigenous or brought in from outside. He would, of course, remain ultimately responsible to his own government or to the IRO. The DC would have a number of deputies dealing with each of the following rescue priorities; where no such expert deputies are available, again the IRO would offer its own personnel. Only experience after several disasters would show how this chain of command would work and where there might be a need for improvement.

Reconnaissance. Assessment would be made of the extent of devastation either from survivors, or if necessary, by immediately sending its own disaster experts, engineers, and doctors to the scene. If necessary they would be dropped by parachute.

As precise information will be the most precious commodity during the first hours of any disaster, the DC or the IRO regional centre may well, as its first action, request from the local air force a photographic reconnaissance flight to obtain precise data on which to base its subsequent actions. Natually voice radio contact with such a flight would give prior information, but photographs would be essential a few hours later to plan the siting of mobile emergency hospitals, to locate evacuation routes, and to find surviving land or waterways for the approach of rescue teams.

The pathfinders of the IRO would be its own experts, flown in or parachuted to the site of the disaster. Their function would not be to carry out any rescue at all, but to act as the eyes and ears of the DC or the regional centre who would by now begin to open the warehouse. Here again a planned and often rehearsed procedure would be essential to make sure that the right supplies go on the first planes. Naturally these would vary according to the type of disaster; small mechanical shovels for earthquakes, rubber dinghies for floods. Most likely a central computer for all regional IRO offices would be the best way of recording names of experts, unusual rescue needs, and up-to-date records of the contents in all IRO warehouses.

Communications. The third priority must be contact with survivors or with the IRO disaster experts. Even if all regular telephone lines have been destroyed, radio amateurs can often ensure contact with the outside world (for the first few days). In more primitive areas, the IRO experts would have with them a communications man with a powerful short-wave radio transmitter to keep regional headquarters of the IRO constantly informed.

The International Telecommunication Union, the United Nations agency dealing with all communications, has drawn up specifications for commercial production of small portable ground stations especially for disaster areas which can reach communication satellites. Only "thin line" traffic of about five to six telephone channels would be needed to reach the affected country's capital, the Red Cross in Geneva, and the United Nations in New York. Such ground stations, stockpiled by the IRO, would be parachuted to the site to re-establish communications within hours. They might well be in use for weeks and months.9

Evacuation of the Injured and Living Survivors. The next priority is removal of the injured and living, in that order. Where helicopters are available, they will be ideal but the IRO itself could not own these most expensive and limited-range means of transport. In the case of widespread floods, collapsible rubber dinghies would be thrown out from low-flying aircraft, after having been loaded with them from the IRO's regional stockpiles. Obviously a two-way traffic plan would be established as soon as possible, ferrying out the victims, and bringing in return emergency supplies of whatever kind are most urgently needed. This would come under the co-ordination of the Communication Officer, unless the disaster is of such magnitude or complexity that a separate traffic command for land, sea or air would be essential.

Mobile Hospitals. Twenty-four hours after the first news of the disaster, mobile hospitals would have been set up at safe rearguard positions. These fifty-bed natural-disaster hospitals and their equipment would have come from IRO reserves; the doctors and nurses, all volunteers, would have been flown in.

Disaster Survivors. At this point survivors, either in the area where possible, or at evacuation sites, would now receive full attention. If the disaster exceeds the resources of the regional reserves, extra help would have been flown in from other regions, according to the requests made originally.

Water. For all survivors this is the top priority. Small portable stills now exist which can convert sea-water into fresh water, or if fresh water is available but contaminated, water-sterilization pills by the thousands can be distributed. Stills and pills would of course come from IRO stockpiles. Where droughts take on disaster or even catastrophic dimensions, more drastic rescue operations should be mounted. Although not available on the surface, there may often be rich water layers deep below, as for example in the Sahara, where at a depth of 1,000 metres huge water reserves have been found. Drilling equipment for such an emergency could be housed in one of the IRO's central warehouses, be rented from oil-drilling firms, or purchased from IRO funds.

For more local droughts, it might prove possible to lay 50 or 100-kilometre-long plastic water pipes, say in ten-kilometre lengths from a huge rotating drum strung below a helicopter. Small booster stations would be needed every few kilometres. This operation should not prove more difficult than the petrol pipe laid from England to France during the Second World War from the famous "Conundrum," the floating and rotating drum towed by tugs.

Health and Sanitation. Treatment of the survivors must be a quite independent operation from the treatment of the injured. Vaccines can now be safely stored for years in the dry state and mass inoculation of survivors against cholera and typhus carried out easily by semi-automatic means. Mental health of shocked people is just as important as physical health. Special IRO volunteer experts would use all available media of communication for reassurance of victims and keep up a constant flow of information to them, where they can obtain additional help, how to find lost relatives, and where to resettle.

Food. Once physical communications have been re-established this would provide the least difficulty. There is today a vast variety of storable foods, tinned, compressed, dehydrated or only concentrated, which could be distributed from IRO stockpiles. Local preferences or idiosyncrasies would be well known at regional centres, and where language difficulties might arise, explanatory picture diagrams would be printed on the outside of food containers.

Clothing, Heating, and Shelter. These should have lowest priority when aircraft cargo space is at a premium. Many more natural disasters occur in tropical areas than in higher latitudes, but here again local conditions may make exceptions. Blankets and small portable oil stoves may play a vital role and may need to be flown in even before food where disaster survivors are in danger of freezing to death. The high priority of communications between local experts and regional IRO centre need hardly be stressed in this context. Additional fuel could easily follow later by land or water.

These ten rescue priorities are at present based on purely theoretical, common-sense considerations. Only real experience in the field of disaster rescue operations will show how they stand up to practical demands, and they will no doubt be modified by experience and by individual disaster requirements.

The Future

Hope for better disaster relief, although by no means on an international scale as outlined above, lies with three organizations, the first of which is the United Nations Disaster Relief Organization.

The United Nations Disaster Relief Co-ordinator's Office (UNDRO)

The United Nations Disaster Relief Co-ordinator's Office (UNDRO) was established in 1972 to mobilize and co-ordinate international emergency relief to disaster-stricken areas, and to promote disaster preparedness and prevention.

Three Broad Functions

The first is that of international relief co-ordination: to ensure that in case of natural disaster or other disaster situations, emergency relief activities of all donor sources are mobilized and co-ordinated so as to supply the needs of a disaster-stricken country in a timely and effective manner. Its second function is that of preparedness: to raise the level of pre-disaster planning and preparedness, including disaster assessment and relief management capability, in disaster-prone developing countries. Thirdly, there is the function of prevention: to promote the study, prevention, control and prediction of natural disasters, including the collection and dissemination of information concerning technological developments.*

---

* See UNDRO News, published bi-monthly by the Office of the United Nations Disaster Relief Co-ordinator, Palais des Nations, CH-1211 Geneva 10.

Recent Activities

During 1983, UNDRO was directly involved in 44 major disasters. As a co-ordinating office, UNDRO is not itself a principal source of relief assistance, although the co-ordinator has the authority to make a contribution not exceeding $30,000 for any one disaster (and not exceeding in total $360,000 in one year) to meet immediate emergency needs, such as medicines, food or the transport of life-saving equipment. The co-ordinator has moreover been empowered to receive from donors contributions in kind and in cash which are used for the provision of relief supplies. The greater part of the emergency assistance provided by the international community goes directly to the country concerned, and it is expected that the amount and nature of these contributions will be based upon the information given in UNDRO's disaster "situation reports" which are sent by Telex to donor sources and other interested organizations throughout the world. During 1983, contributions for emergency relief reported to UNDRO, mobilized by it or channelled through it, exceeded $400 million. UNDRO staff members are often sent to a disaster-stricken country to assist governments in the tasks of assessment of damage and needs and in local co-ordination of relief activity In any one year UNDRO organizes or participates in many multi-agency disaster assessment missions.

Disaster preparedness advisory missions are usually undertaken by consultants hired by UNDRO. They advise governments on the best methods of improving their organization to deal with all kinds of disasters, and not just those which arise from natural causes. The recommendations of these missions sometimes call for specific projects to be carried out, and if these cannot be funded by the government, then UNDRO may be asked to seek the necessary financing from donors. Preparedness organizations natually need trained personnel, and UNDRO arranges or takes part in many seminars for disaster managers and others concerned in relief work, in the preparation and issue of warnings, and in the application of new technologies to disaster work generally. UNDRO is also engaged in attempts to remove obstacles to the rapid delivery of international relief; this requires willingness by donors as well as by potential recipients to streamline procedures and to waive normal legal requirements for the movement of relief goods and personnel.

In the area of disaster prevention, UNDRO is engaged in development of techniques of vulnerability analysis and their application: in trying to ensure that precautions against existing hazards are observed in the planning of new development projects, and that the projects themselves should not create new hazards; and in promoting the use of legislation, land-use planning, and other inexpensive methods of reducing or eliminating disaster risks.

The Disaster Prevention Research Institute, Kyoto, Japan

The Disaster Prevention Research Institute, Kyoto, Japan, was established in 1951 to carry out scientific and engineering studies to prevent natural disasters. It has more than 100 research staff members. Although purely theoretical and mainly concerned with prevention, it will undoubtedly contribute to greater knowledge about disasters and thus to speedier and more efficient relief operations.

The Australian Counter-Disaster College, Macedon, Victoria

The Australian Counter-Disaster College, Macedon, Victoria, was established by the Commonwealth Government of Australia following the Darwin Cyclone disaster of 1974 and grew out of the existing Civil Defense College at the same location. Its charter states that it will "contribute to the development of an efficient Australian counter-disaster capability by training selected personnel . . . by fostering understanding and co-operation between appropriate elements of the community and by undertaking research into selected aspects of disaster." Situated about fifty kilometres from Melbourne, the college is residential and has since its beginning held regular courses dealing with almost all aspects of man-made, industrial, and natural disasters. It possesses an excellent library, probably the only one in the world dealing with all aspects of natural and man-made disasters. Apart from cyclones, floods, and droughts, Australia is prone to suffer from disastrous bush fires, although free from earthquakes and volcanoes, at least since records have been kept during the last 200 years. Training courses, normally lasting a week, are organized for professional groups, such as industrial managers, police officers, civil servants, and many others who in case of disasters would have an executive function. The college's motto, *In adversitatem paratus*, speaks for itself, and one can only hope that similar training colleges will be set up in other countries where the need exists. One day, these may well become the nucleus for the International Rescue Organization envisaged above.

NOTES

1. *Red Cross Relief Bureau Circular*, No. 408, Geneva, November 1969.
2. United States Department of State, Agency for International Development, Disaster Emergency Relief, *Ninth Annual Report*, 1969.
3. Ibid.
4. *Red Cross Relief Bureau Circular*, No. 447, Geneva, October 1970.
5. A. Stretton, *The Furious Days*, Melbourne, Sun Books, 1976.
6. Details taken from reports in *Frankfurter Allgemeine Zeitung* and *The Times* (London).
7. A. Wilson, *Nature*, Vol. 201, No. 147, 1964.
8. J. Hollin, 'Wilson's Theory of Ice Ages,' *Nature*, No. 208, 1965, p. 8; 'Antarctic Ice Surges,' *Antarctic Journal of the United States*, Vol. 5, No. 5, 1970.
9. R.. Haviland, 'On Satellites for Communications in Natural Disasters, *Telecommunication Journal*, Vol. 44, No. 17, 1977.

TO DELVE MORE DEEPLY

Balchin, W. *Natural and Man-made Diseases, STrategies for Survival.* Presidential address to Geography Section of British Association. Leicester, September 6, 1972. (Available from Professor Balchin, University College, Swansea, Wales.)

Foster, H. *Disaster Planning, the Preservation of Life and Property.* New York/Heidelberg/Berlin, Springer Verlag, 1980.

Hass, E. Common Opponent Sought and Found? *Bulletin of the Atomic Scientists*, November 1968, p. 8.

Lord, W. *A Night to Remember* (*RMS Titanic*). London, Longmans, 1956.

Michaelis, A. International Rescue, *Daily Telegraph Magazine*, No. 163, 17 November 1977. Wanted, An International Rescue Service, *Sunday Telegraph*, 22 November 1970. Chaos After Catastrophe, *Daily Telegraph Magazine*, No. 380, 11 February 1972. Coping with Disasters, *Science and Public Affairs*, April 1973, p. 25. The Infamy of Disaster Relief, *Interdisciplinary Science Reviews*, Vol. 2, No. 2, 1977.

Mills, E. Emergency Technical Aid Services for Natural Disasters, *Impact of Science on Society*, Vol. 16, No. 3, 1966. Natural Disaster. A Selected List of Publications, *International Unions of Architects*, May 1971. (Available from E. Mills, 9-11 Richmond Buildings, Dean Street, London, W.1, United Kingdom.)

Petrow, T. *The Black Tide* (*Torrey Canyon*), London, Hodder and Stoughton, 1968.

A Review of
How To Make a Mess of a Disaster: Disasters and Development, by
Frederick Cuny, Oxford UP, pp. 278, £25, pbk £12.50

The "Borracho Hurricane" alone is worth the price of admission. In
his account of a hypothetical hurricane in a hypothetical Latin
American nation, disaster consultant Fred Cuny shows how
governments, international aid agencies, and the relief agencies labour
to turn a disaster into a catastrophe. The account has a surreal air.
People are advised to shelter in churches, and the churches collapse on
them. Politicians commandeer rescue helicopters to sightsee over the
disaster area. Relief agencies compete for territory and parcel out
wrecked villages in a "lottery."

Cuny, a Texan town planner who runs the Dallas disaster
consulting firm Intertect, has worked in the Biafra fighting, the
Bangladesh civil war, various bits of the Lebanon turmoil, the 1972
Managua earthquake, the 1976 Guatemala quake, and assorted
catastrophes in Burundi, Peru, and Honduras. It becomes clear as he
describes real disasters that all the surreal events of "Borracho"
(Spanish for "drunk") were real events elsewhere. The cyclone which
struck the Indian state of Andhra Pradesh in 1977 demolished three
"shelters" (churches and schools), killing 400. Hurricane David may
have killed relatively few people in Dominica in 1979 because people
did not have time to get to the churches designated as shelters. Four of
the six main churches were totally destroyed.

But these are anecdotes. Cuny is out to change our thinking about
disasters and "relief." Most disaster relief operations involve an agency
from a wealthy country intervening with little consultation in the
complex workings of an alien society: its food supplies, its building

trades, its business patterns. The agencies doing this intervening are not accountable to the victims. They are accountable to donors, head offices, and the media back home. They are mostly amateurs.

Not only do most traditional blankets-from-the-sky relief efforts do little good, but Cuny details ways in which they often actually set back a developing country. A massive influx of relief goods and money can upset delicate peasant economic systems; they can shatter local coping mechanisms; they can provide a disincentive to initiative.

Most major disasters happen in the tropics where the poorer Third World countries are. Disasters are getting bigger and more frequent and the poor, living in bad shelters on dangerous ground are the ones who die when earthquake and cyclone strike. So the most effective disaster "relief" is development projects which attack this poverty and vulnerability—before as well as after the earthquake.

Cuny describes in detail the Oxfam/World Neighbours/Intertect rehousing project following the Guatemala quake. It did not give people money or material with which to rebuild. Instead, working closely with local groups, it sold building materials at subsidised prices, trained local builders in "quake-proofing" even simple adobe homes, allowed poor families to work for their materials and ploughed money into more roofing tin and better roads.

Added attractions of Cuny's book include detailed accounts of the complex workings of the international relief community and of trends and future directions in disaster management.

Disasters and Development has two main flaws. The first, which Cuny admits, is that as a housing expert he is most concerned with earthquakes and hurricanes. He tends to ignore droughts and floods. The drought now threatening 24 African states—aggravated by overgrazing and overcultivation—and the floods which sweep off the largely deforested Himalayas every year, offer even better examples of the disaster/development links. The book needs a second volume.

Secondly, Cuny seems somewhat restrained. He can be a brash, outspoken Texan in interviews. He knows which agencies foul things up repeatedly and which avoid the classic errors. But he is, after all, in the business. His book was sponsored by Oxfam America. The agencies, like fellow members of any small club, do not detail one another's failings. The reader can almost feel Cuny reining himself in. He does not come to terms with the growing opinion of some "radical" geographers who feel that the high death tolls of many "natural" disasters are caused by political and economical systems which put the poor on the margins—shanty-towns on floodplains, adobe huts on earthquake-prone hillsides. Many relief agencies try to restore the status quo as quickly as possible. In doing so, they must take their share of the blame for the growing number of Third World disasters.

Lloyd Timberlake

Reprinted by permission from *New Scientist*, 3 May 1984, and the author.

The views of Stanford University professors of civil engineering are summarized in 31 precepts for preparing and coping with severe earthquakes.

Chapter 23
What to do Before, During, and After an Earthquake

Stanford University News Service

Reprinted from the *Stanford University News Service,* 13 April 1984.

Earthquake Preparedness

Although engineers and scientists have gained a considerable amount of knowledge about earthquakes since the great Alaskan Good Friday earthquake in 1964 (magnitude 8.4), they are no closer to predicting when or where a quake will occur and, in fact, prediction reliability will not be great for many years.

Every person who lives in an earthquake area should think deliberately and frequently about what to do in the next quake, say Professor Haresh Shah and James Gere of Stanford's Civil Engineering Department, codirector of the John A. Blume Earthquake Engineering Center at Stanford and coauthors of *Terra Non Firma: Understanding and Preparing for Earthquakes*. "You are much more likely to remain calm and react sensibly if you have thought about it in advance, not only at home, but also at work, in stores, on the street or in cars," they advise.

Most people think earthquakes act longer than they really do. Survivors of one quake estimated the quaking lasted 30 to 40 seconds, when in reality it lasted 5 to 10 seconds. Most earthquakes are of a short duration—10 seconds—but the more shaking that occurs, the greater the damage than can result, Shah and Gere say. "Most of the life loss in earthquakes comes from the total or partial collapse of buildings. It is interesting that the ground movement itself causes little direct harm; rather, it is the effect of ground shaking on man-made structures that creates disasters," Gere says.

If an earthquake occurs while driving a car, chances are a person will not feel the actual shaking. Rather, he or she may suddenly have the feeling that all four tires have gone flat. The driver should pull off to the side of the road and stop in a place where there are no overhead wires, and away from tall buildings, overpasses and bridges if possible, Shah says.

What to do Before an Earthquake

Shah and Gere have a list of preparations that can be made before the next earthquake. Some of their recommendations are as follows:

- Store drinking water and canned food at home so that you can survive for a few days on your own. One gallon of water per person per day is suggested for drinking and cooking purposes. An emergency method of cooking is convenient—for example, a camp stove or barbecue.

- Always have flashlights and spare batteries readily available.

- Keep a battery-operated radio at home.

- Keep one or more fire extinguishers in convenient locations. Keep garden hoses attached to faucets.

- Learn how to turn off the gas, electricity, and water at your home.

- Fasten to the walls any bookcases or other heavy pieces of furniture that might topple and cause injuries.

- Put one or more straps around water heaters and gas furnaces and attach them securely to the walls.

- Be sure your bed is not located near a large glass window.

- To protect your home if damage occurs, have available some plywood and sheets of plastic to cover broken windows and other openings.

What to do During an Earthquake

When the earthquake occurs, the ground will shake perceptibly for a relatively short time—perhaps only a few seconds, perhaps as much as a minute in a great earthquake. Act immediately when you feel the ground or building shaking, keeping in mind that the greatest danger is from falling debris, Gere and Shah emphasize, as follows:

- Tell yourself to remain calm and don't do things that upset other people (such as shouting or running around).

- If you are indoors, move immediately to a safe place. Get under a desk, table, or work bench if possible. Stand in an interior doorway or in the corner of a room. Watch out for falling debris or tall furniture. Stay away from windows, chimneys, and heavy objects (such as refrigerators and machinery) that may topple or slide across the floor.

- As a general rule, don't run out of a building. Falling debris around a building is a common hazard. It is better to seek safety where you are.

- If you are in a tall building, don't rush for stairways or elevators.

- Don't be surprised if the electricity goes out or if elevator, fire, and burglar alarms start ringing or if the sprinkler systems go on. Expect to hear noise from breaking glass, cracks in walls, and falling objects.

- If you are in an unreinforced brick building or other hazardous structure, you may feel it is better to take a chance on leaving the building than to stay inside.

- If you are on the sidewalk near a tall building, step into a doorway to avoid falling debris from the building.

- If you are outdoors, try to get into an open area, away from buildings and power lines.

- Don't be surprised if you feel more than one shock. After the first motion is felt, there may be a temporary decrease in the motion followed by another shock.

What to do After the Earthquake

When the shaking stops there may be considerable damage and people may be injured. Shah and Gere suggest the following:

- Remain calm, and take time to assess your situation.

- Help anyone who is hurt. Cover injured persons with blankets to keep them warm.

- Check for fires and fire hazards. Put out fires immediately, if you can.

- Check for damage to utilities and appliances. Shut off gas valves if there is any chance of a gas leak, and electricity if there is any chance of damage to wiring. Shut off water mains if breakage has occurred.

- Do not light matches or use any open flames or turn on electrical switches or appliances until you are certain there are no gas leaks.

- Do not touch power lines, electric wiring, or objects in contact with them.

- Do not use the telephone except to call for help or to report serious emergencies (medical, fire, criminal) or to perform some essential service. Jammed telephone lines interfere with emergency services.

- Do not go sightseeing nor occupy the streets unnecessarily.

- Be certain that sewer lines are not broken before resuming regular use of toilets.

- Be prepared to experience aftershocks.

- Use great caution when entering or moving about in a damaged building. Collapses can occur without much warning and there may be dangers from gas leaks, electric wiring, broken glass, etc.

- If electricity is out, use up foods from the refrigerator that will spoil.

- Open closet doors and cupboards cautiously, because objects may fall outward on you.

"Earthquakes will always cause death, injury, and destruction, and no rules can make us completely safe. Furthermore, some rules will apply only in certain situations and must be altered or abandoned under other circumstances. However, by judicious use of these suggestions, people can greatly reduce the dangers from earthquakes and be of more help to ourselves and others when the next one comes, as it will," Shah and Gere explain.

The burden of this book is to recognize both the scientific nature of nature's violent forces and man's need to forecast, to prepare for and to cope with catastrophic events.

Chapter 24
POSTSCRIPT: In the Service of Curiosity and Concern

Robert H. Maybury

Robert H. Maybury is the editor of this volume. He is presently Consultant to the World Bank, following retirement from Unesco. Educated as a physicist, Dr. Maybury has been especially concerned in recent years with the needs of developing countries.

As the reader can see, the greater part of the papers collected together in this volume are devoted to descriptions of the violent forces of nature. For, several years ago when we were first planning the original issue of *impact* on this theme of nature's violent forces (Vol. 32, No. 1, 1982), our main interest was in providing our readers up-to-date reports from scientists probing the secrets of this violent side of nature. Our search at that time for such front-line reporting was well rewarded: excellent accounts came to us from leaders in research on the major manifestations of nature's violence—fire, cyclonic storms, earthquakes, volcanoes, avalanches, tsunami, and mountain hazards. In expanding that issue into this present book form, we have held to our earlier interest by including additional front-line reports on the phenomena of flooding, land subsidence, desertification, lightning, and wind shear.

In devoting so large a share of this volume to reports describing the violent forces of nature, we are acknowledging the dimension of curiosity in the human response to nature. This stirring of the mind—call it inquisitiveness or the desire to know, if you wish—is spontaneous and childlike, yet is also a force propelling the scientist forward in his methodical procedures of inquiry with nature. Curiosity is evident throughout the reports of this collection as scientists encounter nature in her bewildering variety of awe-inspiring, bizarre and incredible manifestations: Kerry Sieh discovering the peat sediments athwart the San Andreas fault revealing the history of 2000 years of earthquakes (Ingwerson, Chapter 1); Westercamp listening to the rumblings of a "living," awakening volcano; Marbouty observing a cloud of fresh show and air hurtling down a mountainside at 300 km per hour; Krider picturing the luminous processes during a lightning strike.

Curiosity is indeed a dimension of the human response to nature, but when the encounter is with nature's violent side, an additional, quite different dimension becomes aroused—concern for human life and safety. The manifestation of this additional dimension became apparent to us as soon as we began to gather the scientific reports on these violent forces. Right along with curiosity, concern for the life and safety of those encountering a given natural phenomenon gave impetus to the scientist's investigation. This led us to establish Part V in the text as "Preparedness and Rescus," and to include papers dealing with various aspects of society's effort to cope with the violent forces of nature.

Both sets of papers, the scientific accounts and those in Part V are essential to any treatment of the subject of nature's violent forces which seeks to be of service to human society, for as van Essche (Chapter 19) indicates, "science, technology, and objective knowledge can only carry us to a certain point in the decision making process. Ultimately, policy and planning decisions depend as much on human factors as they do on objective scientific criteria and technology. This is an important observation to make to scientists and engineers. Indeed, experience shows us that it is most important and urgent that "hard" scientific data on (—) risk be adapted to the needs and language of planners, architects and those responsible for the protection of the population in times of (—) emergencies."

We are aware that this mere juxtaposing of a group of reports containing this "hard" scientific data with a group of papers describing some of the dimensions and problems of disaster prevention and preparedness can be no more than a beginning to this process of adaptation which van Essche refers to. Fortunately, as Fournier d'Albe, reminds us in his introduction to this volume, the new attitude that this adaptation requires "is gradually, but still too slowly, spreading from the scientific and engineering community to the spheres of government, public administration and public opinion."

One critical step that must be taken in this process of adaptation is described by the UNDRO report in Chapter 18: "much work has been done in the earth sciences to define the physical characteristics of earthquakes, storms, floods, etc. Less has been done to carry the analysis one step further, i.e., to increase the basic understanding of how these natural phenomena, by their severity, can affect lives and property." We are confident that including the Part V papers on Preparedness and Rescue along with the scientific account enables the analysis to be carried this critical "one step further." An excellent example of this is the article by Vickery which makes effective use of case studies on earthquakes in Peru, Afghanistan and Italy to show how better design of school buildings can save lives.

This juxtaposition of accounts on scientific and social response also carries the analysis "one step further" by contributing to the important matter of informing and educating the public, which Fournier d'Albe, in his introduction, calls the "essential though often forgotten element" in attempts to reduce human vulnerability to nature's violent forces. Without this information, the public lacks the very understanding on which they can base action for their own safety.

By taking matters "one step further," this juxtaposition of science and social concern also contributes to the professional preparation of those specialists whose mission is to cope with the violent forces of nature—authorities in agencies like the U.S. Federal Emergency Management Agency, for example, or elected officials in state and municipal governments whose responsibility is to put in place effective legislation for disaster preparedness. The UNDRO "Guidelines for Disaster Prevention and Preparedness in Tropical Cyclone Areas," published jointly by the UN Economic and Social Commission for Asia and the Pacific, the World Meteorological Organization and the League of Red Cross and Red Crescent Socieities (Geneva/Bangkok, 1977) indicate the multiplicity of matters to be covered in effective legislation for disaster preparedness and relief:

(a) The monitoring of natural phenomena, the issue of warnings and the actions that should then be taken;

(b) The conduct of emergency measures (e.g., flood fighting and evacuation);

(c) The operation of measures related to protection, rescue and relief;

(d) Measures for the education and information of the population, including school children, regarding action to be taken in emergency;

(e) Measures for the restoration of building, installations and equipment;

(f) Health measures, including epidemic control, public health and sanitation;

(g) Measures for the preservation of social order, for emergency transport, traffic control and crime prevention;

(h) Measures for rehabilitation;

(i) Financial measures, and

(j) The definition of authority and responsibilities and, if required, the establishment of appropriate agencies.

It will be probable (and it is recommended) that legislation will include as a minimum the procedure for declaring a state of emergency; the emergency-related duties of authorities forming part of the normal structure of government as well as those of bodies specially established to prepare for and deal with emergencies; the powers those authorities will enjoy; and related financial provisions.

The scientific accounts along with the discussion of social organization presented in this book are a rich storehouse of facts about the violent forces of nature and revelations of the play of human opinion and will, social prejudice and emotion in the workings of organizations and communities. Authorities and legislators should find this a useful knowledge base for their public decision-making in the formulation and implementation of effective programs of disaster preparedness and prevention.

Robert H. Maybury

Appendix
A Selected Bibliography on Natural Disasters and Hazard Mitigation

Dennis King

Dennis King received his Masters Degree from Columbia University and has also attended the University of Florida and George Washington University. He is currently working as a librarian and information specialist for the Office of Foreign Disaster Assistance, Agency for International Development, U.S. Department of State.

A.I.D. Policy Paper: International Disaster Assistance. Issued by Bureau for
Program and Policy Coordination, U.S. Agency for International
Development, Washington, DC 20523, May 1985.

American Seismology Delegation. "Earthquake Research in China" *EOS
Transactions* American Geophysical Union. 56 (II). pp. 838-881.

Ayre, Robert S. *Earthquake and Tsunami Hazards in the United
States: Research Assessment.* Boulder: University of Colorado Institute of
Behavioral Sciences. 1975. 150 p.
Research into the use and application of simulation modeling in predicting
and mitigating earthquakes and tsunamis.

Blundell, D.J. "Living with Earthquakes" *Disasters* Vol. 1, No. 1 (1977)
pp. 41-46.

Bolt, B.A., et al. *Geological Hazards.* New York: Springer-Verlag. 1977.
330 p.
Overview of the causes, risks and effects of earthquakes, volcanoes,
tsunamis, landslides, ground subsidence, snow avalanches and floods. Book
includes case histories of natural disasters and concludes with a chapter on
hazard mitigation and control.

Brinkmann, Waltraud A.R. *Severe Local Storm Hazard in the United States:
A Research Assessment.* Boulder: University of Colorado Institute of
Behavioral Science, 1975. 154 p.
Assessment of the damage dimensions, mitigation efforts, and research on
tornadoes, hail and lightning hazards in the United Sates.

Burton, Ian, Kates, R.W. and White, G.F. *Environment as Hazard.* New
York: Oxford University Press. 1978.
This book examines natural hazards and occurrences and how they affect
mankind. Book includes numerous case studies of earthquakes, floods,
cyclones and droughts and explores how man might prevent, reduce and
adjust to these natural hazards.

Clark, Champ. *Planet Earth: Flood.* Alexandria, Va.: Time-Life Books, 1981.
176 p.
This volume from the Time-Life series, examines the history of flood
disasters throughout the world, specifically how different areas of earth
react and adapt to recurrent flooding.

Cochrane, Harold C. *Natural Hazards and their Distributive Effects.* Boulder:
University of Colorado Institute of Behavioral Science, 1975. 135 p.
Examination of the effects, implications, relationships and impacts of
natural hazards, based on case studies of actual disasters and simulation
exercises.

Cuny, Frederick C. *Disasters and Development.* Oxford: Oxford University
Press, 1983.
A comprehensive and thoughtful examination of the ways in which

international relief agencies and organizations respond to natural disasters in developing countries.

D'Albe, Fournier. "Natural Disasters, their study and prevention" *UNESCO Chronicle*, 16 (1970) pp. 195-208.

Dey, A.K. "Earthquake and Earthquake Prediction" *Disaster Management Quarterly*. Vol. 3, No. 1 (January-March 1983) pp. 30-40.

"Earthquakes and Risk in California" *Earthquake Information Bulletin*. Volume 14, No. 3 (May-June 1982) pp. 98-107.

Earthscan. *Natural Disasters: Acts of God - or Acts of Man?* London: International Institute for Environment and Development, 1984. 116 p.
In-depth study into the causes and effects of natural disasters and ways in which governments, relief organizations, and voluntary agencies respond to catastrophes in Third World societies.

Ericksen, Neil J. *Scenario Methodology in Natural Hazards Research*. Boulder: University of Colorado Institute of Behavioral Science, 1975. 170 p.
Analysis of the use and applications of scenario methodology, computer simulations and modeling in disaster research.

Fiske, R.S. *Volcanologists, Journalists, and the Concerned Local Public: A Tale of Two Crises in the Eastern Caribbean*. In *Explosive Volcanism: Inception, Evolution, and Hazards*. Geophysics Study Committee. National Academy of Sciences. Washington. 1984.
This paper describes the very real differences that are found between the relationships developed among scientists, civil authorities, and journalists during the volcano on Guadeloupe in 1976 and those developed among these same actors at the time of the volcano on St. Vincent in 1979. This comparison leads to lessons that are useful for improving these relationships during such crises arising elsewhere at future times.

Fried, Don G. *Computer Simulation in Natural Hazard Assessment*. Boulder: University of Colorado Institute of Behavioral Science, 1975. 192 p.
Examination of the uses and applications of computer simulation methodology in assessing and predicting the hazard potentials of earthquakes, hurricanes, floods and drought.

Funaro-Curtis, Rita. *Natural Disasters and the Development Process: A Discussion of Issues*. Washington: Office of U.S. Foreign Disaster Assistance, A.I.D. 1982. 33 p.
A report documenting the effects of natural disasters on the economic development of developing nations.

Hagman, Gunnar et al. *Prevention Better Than Cure: Report on human and environmental disasters in the Third World*. Stockholm: Swedish Red Cross, 1984. 187 p.
This report, prepared for the Swedish Red Cross, examines the vulnerability

of Third World populations to the devastating effects of earthquakes, cyclones, floods and drought.

Hall, P.S. and Lendreth, P.W. "Assessing some long term consequences of a natural disaster" *Mass Emergencies* 1 (1) (1975) pp. 55-61.

Howard, J.A. "The Application of Satellite Remote Sensing to Monitoring of Agricultural Disasters" *Disasters* Vol. 2, No. 4 (1979) pp. 231-240.

Jones, Barclay G. and Tomazevic, Miha. *Social and Economic Aspects of Earthquakes: Proceedings of the Third International Conference* held at Bled, Yugoslavia, June 29-July 2, 1981. Itahaca: Cornell University Press, 1982. 654 p.

Proceedings and papers from third annual conference sponsored by US-Yugoslav Joint Board on Scientific and Technological Cooperation, dealing with risk assessment, hazard reduction, seismic engineering and socio-economic impact of earthquakes.

Kates, Robert W. *Risk Assessment of Environmental Hazard.* Toronto: John Wiley & Sons, 1978. 112 p.

Comprehensive study of the application of risk assessment methodology in mitigating the effects of natural hazards, based on case studies of Canada, East Africa and Sweden.

Kerr, Richard A. "Volcanic Hazard Alert Issued for Long Valley-Mono Lake Area of California," *Earthquake Information Bulletin* Volume 14, No. 3 (May-June 1982) pp. 84-93.

Lipman, P.W. and Mullineaux, D.R. Eds. *The 1980 Eruptions of Mount St. Helens, Washington.* (Geological Survey Paper 1250). Reston, Virginia. U.S. Geological Survey. 1982.

The events of 1980 are described and interpreted in over 60 papers by authors from the Geological Survey and from the academic community. Describes the following: the geological evolution of the volcano; chronology of the eruption; seismic activity and deformation, gas emissions, thermal anomalies, and various types of monitoring; pyroclastic eruptions and debris flows; and effects of ash falls and mudflows. The problems of assessing and alleviating hazards are discussed.

Melson, William. *Plant Earth: Volcano.* Alexandria, Va.: Time-Life Books, 1981. 176 p.

A well written account of the underground forces at work that cause volcanic eruptions and how volcanoes have shaped the earth's landscape. This volume includes many spectacular photographs of volcanic eruptions and an account of the cataclysm on Mount St. Helens.

Mileti, Dennis S.; Hutton, Janice R.; and Sorenson, John H. *Earthquake Prediction Response and Options for Public Policy.* Boulder: University of Colorado Institute of Behavioral Science. 1981. 152 p.

This work reports on the history and status of earthquake prediction, based on actual case studies and hypothetical scenarios and proposes a methodology for studying human response to earthquake prediction.

National Research Council. *Earthquake Prediction and Public Policy.* Washington: National Academy of Sciences. 1975. 142 p.

This report, put out by the special Panel on the Public Policy Implications of Earthquake Prediction, analyzes the role of government agencies in responding to earthquake prediction and discusses some of the economic, psychological, legal and political issues involved.

Office of the U.N. Disaster Relief Coordinator. *Disaster Prevention and Mitigation. A Compendium of Current Knowledge: Volume 1 - Volcanological Aspects.* Geneva: United Nations, 1976. 37 p.

This volume of the UNDRO series describes the various types of volcanic destruction, the ways of predicting and preventing some of them and suggests measures to return the affected land to profitable use.

Office of the U.N. Disaster Relief Coordinator. *Disaster Prevention and Mitigation. A Compendium of Current Knowledge: Volume 2 - Hydrological Aspects.* Geneva: United Nations, 1976. 100 p.

This volume explores the many different causes of flooding and the use of land management, flood forecasting, civil engineering and environmental monitoring to mitigate flood hazards.

Office of the U.N. Disaster Relief Coordinator. *Disaster Prevention and Mitigation. A Compendium of Current Knowledge: Volume 3 - Seismological Aspects.* Geneva: United Nations, 1978. 127 p.

This volume examines the many seismological aspects of earthquakes and tsunamis, including seismic mapping, macrozoning and microzoning, earthquake prediction and protection.

Office of the U.N. Disaster Relief Coordinator. *Preparedness Aspects,* Vol. II in *Disaster Prevention and Mitigation,* Geneva, United Nations, 1984.

Intends to provide a summary of the best current practice and to serve as a signpost pointing the way to other, more detailed sources of information which should be readily available to emergency planners.

Office of the United Nations Disaster Relief Coordinator. Natural Disasters and Vulnerability Analysis. Report of Expert Group Meeting, July 9-12, 1979.

Our Violent Earth. National Geographic Society, P.O. Box 2895, Washington, DC 20013.

A National Geographic Society book on the subject of natural disasters for the younger reader. Lavishly illustrated: contains an excellent bibliography on the subject for school libraries and a chapter entitled "Thinking Ahead: Careers in Earth Sciences."

Quarantelli, E.L. and Dynes, R.R. "Community conflict: Its absence and presence in natural disaster." *Mass Emergencies* 1, (1976) pp. 139-152.

Richards, Paul B. "Space Technology Contributions to Emergency and Disaster Management." *Advanced Earth Oriented Space Technology* Vol. 1, No. 4. 1982. pp. 215-221.

Robinore, Charles J. "Worldwide Disaster Warning and Assessment with Earth Resources Technology Satellites." Geological Survey, U.S. Department of Interior. 1975.

Simpson, Robert H. "Hurricane Prediction." *Geophysical Predictions.* Washington, D.C.: National Academy of Sciences, 1978. pp. 142-152.

Stanford Research Institute. *Earthquake Prediction, Uncertainty and Policies for the Future: A Technology Assessment of Earthquake Prediction.* Washington: National Science Foundation, 1977. 312 p.
This special study examines the implications, benefits and liabilities of earthquake prediction and explores the prospects for improving forecasting capabilities in the future.

Steinbrugge, Karl V. *Earthquakes, Volcanoes and Tsunamis: An Anatomy of Hazards.* New York: Skandia America Group. 1982. 392 p.
Study of risk assessment and insurance issues involved in earthquakes, volcanic eruptions and seismic sea waves.

UNESCO. *Annual Summary of Information on Natural Disasters.* Paris, UNESCO.

UNESCO. *Avalanche Atlas.* An illustrated international avalanche classification. Paris. UNESCO. 1981.
Using morphological and genetic criteria this book presents a classification scheme for avalanches based on the recommendations of the International Commission on Snow and Ice (of the International Association of Hydrological Sciences).

Walker, Bryce. *Planet Earth: Earthquake.* Alexandria, Va.: Time-Life Books, 1981. 176 p.
This book examines the disastrous effects of earthquakes throughout history, how different societies have monitored, reacted and adjusted to earthquakes and the current efforts to improve the methods of seismic prediction and disaster mitigation.

Waltham, Tony. *Catastrophe. The Violent Earth.* New York: Crown Publishers, Inc. 1978. 170 p.
Examines the geological and man induced causes of earthquakes, volcanoes, landslides and subsidence and explores man's efforts to predict, prevent and mitigate disasters.

Ward, Peter L. "Earthquake Prediction." *Geophysical Predictions.* Washington, D.C.: National Academy of Sciences, 1978. pp. 37-46.

Warrick, Richard A. *Drought Hazard in the United States: A Research Assessment.* Boulder: University of Colorado Institute of Behavioral Science, 1975. 199 p.

Assessment of the social consequences, responses and research opportunities on droughts in the United States.

Warrick, Richard A. *Volcano Hazard in the United States: A Research Assessment.* Boulder: University of Colorado Institute of Behavioral Science, 1975. 144 p.
Study of volcanic risk assessment, with an emphasis on environmental monitoring of volcanoes, predicting of volcanic eruptions and human adjustments to volcanic hazards.

Whipple, A.B.C. *Planet Earth: Storm.* Alexandria, Va.: Time-Life Books. 1981. 176 p.
This volume looks at the different types of storms-hurricanes, typhoons, tornadoes, hailstorms, blizzards and thunderstorms and discusses the meteorological advances that have been made in tracking and predicting storms and controlling the weather.

White, Gilbert F. *Flood Hazard in the United States: A Research Assessment.* Boulder: University of Colorado Institute of Behavioral Science. 1975. 141 p.
Another University of Colorado study into the causes, effects and adjustments to flood hazards in the United States, incorporating a case study of the 1972 Rapid City, South Dakota flood and a simulation study of Boulder, Colorado.

White, Gilbert F. and Haas, J. Eugene. *Assessment of Research on Natural Hazards.* Cambridge, Mass.: M.I.T. Press, 1975. 487 p.
Reports research done at the University of Colorado on various kinds of natural hazards, ways of coping with them and ways of simulating these hazards.

Whittow, John. *Disasters, the Anatomy of Environmental Hazards.* Athens: University of Georgia Press, 1979. 411 p.
A comprehensive discussion of natural disasters throughout history to the present day, emphasizing earthquakes, volcanic eruptions, tsunamis, hurricanes, floods, blizzards and droughts. The volume includes a case study of Los Angeles and concludes with a chapter on disaster research.

Wijkman, Anders and Lloyd Timberlake. *National Disasters: Acts of God or Acts of Man.* London: Earthscans. 1984.

Wisner, Ben. "Flood Prevention and Mitigation in the People's Republic of Mozambique." *Disasters,* Vol. 3, No. 3 (1979). pp. 293-306.

Wyrtki, Klaus et al. "Predicting and Observing El Nino." *Science.* Vol. 191, No. 4225 (January 30, 1976) pp. 343-346.

Index